TRAIL OF THE FOX

Thomas Devins: From his L.A. car-parking days, he had hustled his way successfully through countless real-estate deals. Handsome, smooth and utterly charming, he conned Norma Wilson into a European jaunt. Somewhere in the Swiss Alps, he allegedly shot her dead—and scattered her body throughout the mountains . . .

Norma Wilson: Her marriage to a younger man wasn't enough, and for Devins, she was easy prey. She trusted him with her money and her affections—and Devins was the last person to see her alive . . .

Robert Forget: The tough, not-too-bright Canadian was Devins' perfect pawn. He went to Europe as Norma's bodyguard, but chickened out of the murder plan. And when Devins gave him Norma's jewels, he was greedy—and stupid—enough to keep them . . .

Bill Burnett: In the D.A.'s office, they called him "cowboy." Lanky, easygoing, Burnett was a bloodhound of an investigator—and nothing could shake him off Devins' trail . . .

Steve Trott: He had to make a case that was a prosecutor's nightmare—uncertain jurisdiction, no body and the shiftless Forget as his star witness. Working closely with Burnett, he achieved the impossible: putting Devins on trial for murder . . .

***"TRAIL OF THE FOX* is a real spellbinder . . ."**
—Library Journal

"Facts top fiction! *TRAIL OF THE FOX* combines the gripping tempo of a thriller with fascinating insights into painstaking police work . . . Authentic and fast-paced . . . COMPELLING!"
—Flora Rheta Schreiber,
author of *Sybil*

TRAIL OF THE FOX

LAWRENCE TAYLOR

POCKET BOOKS

New York   London   Toronto   Sydney   Tokyo

The photographs on the inside covers are from police files or from the personal files of Steve Trott, Bill Burnett, and the family of Norma Wilson; they are used by permission.

POCKET BOOKS, a division of Simon & Schuster Inc.
1230 Avenue of the Americas, New York, N.Y. 10020

*For Linda, my wife and best friend,
who gave me the courage to venture from
the logical world of the lawyer into the
Alice-in-Wonderland of the writer*

Contents

The following is a true story. The information was obtained from trial transcripts, Los Angeles County District Attorney files, Los Angeles Superior Court case files, and personal interviews. None of the names, places or dates have been changed.

Prologue

SHE HURRIED ACROSS the terminal as the voice from the loudspeaker announced that her flight was in its final boarding stages. She glanced quickly at her diamond-studded watch, then tightened her grip on the handle of her leather briefcase and hurried on.

She was an older woman, perhaps in her mid-fifties, with brilliant silver-blonde hair carefully lacquered into an immaculate but old-fashioned hairstyle. Her face was heavily powdered and rouged, yet beneath the layers of makeup lay the lines of classic beauty—a delicate aquiline nose, large pale blue eyes, high cheekbones, a fine jawline, slim, gentle lips. She was an attractive woman—and had been a beautiful one.

She wore a knee-length white mink coat that seemed oddly out of place in the Southern California milieu of T-shirts and hip-hugging jeans. The heavy fur coat was unbuttoned, flapping open as she walked to reveal a powder blue wool knit dress. Diamonds fell from her ears, and a double strand of large white pearls hung loosely around her powdered throat. A giant emerald on her finger added to the impression that she had just emerged from a Pasadena society tea.

Walking next to the woman was a younger man, dressed neatly in gray slacks and a golf shirt. He appeared to be in his thirties, and had the tanned, fleshy good looks of weekends in Palm Springs. He was carrying a woman's pink overnight case and staring ahead down the corridor with an expression of resigned boredom.

At the passenger entrance the woman stopped and turned toward the man at her side. She smiled slightly, a strained smile, then closed her eyes as he leaned forward and kissed her indifferently on the cheek. When he had drawn back, she opened her eyes and studied his face. The forced smile had not changed, but there was a look in her eyes of indecision, of regret, of pain.

She turned quickly away, picking up the briefcase and pink overnight case.

"I'll see you in a few days," she said.

But the attractive woman in the white mink coat would never return.

Part I

THE SCENT

Chapter 1

WHEN THE CALL CAME, District Attorney's Investigator Bill Burnett had been dictating into his recorder, summarizing new evidence on the latest pier killing. It had been a particularly gruesome murder, involving a small-time drug pusher who had stabbed a young girl in the lonely darkness under the old Santa Monica pier; the killer had cut her body into pieces and thrown them to the swarming crabs. Burnett had finally found the link between the girl and the killer: an old wino, half-asleep on the beach that night, had seen the suspect throwing something into a trash can. The garbage man's route had been traced and finally, after hours of searching through tons of trash, Burnett found a knife—complete with fingerprints and type A blood. When Burnett finished his tape, it would be transcribed into a memo and forwarded to the prosecutor for the trial.

The phone call was an irritating interruption. It was Joe Chandler, head of the L.A. County D.A.'s office at Santa Monica.

"Bill?" Chandler asked.

"Yeah, Chief."

"I want you to do me a favor. I've got a Mr. Wilson, Bill Wilson outside and his brother-in-law, a Thomas Bell. It seems Mr. Wilson's wife has, uh, disappeared." There was silence for a moment. "Bill, look, I know you're snowed under. I know you got that pier case and the gang thing and all, but just talk to them, okay?"

"Chief—"

"As a favor, okay? Gilber over at F.B.I. sent them. No federal jurisdiction, he says. Asked me as a personal favor, would we look at it. And you know what Gilber does for us. Hell, we owe him. And all you gotta do is talk to Wilson. Calm him down, stroke him a little. The old lady probably skipped for a few days of fun and games; she'll be back, everything'll be okay—you know how it goes."

"Jesus."

"Good, I'll send Wilson down right away."

Another missing persons case, Burnett thought. Another pile of forms to fill out, another file to add to a mountain of long-forgotten cases. Los Angeles was nothing but a huge collection of missing persons. In Southern California, that never-never land of dreamers and drifters, a missing persons report was nothing but a bad joke.

Burnett leaned back in his metal folding chair and propped one of his dark brown caribou hide cowboy boots on top of the scarred wooden desk. The boots stuck out incongruously from his baggy gray flannel trousers, part of the gray uniform he always wore. Burnett owned three suits, all in gray flannel; they had earned him the nickname "The Gray Ghost." Today he also wore a clean white button-down oxford shirt, short sleeved and badly frayed at the collar. A red-and-gold ivy rayon tie hung at an angle, pulled loose from the opened collar. Behind him, on an old wooden coatrack, a wrinkled gray flannel coat hung limply. The drab, loose-fitting clothing suggested a shoe clerk or a brush salesman. It was an impression countered only by the incongruous cowboy boots and the snub-nosed Colt .38 tucked into a small leather belt holster on his left side.

Burnett was not a particularly handsome man. He was average, ordinary looking, unnoticeable in a crowd. Thirty-four years old, about five feet ten and a bit on the lanky side, he had medium-length straight black hair that fell onto his forehead and a schoolboy's cowlick sticking up behind. A black mustache was roughly trimmed, and a favorite black briar pipe usually jutted out below it. His nose was slightly bent—an Army souvenir from a drunken night in a Korean whorehouse. It was his one distinguishing feature, though his hazel eyes had a mischievous twinkle and his thin mouth was often curled into an incomprehensible grin—a vague Mona Lisa smile, which made you think he was remembering some private joke. In a world of murderers, thieves, rapists and drug pushers, Burnett's gentle country-boy manner tended to create a feeling of uneasiness in those around him.

And Burnett really was a country boy, the genuine article. Easy-going, soft talking, he was born and raised on a small horse ranch in southern Illinois, near the small coal-mining town of Benton. As in the storybooks, Burnett had to walk a mile to catch the bus into town, where there were five kids in his class. After half a day in school, he would return to the ranch to break horses and cut grain while his dad, an ex-bronco buster from Texas, worked in the local mines to help support the family. The mines exploded on Christmas day, 1951, in the infamous Orient number 2 mining disaster; miraculously, Burnett's dad had changed shifts and was working on the ranch at the time of the calamity, which took the lives of hundreds of miners.

Burnett was still tilted back in his chair, his boots on the desk, when a man appeared at the open door to the office, knocking tentatively on the door frame. The lanky investigator slowly rose from his desk and extended his hand. "Bill Burnett," he said. The man's hand felt soft, clammy, delicate. "Grab a chair."

The man entered the office hesitantly, looking around the room. The brown formica sign on the office door read "Bureau of Investigations," but the room looked more like a small-time bookmaker's office. Three worn-out wood desks were arranged in haphazard fashion, each with an unpadded wood chair or a metal folding chair behind it and another in front. The desks were covered with faded green blotters, names and phone numbers scrawled across them. Thick Manila files were scattered across the desks in confusion, and more files were stacked on the floor against the dingy white walls. A gray steel filing cabinet stood in one corner, its three open drawers disgorging its papers in every direction. Next to the open door was a small wood end table holding a percolator, a can of coffee, sugar cubes, and four or five dirty ceramic mugs; one was labeled "George"; another displayed a bulldog with a campaign hat. The walls were bare, except for a large calendar with a fishing picture, an airline poster, and four sheets of scribbled notepaper scotch-taped to the dull plaster.

A good-looking young man in a flashy green shirt and a black tie stood next to one of the desks and fiddled with a small tape-recording device. There were straps fastened to the unit, with long thin wires and a small round microphone at the end. The man's right trouser leg was rolled up, and he was busily trying to attach the device to the inside of his ankle. A wire ran up his leg, taped to the skin, and the microphone hung loosely from a large brass buckle on his belt. He was silently muttering obscenities to himself as he struggled with the equipment.

The third desk was empty, but next to it, in the far corner, a large automatic rifle, a sub-machine gun, a few clips of ammunition, and three hand grenades rested ominously among the surrounding litter of files and papers. A Manila tag, with red ink writing, was tied to each of the weapons.

Burnett walked back to his chair behind the sloppiest of the three desks and sat down. He reached into his shirt pocket, pulled out a small box of wood matches and lazily lit his old briar pipe. Clouds of sweet gray smoke began filling the office. He leaned back in the chair again and studied the man sitting across from him.

Bill Wilson appeared to be about thirty-five years old, clean-cut and meticulously casual in a cashmere sport coat. Underneath the coat he wore a white silk shirt, opened into a V-neck, with monogrammed initials barely visible on the chest pocket. He stood about five feet ten, and weighed maybe a hundred and seventy pounds; he was fashionably tanned but soft, almost flabby. Evidently he was striving for that look of having just stepped off a Beverly Hills tennis court but not quite making it. The blue eyes, the delicate features, and the roundish face reminded Burnett of the carefully scrubbed 1950s all-American look. That was it, he thought: Wilson reminded him of an aging, slightly chubby boy scout who was trying hard not to grow up.

Burnett was the first to speak. "When was the last time you saw your wife, Mr. Wilson?"

"I . . . well, she . . . the airport—L.A. International. It was November 8th. Norma had bought a round-trip ticket to Montreal. I saw her get on the plane; I saw it take off." He shrugged slightly, his eyes fixed on the manicured hands resting on his crossed knee. "I never saw her again."

"November 8th," Burnett said, nodding. "Three months ago. When was she due back from Montreal?"

"In three days. It was a three-day trip. She was just flying up to take care of some business and then coming right back."

Burnett nodded absently. "What did . . . Norma?"

"Norma Bell Carty Wilson."

"What did Mrs. Wilson take with her?"

"A weekend bag, that's all. She packed only a few things. As I said, she was coming right back. She said she might stop off in Texas on her way back, but still—she was to be gone no more than three days."

"Texas?"

"Norma has a few oil wells there. We're . . . Norma's rather wealthy. Real estate, oil—that type of thing." Wilson began staring blankly out the window at the view of the Santa Monica City Hall. The tall, elegant old tile and stucco Spanish architecture clashed with the modern drab of the County Courthouse that housed the D.A.'s branch office. Just to the left of City Hall, maybe three or four blocks away, Wilson could barely make out the hazy blue of the Pacific through the smog.

"How much money did she take with her on this trip?"

Wilson looked back, as if awakening from a dream. "She . . . I don't believe she took very much. Norma preferred credit cards. American Express mostly."

"You got any bills from American Express since she . . . disappeared?"

"Only for a few things bought before she left, and the

Montreal tickets. But the card hasn't been used since she . . . left."

"Were you and Mrs. Wilson having any marital problems before she left?" Burnett asked.

Wilson shook his head. "No, not really. Oh there were a few arguments maybe, the normal spats. But nothing to . . . there was no reason why she would simply leave."

"The trip to Montreal, what was the purpose?"

Wilson shifted uncomfortably. "Norma told me she had to meet with some financiers, to get a loan. She was planning to build a medical office building here. And Devins told her—"

"Devins?"

"Tom Devins. Her financial adviser. A real estate broker, I believe. He's handled her business dealings for the past few years. In any event, Devins told her—about a month before—that he'd met some gentlemen from Biafra. In Africa. He told her they'd taken millions of dollars out of the country—sacked it before the takeover. And they were looking for places to invest it. So Norma said she had to go to Montreal to meet with them, and with Devins and his wife. They were interested in financing the office building— with a one-million-dollar loan. And perhaps buying the hospital as well."

"What hospital's that?"

"The Brentwood Convalescent. Norma owns it, too. She took the deed with her, in the event they could close the deal right there. And, well, then I saw her off at the airport."

"Devins was with her?"

"No. No, he was going to meet her in Montreal."

"And you never heard from her again?"

"I never saw her again. But I received a phone call the next day, November 9th, at about nine in the morning— noon there, I guess. She was in Montreal and wanted me to know she was all right. And she said there were some complications in the deal. She had to fly to Lisbon to get the loan."

"Was she alone in Montreal?"

"No. Devins was with her. But his wife wasn't there. And there was another fellow. Bob Forget. Norma said he was hired to be her bodyguard."

"Did she say why she needed a bodyguard?"

Wilson shrugged. "The money, I suppose. A million dollars. And the deed."

"A million dollars in cash?"

"I don't know. I don't know what the arrangements were. Norma was, well, rather quiet about her financial dealings."

"You know anything about this guy Forget?"

"He worked for Norma in one of her buildings. A carpenter. He does odd jobs—maintenance, that kind of thing. A French Canadian, I believe."

"Okay, did you ever hear from Mrs. Wilson again?"

"That was the last time I talked with her. But two, maybe three days later, I did receive some mail—a second insurance policy, for a round trip to Madrid. It was alone in the envelope."

Burnett took the pipe out of his mouth, absently studying the ashes. He tamped at it with his finger. "You were the beneficiary?"

Wilson nodded.

"You said there was a second policy?"

"Yes, at the airport. She bought one for the Montreal trip. From one of those machines in the lobby. She was always buying trip insurance whenever she would fly anywhere."

"How much were the policies for?"

Wilson shrugged. "I really don't recall."

"Did she have any other life insurance?"

"Uh, I don't believe so." Wilson looked up suddenly. "Mr. Burnett, if you're suggesting that I—"

Burnett held up his hand, grinning. "Just trying to get the whole picture." He continued tamping at the ashes, then struck another wood match to it.

"Anyway," Wilson continued, "three days later I received a postcard." He reached into his coat pocket and pulled out two cards, placing one on top of some scattered files on the desk.

Burnett picked it up. On one side was a black-and-white photograph of a big, expensive hotel. He turned it over. "The Castellana Hilton Hotel, Madrid, Spain" was printed on the back. The card was addressed to Bill Wilson. He noticed the Madrid postmark and the stamped date of November 10, 1968. Then he read the delicately scrawled writing.

6:30 PM, Sunday, '68
Bill, sure seems strange to be in this hotel without you. Had a few hours of sleep. No sleep on the plane, all night on the plane. I think we are leaving in the morning for Malaga. Everything coming along—know what I mean? Love, Norma.

Burnett looked back up at Wilson. "*Did* you know what she meant?"

Wilson shrugged. "The business deal, I suppose." He looked at the second postcard in his hand, then passed it to Burnett. "I got that about a week later."

It was postmarked Tangiers, Morocco, November 14, 1968. The writing was in the same hand. The face of the card was split into four equal-sized photographs of a yacht harbor, a business district, a large Moorish building and a street scene of men in Arab dress.

November 14
Bill, I really get around, don't I? Been in the "Casbah" all afternoon. From here to Lisbon, meeting with people tomorrow. I am fine, but was very sick in Spain. Too much to tell you. Love, Norma.

"And that appears to be your wife's handwriting?"
"It's hers."
"Okay. When was the next contact?"
Wilson looked out the window at the old City Hall. "I

never heard from her again," he said softly—almost melo-dramatically, Burnett thought.

"Mrs. Wilson got any relatives?"

"Oh, yes. She was very close to them. And she had some very good friends. Tom Bell is waiting out in the lobby now. Her brother."

"Any of them hear from her?"

"They received postcards, too. Then nothing. We all stopped hearing from Norma at approximately the same time."

Burnett stared at his pipe for a moment, then looked directly at Wilson. "Mr. Wilson, did your wife have any . . . male friends?"

Wilson looked back down at his hands. For a few seconds he said nothing. "I don't know. I really don't know. Tom Devins, well, they were pretty close. How close, I don't know."

"Anyone else?"

Wilson breathed deeply, then exhaled slowly. "After Norma had been gone for a while, and there was no communication, I naturally became worried. When she hadn't returned by her birthday, November 19th—there was always a party with her friends and relatives, a big birthday party—well, I started calling her family. And they were becoming rather worried, too. Anyway, the days passed and still nothing. So I decided to call Devins." Wilson paused to study his fingernails. "I found his number in Norma's telephone book. It was his business phone, but all I reached was an answering service. I finally found another number in the book and dialed it. Devins answered. Well, I was pretty surprised—I mean, to find out he was back without Norma."

"Did you recognize his voice over the phone?"

"Well, he said it was Tom Devins. I assumed it was him. And I asked him where the hell Norma was and when he had returned—I was excited and asking him three or four questions at the same time. He said, 'Oh, I've been back a week or so.'"

"When was this?"

"December 11th. And he said he'd been back a week, maybe two. But he sounded evasive. And again, I asked him where Norma was. Well, he said, he'd left her in Geneva, and she was going to Sweden—to some health spa in Sweden, he said. And she was going to meet Tom McSpadden." Wilson looked up, trying to read something in Burnett's maddening smile. "McSpadden was a former friend of Norma's, before I married her. My understanding is that they were . . . close."

Burnett nodded slightly. There it is, he thought. Your garden variety L.A. missing persons case. The neglected woman, lonely, aging. The husband's attentions wane, reality sets in with the wrinkles, and she desperately grabs at one last amorous fling with an old boyfriend. Norma Wilson and this guy McSpadden are probably shacked up somewhere in romantic Switzerland.

"Mr. Wilson," Burnett said slowly, "you do understand I'm just an investigator for the D.A.'s office? I mean, this isn't really a matter for the D.A. If your wife is missing, you should go to the L.A. police, or maybe the Sheriff's office."

"I've *been* to the police," Wilson said. "They told me that because she was seen flying out of Los Angeles, she didn't 'disappear' here. So they don't have jurisdiction."

Passing the old buck, Burnett thought. "Well, then, the F.B.I."

Wilson nodded, his eyes again cast down to his hands. "The police sent me there. But it's not a federal matter, they said—it's for the local authorities." He shrugged. "So they sent me here."

"Mr. Wilson, I'm sorry you've been given the runaround. But the problem is, our office only investigates cases the D.A. is prosecuting—you know, getting them ready for trial, digging up evidence, checking out defense testimony. Sometimes we go out and work up a new case but locating missing persons—it just isn't what we do here."

"Mr. Burnett," Wilson said slowly, "my wife isn't just a missing person. Norma is dead. She's been murdered."

Burnett was not intrigued. He looked at the files scattered over his desk and thought of the work he still had to do on them. The Avila robbery, the Malibu rape, the pier murder, the "juvie" gang job, the Navy killing . . . He just had no time for a geriatric love triangle.

"Mr. Wilson," he said in his slow rhythmic drawl, "what we've got here is a missing persons case. Pure and simple. Now, I don't know where your wife ran off to, or why, or with who, but . . ."

"She didn't run off, Mr. Burnett."

"All right, she's missing. But this is the D.A.'s office. We prosecute for provable crimes. I don't see any crime here. No evidence of murder. Only a missing person."

"It's been three months without a word and Norma always writes when she's away—every day. And what could she be living on? There've been no withdrawals from our account, no charge on her credit cards. . . ."

"This guy Devins seems to think she's in Switzerland or Sweden with . . ."

"I called McSpadden! He says he hasn't been to Europe, and he hasn't seen Norma. And the idea of her going to Switzerland or Sweden, to a spa in the winter, is nonsense. Norma hated the cold weather. She moved out here from D.C., to get away from the cold. It's ridiculous—she'd never travel to northern Europe in the winter. Norma's dead. I'm sure of it."

Burnett nodded wearily. "We don't know that, Mr. Wilson. We just don't know that. She may just be on some kind of long, impulsive vacation."

"Mr. Burnett, I've done everything I can. I've been to the State Department, I've been to the police, I've been to the F.B.I. My wife disappeared three months ago. I think she's dead. And no one will lift a finger to find out."

Jesus H. Christ, Burnett thought, I don't need this. "Look, Mr. Wilson, even if she were dead, unless it happened in L.A. County, there's not much I can do. I can't go around investigating crimes in Spain or Morocco."

Wilson continued studying his hands. It was becoming

15

clear to Burnett that this man was not going to budge until he got what he came for.

"All right," he said finally. "All right, we'll give it a shot."

"Thank you," Wilson replied simply. "Thank you." Somehow, Burnett observed, Wilson's sense of relief lacked feeling. He seemed anxious to find her, and yet . . . Well, he'd make a few short inquiries, make everybody happy, and then bury it where it belonged.

"I'll need Devins' address and phone number, and also the names and addresses of Mrs. Wilson's relatives and close friends, including Mr. McSpadden."

"Of course."

"And let us have a list of Mrs. Wilson's credit card accounts . . ." Burnett dug through the stack of papers and files for a blank legal pad. "Did she have anything of value with her when she left Los Angeles?"

"No, but Devins says she received a large amount of money in Europe."

"I mean personal items—jewelry, like that."

"She was wearing a long fur coat—a white mink. And she had a ring, with a large emerald and two diamonds set in it. There was a pearl necklace. And, oh yes, her watch; it had diamonds in it."

Burnett nodded as he wrote. Maybe she was jumped by some thugs in a back alley in Tangiers. But more probably the whole thing was just a romantic lark, a kissing-off of this fortune-seeker.

"And do you have any pictures of Mrs. Wilson?"

Wilson reached into his coat pocket again and handed over a 3 x 5 black-and-white photo of a woman with fair skin, platinum blonde hair, finely structured features, a perfect nose, light warm eyes, and a pleasant smile. An attractive woman, Burnett thought—and a good twenty years older than Wilson.

"Uh, how old is your wife, Mr. Wilson?"

"She would have been fifty-seven." There was silence for a moment as Burnett continued puffing quietly on his pipe.

"You're probably wondering, Mr. Burnett, exactly how old I am. I'm thirty-one."

"And when were you and Mrs. Wilson married?"

"Nineteen sixty-four. May 27, 1964."

Burnett did some mental subtraction. Norma would have been fifty-three years old that year, and Wilson only twenty-seven. A smooth, dapper, good-looking young man, and he marries a woman already into old age. But wealthy. Very wealthy. No wonder Wilson was anxious to have her pronounced dead.

"Okay," Burnett said finally. "You say this guy Devins told you Mrs. Wilson got hold of a pile of money somewhere in Europe?"

Wilson nodded. "I asked him, 'Did she get any money? Did she get the loan?' And he said, 'Oh, yes, she got a great sum of money.' And he also said something else— something about having trouble getting the money out. 'We had to go to Spain,' he said, or 'We had difficulty in Spain.' Something like that."

"Did you ask him where he and Mrs. Wilson had been?"

"Oh, yes. He said they'd gone to Tangiers, Casablanca, Malaga, and also Madrid. And then he'd left Norma in Geneva, at the Intercontinental Hotel. And that was the last he'd seen of her. Or so he said."

Burnett pulled out a pipe cleaner and began running it through the briar stem. "Did you and Devins discuss anything else?"

"Well, I told him I was worried, we were all worried, and I asked him to help us find her. And he said all right. I informed him I had to leave on a cruise in a week, and I—"

"A cruise?"

"Yes, to Hawaii. Norma and I always go for the holidays." He looked up. "Well, I thought . . . I mean, if she returned, she could certainly fly over and meet me in Hawaii. I saw no reason to cancel the trip."

The mourning husband, Burnett thought. "Go on."

"Apparently Devins flew to Europe and began looking for Norma right away, or so he claims. A few days after I'd phoned him, I received a telegram. It was from Devins but it was sent from here." He began patting his pockets, then pulled out a yellow paper.

Burnett read the telegram:

MANY SUCH PLACES IN SWEDEN. WILL CONTINUE UNTIL I CONTACT NORMA. IF YOU ARE LEAVING ON A TRIP AS PLANNED, PLEASE MAIL ITINERARY TO ME. FURTHER USE. COULDN'T REACH YOU BY TELEPHONE. THOMAS DEVINS, 15752 VALERIO STREET, VAN NUYS, 91406.

"After that I had a meeting with Norma's friends and relatives, and we decided to call the F.B.I. and the State Department. We were all extremely concerned for her safety. So we—"

"Did you go to Hawaii?"

"Uh, yes. Yes. As I said it seemed pointless to—I mean, it was already planned. The Moana Hotel. December 21st to January 2nd. It was our custom."

"You went alone?"

"Of course! I hoped Norma would return, as I told you, and join me there. . . . That's all, really. As I said, no one's heard from her for three months."

"What's your business, Mr. Wilson?"

"Business?"

"What do you do for a living? Who writes your paycheck?"

"I . . . well, I'm a writer."

"A writer? Well, I'll be damned. First one I ever met. You write for TV, or the movies, or what?"

"No. No, I . . . write books."

Bill shook his head. "No shit. Now, that's really something. Books. Which ones did you write? Maybe I read one."

"Ah, well—I, ah, I haven't exactly—I mean, I'm still

working on it—on the book, I mean. It isn't finished yet, you see."

"Oh," Burnett said, the pipe-clenched grin not changing. "Well, what did you write before?"

"I . . ." Wilson shifted in his chair. "This is the first one. I'm just getting started."

"Ah, I get you. Well, what was the handle before?"

"Handle?"

"Job—what did you do before?"

"Oh, well, I . . . I was a salesman for a while."

"What did you sell?"

"Cars. I sold cars."

"Uh-huh. When was that?"

Wilson coughed. "Say, is all this really necessary? It's my wife who's missing, not me."

"Yes, well, I need to ask a lot of questions, Mr. Wilson. It all kind of helps, somehow. In the end."

"Nineteen fifty-seven," Wilson answered finally. "Twelve years ago. I've had a few odd jobs here and there, of course. I taught dancing for a while at the Arthur Murray Dance Studio—the one at the Hollywood Roosevelt Hotel. And other things. You know . . . odd jobs."

Studying her young gigolo across the desk, Burnett felt he knew who Norma Wilson was. She was a woman who believed that time in the land of angels was suspended, who was adamant that her life would not end as it had been spent—without meaning. She was another of the countless who wanted desperately not to die without having *lived*. And to live, for her, was to act out the role she had seen Myrna Loy play so many times. But the truth soon gripped those like Norma Wilson. Having committed the offense of growing old, she would have no place in the California sun. And the older she got, the more desperate she became for youth, at any price.

"Okay," Burnett said finally. "Okay, Mr. Wilson. Now, let's just say for a minute that Mrs. Wilson did run into some foul play. Is there anyone you know of who would want to do her harm?"

Wilson looked back at Burnett and swallowed. Then he reached into a pocket, pulled out some papers, and handed them to Burnett.

"It's a copy of a deed," Burnett said, studying the papers.

"Yes. A grant deed. For the Brentwood Convalescent Hospital."

"And this is Mrs. Wilson's signature?"

"It certainly appears to be. Now look at the date and place of execution." It read: *Maurice Oberweger, Queens, New York, November 9, 1968.*

"That's the day Norma left Montreal for Europe," Wilson added.

Burnett nodded. "So it seems she had a stopover in New York and signed a deed there."

"And look at the grantee—the individual to whom she conveyed a million-dollar property."

Burnett read the name out loud. "Thomas Devins."

"The last man to see my wife alive."

Dark smoke drifted from Burnett's pipe bowl. "You tell me Devins was her business adviser, Mr. Wilson. It's no big deal to sign property over to your business adviser, to be held in trust."

Wilson said nothing.

"Well, we'll check it out," Burnett added as he rose to his feet. "We'll be sure to let you know if anything turns up. Meanwhile, if you have any more news, give me a call."

As he accompanied him down the hall, Burnett was still trying to understand the attitude he sensed in Wilson: a desire to have her found but beneath it, a lack of real concern. Probably he was just anxious to get his meal ticket back. Or maybe he was paving the way to claiming her estate. But more and more, something about the whole case was whispering foul in the back of Burnett's mind. What if Norma Wilson really was dead? A wealthy older woman, a young fortune-hunting husband—it was the classic setup. Knock off the old lady; then report it to the police to cover your tracks. It was almost a cliché—a story as old as greed.

Too many murders on your mind, Burnett said to himself; you're beginning to see them behind doors. An aging, pampered gigolo comes crying that his score dumped him for a newer model, and you smell a murder.

Okay, Mr. Wilson, he thought as he shook the man's hand once again. Okay, I'll make a few calls. But then you're on your own.

Chapter 2

Raymond Chandler had called it "Bay City." It was a town that was born in a time of orange groves and Charlie Chaplin, of swaying palm trees and stucco Arabian. Comfortably nestled into the merger of the coastal mountains and the silver-blue Pacfic, Santa Monica presided serenely over a gentle twenty-mile arc of sand that stretched from the movie colonies of Malibu on its north to the moneyed ranchos of the Palos Verdes Peninsula in the south. And lying directly across the bay on the hazy horizon as if in a faraway dream, Catalina drifted sleepily in the sun. Dominated by the grand Avalon Ballroom, the benevolent island fiefdom of Philip Wrigley rose every morning from the past as a reminder to Bay City of her days of Muscle Beach, merry-go-rounds, and offshore casinos.

Santa Monica was a city that did not wish to change. She had cultivated a lazy grace in her golden years, and now she resisted the pull of the dizzying present. Politely but firmly, Bay City declined to take part in Southern California's new, fast-lane living; she preferred to isolate herself from her frantic neighbors and to bask discreetly instead in the warm sands of memory. But was she winning her battle against reality?

The tide was turning in the south. Like an insidious disease, the ghettos of Venice and Mar Vista were reaching up into the city's unprotected flank, pushing the residents northward to the mountains. Battle lines had been drawn at Pico Boulevard, then at Olympic, and finally at Santa

Monica Boulevard, bisecting the city from Westwood to the ocean. Then a freeway had been thrust through Pico to the coast, linking up the dreaded inner city of Los Angeles with Santa Monica's quiet beaches. Thus, the southern half of Bay City withered, died.

Grace Barnum's house rested near the brink of the canyon, the city's northern edge, in the area farthest removed from the harsh realities of life to the south. The streets were quiet and gracefully lined with old, well-kept Spanish-style homes and set back under immaculately manicured trees. The air smelled good—a mixture of sweet-smelling greenery and the salty briskness of the ocean. There was a serenity here, a pastoral peacefulness—a commodity that brought high prices in the smoggy marketplace of Los Angeles.

Burnett sat uncomfortably on the edge of an antique chair in Grace Barnum's front room. The room was expensively furnished with antiques, each piece carefully polished and in perfect condition. Persian rugs covered hardwood floors. Mahogany shelves and etched glass cabinets were filled with old photographs, faded mementos, and fine china figurines. The arms of the heavily padded sofa and matching lounge were covered with intricate white doilies. In front of the sofa, on a deeply glowing hardwood coffee table, was an engraved silver tray filled with china cups and saucers, and a silver coffee service.

Burnett looked around the room at the people politely sipping their coffee and smiled. Grace Barnum, about seventy years old, sat in the overstuffed chair across from Burnett; she was one of Norma Wilson's sisters. Next to her, in an ebony chair, was the older man who had come to the D.A.'s office with Bill Wilson, Tom Bell—Norma's brother. On the embroidered couch sat sixty-seven-year-old Hilda Eacho, another of Norma Wilson's sisters; she had flown out from Washington, D.C., for this meeting. Ben Ratner, a short, fastidiously dressed gentleman in his sixties or seventies, sat benignly in the center of the couch; Ratner had just been telling Burnett about some of his experiences as a concert pianist on the East Coast. Beside him was his wife, Bernice Ratner. Behind the couch, next to the lace-draped window, stood Diane Roth, an anomaly in this room of gracefully aging wealth; the Ratners' attractive daughter, she gave Burnett the feeling of a fresh breeze—a touch of youth in a world of old doilies and bric-a-brac. He looked around again. Everything was pleasant, polite, proper.

He listened as Hilda Eacho told him about Norma. The Bells apparently had been a very close family with nine children, and they all still kept in touch. Burnett concluded from some of her comments that the Bells had been stinking rich and rated rather high in the strata of Washington society. And Norma, in her youth, had married well. Roy Carty, her former husband, had been a wealthy contractor in Washington before they decided to leave the cold weather for the sunny climes of Southern California; Carty had died of a heart attack after a few seasons of L.A. warmth.

"Oh, my, yes," Mrs. Eacho said, "we were all very close. We're still very close." She looked around pleasantly. There were nods of agreement from the others. "We exchange letters, cards—we get together whenever possible. Christmas, birthdays, you know. That's what's so strange, you see—Norma not being here for her birthday, November 19th. It was always one of our favorite parties."

"Was there a definite agreement on this party?" Burnett asked. "I mean, did Mrs. Wilson definitely understand it was to take place?"

"Of course! It was a standing arrangement. Every year."

Burnett sipped some coffee from his bone china cup. "And when was the last time you all heard from Mrs. Wilson, ma'am?"

Mrs. Eacho looked around at the others. "Well," she said, "we all received a postcard or two from Norma when she went to Canada and Europe."

Bernice Ratner coughed. "The last one I received," she said quietly, " was from Madrid. It was quite a surprise. I thought she was just going to Montreal for two or three days."

"What did she say in the card, Mrs. Ratner?"

"Oh, something about being tired and sleepy—from the time change and all, I should imagine. But she said—I remember she said—'I'll see you soon.'"

"Do you have the card?"

"I'm afraid I threw it out. I'm terribly sorry."

Hilda Eacho crossed the room and handed a postcard to Burnett. He read the Tangiers postmark, the November 14th date. In the same handwriting he had seen before was a short message:

> *Hi. Been in the Casbah all afternoon, from here to Lisbon, you really should come to Tangiers. It is my first visit. If I stop in N.Y., will call you. Love, Norma.*

"May I keep this?" Burnett asked.

Mrs. Eacho smiled. "Of course."

"So there's been no communication since these cards?" he asked.

Mrs. Eacho shook her head.

"I . . . we all exchange Christmas cards, Mr. Burnett," Ben Ratner interjected. "And Norma did something else. She always mailed each of us a fruitcake—from Corsicana, Texas. But none of us received cards from her, or fruitcake, this past Christmas. Or presents, for that matter."

"I see. Mr. Ratner, I'm not sure I understand your relationship with Mrs. Wilson."

"We—my wife Bernice and I and the children—are probably Norma's closest friends. Next to her relatives, of course. We've known Norma for thirty years, maybe more. Back in the thirties, in Washington, I used to give Norma piano lessons and, well, we became very close. When our son was born, we named him Norman—after Norma. That's how much we thought of her. And when Diane here was born, why, Norma was the godmother."

"She carried me home from the hospital," the young woman behind the couch added quietly. "She was always like a second mother to me. I'd always run to Norma when I wasn't getting along with mother. And when I got married, I asked her to be my matron of honor. Since then, she's opened trust accounts at the bank for my children's college education."

"And Bill Wilson," Burnett asked, "was he a part of this . . . closeness?"

There was an immediate stiffening in the room, a sudden chill. It was Grace Barnum who finally spoke. "As you may gather, Mr. Burnett, we don't really approve of Bill. We feel Norma's choice was . . . unfortunate. Roy's death—that was in 1959, June of 1959—affected her rather deeply. She became obsessed with business dealings after that; she buried herself in business matters. Investments and such. To answer your question, no, Mr. Burnett, Bill Wilson did not share in this closeness. We almost always saw Norma alone, at our homes. Perhaps I should . . . " She paused. "Let me explain something. Norma . . . You see, after Roy passed on—"

"She changed, Mr. Burnett," Diane Roth interrupted. "Norma was a sophisticated woman, very gracious, very cultured. She always acted with restraint and dignity. But when Roy died in 1959, she took it pretty hard. She felt alone suddenly, unsure of herself. She and Roy had been very close, they'd loved each other very much. And when he died, I guess it hit her pretty hard. I don't know, maybe it was loneliness; maybe she realized that her years would be coming to an end, too. But whatever the reason, her personality changed."

"What do you mean?"

"After she got over the initial shock of Roy's death, she became interested in men who were much younger than herself. Men like Bill Wilson. She began seeking out younger men, going to nightclubs and places like that, going out on dates with men half her age. And—"

Ben Ratner cut in. "Diane, I don't—"

"No!" she continued. "It's true! She became very concerned about her appearance, Mr. Burnett. She would spend hours putting on makeup, having her hair done, her fingernails, skin treatments. She began wearing different clothes—younger women's clothes. I mean, she still dressed with good taste, but it was . . . younger, more attractive, more . . . revealing. And she began acting younger, too, almost like a little girl. She'd giggle, and act naive, and . . . It was as if Norma was trying to pretend she hadn't grown old. And she became very worried about her future security. With Roy gone, she just felt very alone. She wanted so much to be taken care of, to have someone take care of her. Then she became obsessed with financial matters, business deals, real estate and all. I don't know, maybe it was her way of forgetting about Roy."

"And it was during this time that she met Bill Wilson?" Burnett asked.

"Yes," she replied, her lips tightening. "Bill Wilson. He was young; he paid attention to her, made her feel cared for . . ." She shrugged. "That was before the marriage."

"I understand Mrs. Wilson wore jewelry, fur—that kind of thing?"

Diane Roth spoke again. "Norma always dressed well but with good taste. She was a lady to the nth degree. She looked like a queen, and she acted like a queen. If you ever saw her, Mr. Burnett, you'd know what I mean. She was a beautiful woman—and a lady. At all times, a lady."

"Yes. But what kind of things did she wear? Things that someone might be interested in taking?"

"Norma had an extensive collection of jewelry and furs," Hilda Eacho said. "She might have been wearing anything, but . . . oh, yes, I remember. I told her, before she left, I said it was going to be cold in Montreal, and she said she was going to take her full-length mink, a beautiful white mink."

"Any jewelry?" Bill asked.

Mrs. Eacho looked up, almost startled. "Jewelry? Yes, I'm sure. Norma always wore jewelry."

"Any special pieces?"

Diane Roth cut in. "The watch. And the pearls."

"Oh yes," Mrs. Eacho said. "She always wore a pearl necklace." She fingered her own pearl necklace, then lifted it slightly. Beneath it was the faint outline of a thin scar. "You see this? It's from a thyroid operation some years ago.

Norma had the same operation, you see. The same scar. We both wear pearl necklaces to cover the scar. Norma never went anywhere without a pearl necklace."

"And the watch?"

"Oh, yes. She always wore it. Let me see, I don't really recall the brand, but there were a number of diamonds set into it. And she always wore her emerald ring. A very large, beautiful emerald. Roy had purchased the emerald for her on a trip to South America. She had it set in a ring with two diamonds, and it held memories for her."

"Did Mrs. Wilson tell any of you why she was going to Montreal?"

Bernice Ratner spoke up. "Norma told me she needed to raise some money for the medical building she wanted to put up. That medical building was an obsession with her. She felt very sorry for the older citizens here; she felt they were neglected. She wanted to do something for them, leave them something. That's why she owned the convalescent hospital, the one in Brentwood. And that's why she wanted to build the medical center. It was going to be her contribution, her monument."

"I understand," Burnett said quietly. So far, Bill Wilson's story was being confirmed.

"Norma said she could get only $135,000 here to build it, but she could get much more from some foreign investors in Montreal. And then, suddenly, we heard from her in Europe."

"Was there any mention of Tom Devins?"

"Tom Devins," Grace Barnum repeated. "Yes, Norma mentioned she was going to Montreal to meet Mr. and Mrs. Devins. After our meeting at Norma's, Mr. Devins—"

"Meeting?"

"Why, yes. All of us—we met at Norma's apartment sometime in December, or perhaps January. Bill was there, of course. We were all concerned about her disappearance, and we were trying to decide what to do. But Mr. Devins wasn't there. We met him at a later time, though. . . ."

"And what did he have to say?"

"That he'd been to Sweden, looking for Norma, and that

he'd placed ads in the Swedish newspapers, offering a $5,000 reward for information. But he said he'd found nothing."

"I'd called him before that," Ben Ratner cut in. "He said not to worry, that she'd be back. He said I'd hear from her in two or three days. He told me he thought she might be in Rolle—that's in Switzerland someplace. And I asked him why Switzerland, and he said she was carrying about $135,000 and—"

"Cash?"

"Yes, yes—in cash. And she wanted to deposit it in a Swiss bank. Anyway, he said he called some places in Rolle, but there was no record of her."

"So he'd gone on to Sweden?"

"Sweden!" Ben Ratner snorted. "Ridiculous!"

Burnett looked at the elegantly dressed old man. "Mr. Ratner?"

"It's ridiculous. Norma going to Sweden for plastic surgery—a face-lift, he called it. Ridiculous! Norma's a beautiful woman. Beautiful. A perfect face—nothing could be done to improve it!"

"Well," Burnett said, "maybe to a Swedish spa for a vacation?"

"Ridiculous," Ben Ratner repeated. "Young man, Norma contracted pneumonia four or five times while living in Washington. She and Roy moved out here to get away from the cold. She couldn't stand cold weather. Sweden in December? Sheer nonsense!"

Burnett looked down at his coffee. "Do any of you know Tom McSpadden?"

It was Diane Roth who answered. "I believe they were friends some time ago, Mr. Burnett."

"Do you know if she was 'seeing' this Mr. McSpadden recently?"

"I wouldn't know," Diane Roth said coolly. "But I certainly wouldn't blame her if she did."

Burnett looked around the room at Norma's friends and relatives, their graying heads bowed now in a heavy silence. He sensed a genuineness here, a real concern for Norma

Wilson—something he hadn't felt with her husband. "Well," he said, finally, "is it possible Mrs. Wilson had a health problem? Maybe her heart?"

"Mr. Burnett," Hilda Eacho answered, "Norma was in perfect health. She's a healthy, beautiful, vibrant woman. She never grew old. Oh, I know, you're looking at all of us and thinking Norma must be a doddering old fool, like the rest of us. But she's not. Norma's a very healthy . . . *young* woman, and anyway, the Corcorans said there appeared to be nothing wrong with her in Madrid. She seemed in fine spirits and—"

"The Corcorans?"

"Oh, yes. Margaret Corcoran. I thought you knew. My husband's sister. She married Laurence Corcoran, and they've lived in Spain now for twenty years or so."

"And the Corcorans saw Mrs. Wilson in Madrid?"

"Of course! Norma wouldn't dream of traveling through Spain without visiting Margaret."

"Did they say if anyone was with her?"

"They told us she was with two men. Well, the two men were at the hotel, actually—the Hilton, I believe. They didn't actually see them. Norma went to visit Margaret alone."

"Did they tell you who the two men were?"

"Well, I assume one of them was Mr. Devins. Anyway, Norma told Margaret she was traveling with her business manager and a bodyguard. Margaret thought that was quite dramatic—a bodyguard!"

"What else did Mrs. Corcoran tell you?"

"Well, she said Norma could talk only for an hour or so, and then she had to go south. She was making a deal with some foreign government, she said. But she couldn't reveal the name of the government. Very secret. And then she asked Margaret how to open a Swiss bank account."

"Did she say she was carrying a large amount of cash?"

"No. She simply asked Margaret how to go about opening a Swiss bank account. And Margaret told her."

"Anything else?"

"Only that after the deal was finished, she had been

invited out on a yacht trip with some important people."
Mrs. Eacho raised her palm and shrugged. "And then she
left."

"So the Corcorans never heard from Mrs. Wilson again?"

"No. But Laurence made a number of telephone calls to
Swedish health spas. None of them had ever heard of
Norma, though. Or of Sophia Loren."

"Sophia Loren?"

"Well, Mr. Devins mentioned that Norma said the spa
she was going to was the same one Sophia Loren went to.
But none of them seemed to remember Sophia Loren being
there."

Burnett nodded politely. "By the way, how did Mrs.
Wilson get along with her husband?"

"Mr. Burnett," Grace replied, after a brief silence, "I'm
sure you can see we are not overly fond of Bill. You see, Bill
has been . . . cruel to Norma."

"Cruel?"

"Well . . ."

"He beats her," Diane Roth interjected angrily. "Bill
Wilson beats her up, and regularly! He kicks her and hits
her in the face!"

"It's true, Mr. Burnett," Ben Ratner said. "He's been
abusing her for some time now. None of us can understand
why she hasn't divorced him—any more than we can
understand why she married him in the first place."

"Has anyone seen Mr. Wilson strike her?"

"No, we rarely see Bill at all," Grace Barnum answered.
"But I've seen the bruises on her legs. And a week or so
before she left, I saw her nose bleeding. She was crying and
she admitted Bill had hit her."

"I've seen plenty of marks and bruises," Diane Roth
added. "The last time I saw Norma, before she left, we were
having lunch. Her face was all red and swollen, and her eyes
were puffy. She said it was just an allergy, but I knew better.
She was just too embarrassed to admit the truth."

The room was quiet until Ben Ratner said, almost in a
whisper, "I suppose Devins told you about the will?"

"The will?"

"Devins said she asked him to draft a will during the trip, and so he did. He wrote it by hand and gave it to her, just before she disappeared." The white-haired old man looked directly at Burnett, his eyes bright and crystal clear. "Devins said the will would have cut Bill Wilson out completely."

Chapter 3

BURNETT WALKED INTO the Bureau Monday morning, nursing a sore shoulder. He had spent a three-day weekend in Mexico, racing his BSA 500 dirt bike through the Baja California deserts and mountains with his riding buddies. Among them had been race car driver Parnelli Jones and national dirt track champion Skip Van Leuwen—both of whom Burnett had introduced to the wild pleasures of Baja's desolate countryside. In between flat-out riding across the rugged desert terrain, the men played poker and drank tequila. It had been after a prolonged "tequila stop" that Burnett had taken a particularly spectacular crash and injured his shoulder.

Calm and easygoing as Burnett was, he had a driving need to get out in the open and "cut loose." In his childhood days growing up on the small ranch near Benton, he was known as a wild, uncontrollable boy who was "going to hell sure as sin." He tore up the country with an old BSA motorcycle, got into fights constantly, and infuriated more than one local girl's father.

When it had come time to leave home, Burnett had enlisted in the Marine Corps and asked to be shipped to Korea; it was 1952, and there was plenty of action there for him. He liked the hard-driving Australian soldiers and became good buddies with a few of them—an association that led to a series of wild adventures. He still remembers one harrowing night when five of his Aussie buddies, still

33

drunk, put on their black sweaters and hoods, grabbed Sten guns, and took him on a patrol behind the North Korean lines. It was a few days later in Seoul, sober and still thankful to be alive, that Burnett had a run-in with a Turkish soldier who happened to be in bed with Burnett's favorite whore. As the Turk was only a runty five feet tall, the country boy decided to eject him; the little Turk turned out to be a buzzsaw, and Burnett's nose was permanently rearranged.

After the war, Burnett reenlisted and was sent to Ethiopia as an embassy guard. The fighting and girl chasing continued, but he was lucky enough to enjoy the special protection of Emperor Haile Selassie; the Emperor had taken a liking to the small contingent of hard-drinking Marines and made it a point to invite them to all of his dinners. In Addis Ababa, Burnett met and married Ann Elizabeth Fitz, the daughter of Dr. John Allen Fitz, head of the State Department's economic development program; the wedding was the biggest foreign celebration Ethiopia had ever seen.

Burnett, a sergeant by now, was then reassigned to boot camp at San Diego as a drill instructor. He was put in charge of the "Incentive" Platoon—filled with all the "bad asses" and rejects. It was his job to "rearrange" their attitudes.

When his second enlistment was up, Burnett entered the University of Southern Illinois on the GI Bill. A son was born to him and Ann at the end of the first semester—about the time the government told him the GI Bill applied only to his first enlistment, and had expired six days before his entering the University.

Burnett was forced to drop out of college. He sent his wife and son to live with her father in Pennsylvania while he returned to Southern California to take the entrance exam for the L.A. County Sheriff's Department. He quickly passed and was accepted. But suddenly, Burnett was called back to Pennsylvania: the baby was seriously ill. When he arrived, the doctors told him it was a urinary infection, and the child would be all right. Four hours later the baby died.

Ann in her grief withdrew from the world, becoming

quiet and vacant-eyed and muttering incomprehensible phrases to herself. Burnett couldn't bring her out of her despair.

He began walking alone through the country, thinking, trying to understand why everything had fallen apart, wondering how to start over. One evening, he returned from one of his walks to find a letter from the L.A. Sheriff's office waiting for him: he was ordered to report to the Sheriff's Academy the next morning at eight-thirty. Burnett thought long and hard that evening. Then, after arranging with his father-in-law for Ann's care, he flew back and reported to the Academy.

Burnett eventually graduated third in a class of seventy and was immediately assigned to the County jail. Ann came out to join him, but she was not the same woman he had known before the baby's death. Within months they were separated.

In time Burnett became bored with the dull routine of guard duty at the jail and accepted an offer to transfer to the District Attorney's office as an investigator. One of his earliest assignments was posing as a broke and disgruntled ex-Marine, while infiltrating a huge narcotics and bookmaking ring that was paying off high city officials. Burnett became the "bag man" for the big boss and eventually set up the arrest leading to the indictment of thirteen people and the resignation of the city's police chief.

In 1967 Burnett was assigned to the D.A.'s Santa Monica branch office. He had been divorced for two years and had met Ann Elizabeth Holbrook, a vivacious young Anglo-Armenian beauty. The new Ann Elizabeth had a calming influence on Burnett, and the hard drinking and wild living began to subside. The two were married in 1968, the year Bill Wilson walked into the D.A.'s office with his story of a wife who had disappeared.

Burnett took off his gray flannel coat and winced as he raised his arm to hang it on the coatrack. He sat down at his desk and looked disgustedly at the messages, files and mail that had accumulated during his short vacation. He had a particular dislike for paperwork. Like most people, his image of an investigator's job had been a romantic one; in truth, he spent almost half of his time reviewing case files, dictating memos to the chief of investigations or to a prosecutor, making phone calls, and sorting through a never-ending variety of letters, memos and documents.

As he shuffled through the telephone messages, one caught his eye. It read, "From RCMP Montreal—have info on Wilson, Forget has record." The note was in the handwriting of George Cooper, Burnett's partner and the senior investigator in the Santa Monica office.

"Hey, George. What's this message from the Canadian Mounties?"

Cooper was busily sorting a series of 8 x 10 black-and-white photos from the County Coroner—grisly close-ups of a mutilated corpse. Another ex-sheriff, Cooper was the clean-cut athlete of the office. He was forty years old but still in rock-trim shape from skiing, tennis and mountain climbing. "This morning," he replied, not looking up. "They got something for you on that Wilson lady."

"Fast work! And how about this one from the Consulate in Tangiers?"

"Came in Friday," Cooper replied absently. "The Wilson lady entered at Tangiers from Algeciras. On the date I wrote there. Checked into the Rif Hotel. Left Morocco two days later, headed back for Algeciras."

"Nothing else?"

"That's all they said." He looked up for a moment, grinned. "That runaway wife's gonna cost the County, ol' buddy. You're getting calls from everywhere but China—all collect."

Burnett nodded, then turned to his pile of mail. He sorted through the letters quickly, then pulled out an official-looking envelope from the Police Department, City of Dorval. Dorval was the suburb of Montreal where the Hilton Hotel was located. Burnett had called the police chief and asked for help on tracing the movements of Norma Wilson, Tom Devins and Robert Forget.

He tore open the envelope and read the letter. It was from a J. McDougall, Captain Detective, Investigator's Division, and related that Norma Wilson had checked into the Hilton on November 8 at 6:20 P.M., taking room 361. Her anticipated departure had been listed as November 10, but she had checked out on the 9th at 1:37 P.M. She had paid cash; there were no records of any American Express purchases. Before checking out, she had called a Los Angeles number at 11:19 A.M.; the number called was listed in her own name. Another room was jointly occupied by Tom Devins and Robert Forget. Records reflected telephone calls from their room to Ottawa, and their rental of a car which was taken to Ottawa, on November 8. A local check revealed that neither man had a criminal record in Dorval.

Burnett put the letter down. It squared with Bill Wilson's story—even the phone call. But so far it was still nothing more than a skipped wife. He sorted through some more mail, then pulled out another envelope. The return address indicated it was from the Honolulu Police Department. He opened it—it was a brief report that a William Wilson had indeed checked into the Moana Surf Rider Hotel on December 21, 1968, and checked out on January 2, 1969. He had apparently been alone in the room; none of the hotel employees recalled his having had any companions or visitors.

Burnett finished a brief look at the mail, then picked up the message from the Mounted Police in Montreal. After a few minutes with the operator, Burnett found himself talking to a deep-voiced man with a slight French accent.

"Yes, Mr. Burnett. Sergeant Poulin, C Division. About Mrs. Norma Wilson. A preliminary investigation indicates Mrs. Wilson entered Canada at Montreal, Air Canada flight 620, on November 8 of last year. She resided at the Hilton Hotel and departed the following day, leaving the country on Air Canada, flight 768, destination New York."

"Anything on—"

"Thomas Devins. Arrived the same day on an earlier flight, departed the following day on Mrs. Wilson's flight.

The same is true of Mr. Forget. Devins is an American citizen and appears to have no record in Canada. Forget, however . . .''

"Yes?"

"Robert Jerry Forget. Five feet ten inches, 170 pounds. Brown hair, brown eyes. Born July 20, 1938, Montreal. Raised in an orphanage. Occupation, carpenter. Canadian citizen. Issued Canadian passport November 8, 1968, at Ottawa." November 8. That explained the calls to Ottawa and the rental car. "The application indicates that the passport was issued on the same day as applied for. Apparently, a walk-through. This is sometimes done in emergency situations."

"And does he have a police record?"

"It seems Forget entered the United States illegally in 1959. The Los Angeles office of your Immigration Service developed a file on him and forwarded it to the New York office on February 16, 1968. He was arrested and subsequently deported back to Canada. Later he married an American citizen—the daughter of a retired Los Angeles Police Department officer, Robert F. Tesmer. Apparently, he returned to the United States as the husband of an American citizen. His passport lists his present residence as Vancouver, but a check indicates that he is, in fact, residing in Sedro Woolley, State of Washington."

Burnett was scribbling down notes on the back of a file. He usually wrote things down on whatever was handy. As a result, his notes on a case could be found scrawled on various files, scratch pads, and paper napkins scattered throughout the office.

"That it?" Burnett asked finally.

"End of report," the telephone voice said.

Burnett pressed the telephone receiver lever down for a few seconds, then dialed a number that was written on a piece of paper he had pulled from his pocket. Within a minute he was talking to Robert Miles, passenger office manager for Air Canada in Los Angeles.

"Yeah, Mr. Burnett? We got that information you asked for. Let's see now. Uh, Norma Wilson, ticket number

H014301336860, one-way to J.F.K., flight 768. It left Montreal at 3:00 P.M., November 9, and landed at J.F.K. at 4:15. She had a connection on T.W.A. flight 904, leaving J.F.K. at 7:45 P.M. for Madrid. She bought a one-way ticket and paid with cash."

"You're sure that was one-way? There were no arrangements for, say, an open-ended return flight?"

"Nope. One-way."

"What about the L.A.-Montreal ticket? Was the return ever used?"

"Nope. As of this date, the return on the round-trip ticket hasn't been used or redeemed."

Burnett scribbled something on a piece of paper. "What about Devins and Forget?"

"We can't seem to find any record of those two names on the Montreal-J.F.K. flight."

"Nothing?" The Mounted Police had just confirmed that the two men had left on Norma Wilson's flight.

"Nope. Checked the passenger manifest for that day. Only Norma Wilson. But our records do show one-way tickets issued to Devins and Forget on November 9 at our Montreal desk: Madrid, via New York. Same T.W.A. connection as Norma Wilson. Cash payment. But they don't show up on the manifest. Maybe they used other names."

"Anything's possible." Burnett thought for a moment. "What about the L.A.-Montreal leg? Had Devins and Forget bought round-trip tickets?"

"One-way."

One-way, Burnett thought to himself. How did Devins and Forget know they weren't going to be returning from Montreal, but Norma Wilson did not know?

Burnett's next call was to the District Attorney's office in Queens, New York. In a few seconds, a voice came over the line.

"Inspector Paul Vitrano."

"Bill Burnett here, Paul. L.A. D.A.'s office."

"Oh, yeah, yeah, gimme a minute." Burnett heard scratching sounds, the rustling of paper, some barely audible cursing. "Yeah, here we go. Wilson . . . Norma Wilson.

Like you ask, we send Harrington down, one of our detectives, and he checks out that notary public, . . . Maurice Oberweger. The guy's a registered, bona fide notary public with a clean rap sheet. A side business, in the International Airport pharmacy, J.F.K. International Building—the airport. Anyway, we talked to him, he says yeah, he remembers the deal—the deed transfer. Two men and a woman. The woman fits this Norma Wilson's description. He's not too exact on the two men, but they sort of fit the description you gave me on these guys Forget and Devins."

"Only those three?"

"Yeah. Just the two guys and the woman. She signed it and one of the guys signed it. The other guy just stood around."

"Okay. Thanks a lot, Paul." Burnett hung up the phone and stared blankly at the stack of papers and files on his desk. He unearthed the two colorful postcards from Norma Wilson and picked up some papers and a note attached to them with a paper clip. The note was a memo from the D.A.'s downtown branch, written by Larry Sloan, their handwriting specialist—or "Questioned Documents Examiner" as he was officially referred to in court. The memo briefly informed Burnett that the handwriting on the postcards appeared to be genuine—or, at least, in the hand of the same person who had written the exemplars attached to the cards; for comparison, Burnett had forwarded the signed insurance policy Norma Wilson had bought at the L.A. airport, along with a photostat of her driver's license application and some real estate papers Bill Wilson had brought in.

He was curious to see if the deed to the Brentwood Convalescent Hospital had been recorded yet, and if so, by whom. He grabbed a pad of paper and wrote a note to the Bureau's secretary to have the postcards forwarded to the U.S. Postal Inspector's office in San Francisco. The experts there could identify whether the postmarks and stamped dates on the postcards were authentic.

He grabbed his right shoulder, massaged it for a moment, then stood and walked over to the percolator. He poured some coffee into the mug with the bulldog painted on it and walked back to his desk.

Cooper looked up, grinning. "You still on that Wilson thing?"

"Yep. But it's turning hinky."

"What's hinky about a wife who skips?"

"I don't know. Probably nothing, probably a waste of time."

Cooper laughed. "Hey, Bill, you don't have enough work that you gotta go chasing down lost wives?"

Burnett shook his head, smiling. "Yeah, I know, all we needed was something like this. Still . . . there's something funny going on."

"Yeah, well, Bill, listen . . . I don't have to remind you what our load's getting to be around here. We keep falling further and further behind. I got my own ass chewed out downtown on account of that Henderson case last week. Do what you got to on that Wilson thing, Bill, but wrap it up. We just don't have the time, okay?"

"Yeah, George." Burnett sat down behind his desk. He knew Cooper had to let off a little steam now and then. It was the old chain of command: the D.A. chews out the chief of the Bureau downtown, the chief chews out the branch office heads, and then it's the troops' turn. But Cooper was right: a missing persons case just didn't warrant the time of an already overworked staff.

Burnett took out his personal phone book and looked under "American Express." The credit card companies had been helpful in the past in tracing suspects' movements and developing financial profiles. He called a Robert Conklin, the special agent for American Express in charge of L.A. operations. Burnett asked him to run a quick check on Norma Wilson's account, then waited, thoughts running through his mind. Devins—Forget—oil wells—Wilson . . . a million dollars—McSpadden—mink and diamonds. . . .

Conklin confirmed that Norma Wilson's card had not been used since buying the Montreal round-trip ticket. Further, he indicated that the account was four months delinquent in the amount of approximately $900. He added that it was the first time the account had ever been overdue; Mrs. Wilson had been consistently prompt in past billings.

Burnett thanked Conklin and hung up. Next, he checked with T.W.A.'s Security Operations Department at John F. Kennedy airport. Did the passenger manifest for T.W.A. flight 904, November 9, 1968, New York to Madrid, include the names of Norma Wilson, Thomas Devins or Robert Forget? The chief of security informed Burnett that the manifests are routinely destroyed thirty days after the flight. He made a note to check with Spanish Immigration in Madrid for arriving passengers.

Burnett again sifted through the paperwork and finally found the telephone numbers for Tom Devins that Bill Wilson had left. It would be interesting to see what Devins had to say about the trip arrangements and the deed. Still, there was probably a reasonable business explanation for it all; high finances and real estate transactions were matters that always seemed a little mysterious to Burnett. He dialed the home phone first, but there was no answer. Then he dialed the office number; a woman's efficient voice informed him that Devins was out of the office and was expected back later in the day. Burnett left his name and telephone number.

Next was a record check—to see if either Devins, Forget or Bill Wilson had a "rap sheet." He dialed the number for the Los Angeles Police Department's "R & I" section—Records and Identification. Their computers would instantly report any arrests, convictions or pending charges within Los Angeles County. Burnett identified himself to the operator and within minutes had a clean bill of health on all three men.

Next, Burnett called C.I.I. in Sacramento—the State's Bureau of Criminal Investigation and Identification. Their computerized records would show any criminal history within the State—including Federal crimes. A few minutes later Burnett learned that Devins' file showed only an application for a real estate salesman's license in 1962, requiring a background check. Forget was clean in California. Bill Wilson's file showed an application for a car salesman's license in 1962, a pile of traffic tickets, and a "deuce" in 1967—a conviction for drunk driving. There appeared to be nothing in their California histories to cast suspicion on any of them, but Forget was a Canadian, and Wilson and Devins were very probably like most "Californians"—refugees from cold weather and hard facts.

The Federal Bureau of Investigation in Washington would have records on the three men indicating, with varying degrees of accuracy, criminal conduct within any of the states, and probably Canada. But the F.B.I. wouldn't normally take telephone requests, so Burnett drafted a quick note to the office secretary to send a written request for record checks on the three men. He also asked her to write the chief of police in Sedro Woolley, State of Washington, requesting a thorough workup on Robert Forget.

Burnett looked at the stack of files again. He propped his boots on the table, leaned back in the chair and began tamping at the dead ashes in the black briar. Slowly, he lit the pipe back into life and stared up at the cracked plaster ceiling.

If this was not just a skipped wife, Burnett began thinking . . . if Norma Wilson was not suffering from amnesia somewhere, if she was really dead, if it was not an accident . . . a lot of "ifs." But even "if" it were murder, it probably happened in Europe—"if" she got on the Madrid flight and didn't later return. And that meant no L.A. County jurisdiction. And if she didn't get on that plane, she may have disappeared in New York. Again, no jurisdiction. Or was there? Under California law, if the prosecution could prove that a murder was planned in California, and that initial stages of the plan were executed in California, then jurisdiction for the crime is established no matter where the actual killing takes place. So if this was more than a missing persons case, Burnett knew he would have to prove not only who did it, but also prove that it was conceived and at least partially carried out within Los Angeles.

But if Norma Wilson had been killed, why hadn't there been any reports on a body? Even if there had been no passport or other identification, inquiries would have been made by the local and national police, and photographs of the body would have been circulated. And Bill Wilson said he had notified the State Department. Where was the body?

Burnett puffed deeply on the pipe. Everything kept pointing to just another missing person, a typically fragile L.A. marriage. And yet . . .

Who would have the motive? Husband Wilson: possible insurance or inheritance? Adviser Devins: some high finance shenanigans with the deed? Bodyguard Forget: tempted by the large sum of money in her possession? Boyfriend McSpadden: a lovers' quarrel? Or could Norma Wilson—loaded with jewelry and fur—simply have been the victim of a fatal robbery? Or could she have had a simple accident or a heart attack? Or was she happily skipping around Europe with her old lover?

Burnett looked back at his scratched notes. The word "McSpadden" stared at him, but Burnett had been unsuccessful in trying to reach the Arizona telephone number. "Philip Horrigan" was scribbled next to it. Horrigan was Norma Wilson's lawyer.

Burnett dialed Horrigan's office for the third time. He was put on hold for a few seconds, and then he heard the lawyer's restrained, articulate voice. Burnett quickly explained that he was investigating the disappearance of Norma Wilson.

"Actually," Horrigan said, "I've been meaning to call you. I've only been Mrs. Wilson's attorney for—well, since last year. Roy Carty—that was Mrs. Wilson's former husband—was represented by J. Henry Schweitzer, an associate here in Westwood Village. When Mr. Carty died, Mr. Schweitzer continued to represent Mrs. Carty—now Mrs. Wilson. Then, when Mr. Schweitzer died last year, Mrs. Wilson asked me to assume her legal representation."

"And have you, by any chance, heard from Mrs. Wilson since she left in November?"

"No. No, I haven't. In fact, I advised her against going to—where was it? Montreal?"

"Why were you against it?"

"Frankly, I didn't really trust Mr. Devins. But the entire

setup—the last minute rush out of the country, the mysterious Africans—well, the whole thing was rather disreputable in my opinion. And she and I were also in the middle of trying to sell or trade the Brentwood Convalescent Hospital."

"Oh? I assume you know that the hospital was transferred to Devins?"

"I didn't know. My understanding is that it was part of a triangular escrow by Mrs. Devins, involving a million-dollar apartment complex in San Fernando and cash from a Dr. Abraham, who's been the lessee at the Hospital since 1964. Dr. Abraham has been trying to buy it from Mrs. Wilson for some time, but she's always refused to sell for less than a million dollars. But Devins apparently held title at some point, in trust, and conveyed it to Dr. Abraham for considerably less than a million dollars."

"Did Devins have power of attorney to sign for Mrs. Wilson?"

"A limited power of attorney—only for the sale of the hospital. But I had Mrs. Wilson execute a revocation of that instrument. Perhaps he obtained another one; I don't know."

"Did Mrs. Wilson ever mention a Robert Forget?"

"No."

"Did she tell you, before she left, that she was going anywhere besides Montreal?"

"No . . . she never mentioned any other trips. Only Montreal."

"Have you talked with Devins since he returned?"

"Yes. I believe it was just last month—early in January. I called him because Mrs. Wilson's brother, Tom Bell, told me she was missing, and I asked Devins if he knew where she might be. Devins said there was no reason to be concerned. He said he felt sure he knew exactly where she was, and he'd have no difficulty locating her. He said he'd left her in Geneva, and that she was going to Sweden to have her . . . face lifted."

Burnett puffed heavily on the pipe. "You mean plastic surgery?"

"I assume so. 'Face-lift' was Devins' phrase. She didn't want Bill Wilson to know about this, he said. And he asked me not to tell him. Well, I told Devins her family and friends were worried. He said there was no problem; there were only a few places in Sweden she could be. He said he'd locate her and tell her to contact her family." There was a pause. "Mr. Burnett, I'm afraid I have an appointment, and I'm running a bit late."

"Sure. Can we set up an appointment? I'd like to talk with you some more about all this."

"Of course. Talk with my secretary."

"One other thing, Mr. Horrigan."

"Yes?"

"You handle all of Mrs. Wilson's legal matters, right?"

"That's correct."

"She had a will?"

"She did. I drafted it in . . . I believe it was in May of last year."

"Did she say anything before she left about wanting a new will?"

"No. No, she mentioned nothing about a new will."

"Who were the main beneficiaries of the existing will?"

"In the event of Mrs. Wilson's death, her husband, William Wilson, would inherit the entire estate."

Bill Wilson, Burnett thought. An instant millionaire.

"Unless," Horrigan added, "there was a divorce action pending in court. In that event, Mr. Wilson would receive only $30,000. Now if you'll please excuse me, I really must—"

"Did Norma Wilson ever tell you she was planning to divorce Bill Wilson?"

"Shortly before this trip to Montreal came up, Mrs. Wilson came to my office and advised me that she was contemplating having me file a divorce action, yes."

"But if—hypothetically—she were to die before the action was actually filed . . ."

"Mr. Wilson would still inherit everything. That's correct. Now goodbye, Mr. Burnett."

Chapter 4

Burnett parked the old Plymouth sedan and walked through a maze of cars to the Courthouse. Rain and wind had rinsed the air, and the coolness had temporarily dissolved the smog-trapping inversion layer. The skies were almost blindingly bright and clear, offering a view from Santa Monica's Pacific shore of the towering snowcapped San Gabriel Mountains. It was days like these—maybe no more than a dozen a year—that made life in the normally gray-brown chemical haze palatable.

Burnett walked into the south wing of the Courthouse and down the sterile hallway, glossy from the previous night's machine waxing. L.A. County's West District of the Superior Court was located on the two floors of this wing, having jurisdiction over all felony criminal trials and any major civil matters. There was always an odd assortment of humanity sitting and milling around in the hallway outside of the courtrooms.

Burnett waved to a cop he knew from the Culver City Police Department. The West District covered the jurisdiction of the police departments of Santa Monica, Culver City and Beverly Hills, as well as the western section of L.A.P.D., which included Venice, Westwood, the wealthy Pacific Palisades and a nebulous area vaguely known as West L.A.; finally, the County Sheriff, which controlled the nonincorporated parts of the District, added the colorful areas of Malibu, Marina del Rey and the Sunset Strip to the West District's jurisdiction. It was a totally illogical patchwork quilt, but somehow everyone managed to stay within his own borders.

Burnett turned and walked through the north wing—the other of the L-shaped building's two wings. In this part of the Courthouse were located the municipal courts and the administrative offices. The municipal courts had jurisdiction only over the immediate area—the city of Santa Monica. Other municipal courts were spread around the district, in Malibu, West L.A., Beverly Hills and Culver City. Unlike the superior courts, they handled misdemeanors and smaller civil cases.

Burnett walked up a flight of stairs to the second floor. The Santa Monica city prosecutor was talking outside of Division 2 with a plainclothes officer, probably going over testimony he was about to give in a trial or pretrial motion. Each of the cities—including Los Angeles—had its own prosecutors to handle misdemeanors. But the district attorney had exclusive jurisdiction of all felony cases anywhere in the county, as well as of misdemeanors in areas without a city prosecutor.

As Burnett walked toward the D.A.'s office, he noticed two judges walk by each other without acknowledging the other's presence. He chuckled to himself. A lot of the judges in the building weren't on speaking terms. It was largely a part of political jockeying and infighting. The municipal court judges were scrambling for appointment to the superior court, and the superior court judges were kneeing each other for a better chance at a seat on the court of appeals. He grinned again. Of all the cliché characters in the courtroom's cast—the shady defense lawyer, the ambitious young prosecutor, the clean-cut police officer, the sullen defendant—the least understood among the public was the judge. Hidden from a true view by a cloak of authority and an image of a wise father figure, the judge was very often a vain and petty man who, after years of unrestrained power, had become almost godlike in his own mind. In keeping with this sense of omniscience, the judge often didn't bother staying abreast of developments in the law—adding ignorance to his list of faults. Of course, there were good judges, too—those who didn't feel their political appointment to the bench was tantamount to deification or retirement. But the good ones were few; Burnett could count those in the building on the fingers of one hand.

At the end of the north wing was Burnett's office. He pushed open the door, walked through the reception area and back into the Bureau of Investigations. He grabbed the bulldog mug, poured some coffee into it, then wandered across the room to George Metegka's desk. Cooper was out, in the field on assignment. Metegka leaned back in his chair, a big grin on his face.

"Well, it's our man in missing persons!"

Burnett laughed. "Yeah. Well, it may be a little more than that, amigo."

"Oh?" Metegka said with mock interest. "Don't tell me you've dug up an old traffic warrant on her, too?"

Burnett lit the pipe, then grinned. At twenty-six, Metegka was the youngest of the three Santa Monica investigators. In many ways, he was the opposite of Burnett: a flashy dresser, a born-and-bred city boy. The flamboyant blue-eyed blonde playboy spent most of his waking hours trying to get airline stewardesses into bed. His fancy clothes, colorful mannerisms and one-track interest had earned him the nickname "Ass Bandit." Like Burnett, Metegka drove motorcycles—but his tastes ran to big Harley-Davidsons with plenty of chrome and padding. And like Burnett and Cooper, he had been handpicked from the ranks of the Sheriff's Department. Behind all the flash and girl chasing, Metegka was a clever and hardworking investigator.

"Seriously, ol' buddy," Metegka continued, "I got a call from downtown. They want to know why all the time on the Wilson thing. They want a memo—pronto."

"Stoner?"

Metegka nodded. George Stoner was the chief of the D.A.'s Bureau of Investigations, the head of all the D.A.'s investigators. Only the district attorney himself, Evelle Younger, was higher in the office. But how had Stoner known? Who had told Stoner about the time he was spending on the case? He looked at Metegka.

"Nope," Metegka said, holding his hands up defensively, "not from me, ol' buddy. I didn't say one word."

Burnett knew it wouldn't have been Cooper. Then who? No one else knew, except for the people he'd talked to. Was someone outside trying to pressure him off the case?

Burnett walked back across the room to his desk. A pile of phone messages—only two of which pertained to the Norma Wilson case—awaited him. The hell with the others, Burnett thought. No matter what the top brass thought of this case, Burnett now considered it top priority. His first task this morning was to phone the U.S. headquarters of Interpol—the International Criminal Police Organization—in Washington, D.C., and have them put a trace on the European travels of Norma Wilson and her cohorts Devins and Forget. Next, he noticed that Tom McSpadden had returned his call; he dialed the Arizona number and let it ring eight times before hanging up.

Burnett opened one of the bottom drawers of the desk and pulled out a small tape recorder and a long wire attaching it to a small black rubber suction cup. He set the recorder down next to the phone, flicked a couple of switches and tested it. Then he attached the suction cup to the ear portion of the telephone receiver and dialed Devins' office number. This time he was in.

"Mr. Devins?"

"That's right."

"Bill Burnett, investigator for the District Attorney's office."

"Oh, yeah. I returned your call, but you were out. So we finally got it together."

"Right. Say, Mr. Devins, I was wondering—"

"Call me Tom."

"Tom. I was wondering if we could get together today for a few minutes. I've got a few questions that—"

"Can't do it today, Bill. Really running. Got a couple of big ones in the fire. But I've got a few minutes right now. Shoot."

"Okay. I guess you know we're investigating a missing persons report—Norma Wilson."

"I heard. Strange, real strange."

"What I'd like to know first, when was the last time you saw Mrs. Wilson?"

"Geneva. November 29, last year. I left Europe that day on Swissair, back to L.A. You can check on it. Norma was staying at the Intercontinental. Said she was going to meet an old friend, Tom McSpadden, at a town called Rolle, I think. Personally, I think there was more to it than friendship, Bill. Anyway, she also mentioned something about going to Sweden. A health spa, I think."

"Was Mrs. Wilson carrying a large amount of cash?"

"Sure was—$137,000, to be exact. Plus change. That was the whole point of the trip. Norma was trying to sell off her assets before she divorced her husband."

"She was definitely planning on divorcing Bill Wilson?"

"Definitely. She'd seen her lawyer, guy by the name of Horrigan, I think. And she wanted her will changed—wanted to write Bill out of it. In fact, she asked me to write up a will for her on the plane. Hell, I'm not a lawyer, but I gave her a rough version."

"She kept it?"

"Yeah."

"Where did Mrs. Wilson get the $137,000?"

"From the sale of her interest in the Brentwood Convalescent Hospital."

"Oh? I thought it was worth more."

"It's part of a complicated three-way deal, Bill. Tax benefits and all." There was a pause. "Look, Bill, I really want to help you here. Straight. But let me make a call to my tax lawyer first, before we go any deeper into this hospital deal, okay?"

"Sure," Burnett replied.

"Anything else?"

"Robert Forget. Know him?"

"Of course. He was with us on the trip. Norma hired him as a bodyguard—she knew she'd be carrying around cash. See, Bob works for Norma as a maintenance man in her buildings; plus, he speaks French—so she figured he'd be helpful in Montreal."

"How much did he get paid?"

"Four thousand dollars, plus expenses."

Four thousand dollars, Burnett thought; a lot of money for a maintenance man. Enough to give him ideas of getting more. "He have a gun?"

"I think so. Yeah."

"Was he with her when you left her in Geneva?"

"No. No, we went down to Tangiers, and Bob got sick. He had to fly back to the U.S."

Burnett would have to check with State Department on that. "And where did you and Mrs. Wilson go after Forget left?"

"We rented a car and drove to Casablanca. See, Norma wanted to work in some sightseeing before she returned— Malaga, Casablanca, you know. Anyway, then we flew to Zurich via Air Morocco."

"No trip to Lisbon?"

"No. Zurich. And we rented another car and, well, just drove through the countryside, admiring the sights. And then I dropped Norma off at the Intercontinental Hilton."

"Did you stay in Geneva before leaving?"

"Yeah. At a hotel on the lake. I can't remember the name right off. It'll come to me."

"What was the purpose of going to Zurich?"

"Norma wanted to open a Swiss account with the $137,000 cash she was carrying."

"And did she?"

"I assume so. I took her to the Credit Suisse in Zurich. When she came out, she didn't have the money anymore."

"Okay. Tom, do you have a power of attorney for Mrs. Wilson?"

"Well, see, there we go again. I'm going to have to get back to you on that one, Bill. Tax problem."

Burnett drew deeply on the pipe, let the sweet smoke spill out of his mouth.

"The deed conveyance was notarized in New York, right?"

"Yeah, right. See, part of the deal was in Montreal, but it's a hell of a lot easier to record the conveyance of a U.S.

instrument in the U.S. than it is in a foreign country. You record it in Canada, and there's all kinds of legal problems later."

"Some personal info, if you don't mind, Tom."

"Go ahead."

"Born in California?"

Devins laughed. "Really checking me out, huh? Well, look. I'll give you the whole story—my biography. I was born in Arkansas, July 20, 1940. Fordyce, Arkansas—real hick town. Five kids. My mom and dad were both alcoholics. We moved out to northern California in 1947, and then down here in 1950. I dropped out of school in the eighth grade and left home when I was sixteen. My folks and I didn't get along too well. And then odd jobs. I parked cars for a while at Frascati's on the strip, and then I started selling real estate and here I am."

"Thank you. And what about Forget? Do you know where this Forget is now?"

"I assume he's around here somewhere."

"We have information he lives in the state of Washington."

"I think he used to live up there. May be back there now, I don't know. But he's been here for the last year or so. Say, you really think something's happened to Norma?"

"It's possible."

"And I'm a suspect?"

"We don't even have a crime yet, Mr. Devins."

"Tom. Well, hell, I tell you what. You take a real close look at Bill Wilson."

"Yeah?"

"Yeah. The guy was a hair from being cut off, penniless. But if something happened to Norma on that trip, well, the way things stood before she left, I understand he gets the whole shooting match."

"Oh?"

"Yeah. The guy's a real clown. He met Norma; he told her he was loaded, y' know? I mean, he tells her he's rich. Anyway, they get married, and it turns out he's dead broke. And no job. A writer he says! But he never wrote anything that ever sold. The guy's a bum. A gold-digging bum . . . Hey, Jesus, look at the time. Bill, I gotta go. I really do."

"When—"

"Look, I'll call you back—soon as I get the go-ahead from my tax man. Oh, and one other thing. Bill Wilson, he did write a story once all right, but it didn't sell. Norma told me about it."

"Yeah?"

"Yeah. It was about a guy who murders his rich wife."

Chapter 5

Burnett eased his battered old Plymouth sedan back into the open space on Levering Street, one of the attractively shaded streets on the outskirts of the fashionable West L.A. suburb of Westwood Village. Inland from Santa Monica and at the foothills of Bel Air, it had originally grown as a small business district serving U.C.L.A. But as the popularity of the area grew, and that of the Sunset Strip faded, the Village became the center for chic stores, theme restaurants and first-run movie houses. And as the land values and rents skyrocketed, the college students were forced out into the cheaper suburbs of Palms, Culver City and Mar Vista, leaving Westwood largely to those who could afford to be where the action is. But Levering was one of the quieter streets, only a few blocks from where the stately old fraternity houses still stood.

Burnett walked down the sidewalk to a two-story modern building wrapped around a swimming pool with perfectly groomed tropical plants and shrubbery. He opened the gate, found "Wilson" on the directory and walked up to the second floor.

As he knocked on the door, he was wondering what Bill Wilson's reaction would be when he asked him to accompany him downtown to take a "lie detector" test. Burnett had already set up the test with Ken Scarce, the D.A.'s polygraph expert. The results of the test weren't admissible in court, of course, but they could be very helpful in determining the direction of the investigation. The test was often inconclusive and even more often unreliable. But Burnett had found that the psychological effect of the "lie box" was usually its greatest value: if the subject failed, he sometimes broke down and spilled out the story. If he passed, it often served to give him a false sense of security—leading, maybe, to a slipup later in the investigation. And if he refused to take the test, that would be a pretty good indication he was their man.

The door opened. Wilson stood in the doorway, wearing a beige cashmere sport coat over a blue polo shirt. He had been expecting the investigator; Burnett had called a half-hour earlier.

Burnett stepped into a huge living room, lavishly and expensively furnished. The floor was covered with thick, luxurious white carpeting, and elaborate crystal chandeliers hung from the ceiling. Mahogany, Burnett guessed, as he surveyed the chairs, cabinets and coffee table. Four or five magazines lay neatly in a line on the coffee table, next to a ceramic flower vase. The richly upholstered couch and matching chairs were arranged symmetrically around the table. The walls held original oil paintings, reflecting a conservatively refined taste. The room seemed almost too perfect, like something out of a *House Beautiful* ad.

Burnett noticed the magazines: *Town and Country, Holiday, Business Week, The New Yorker*. He noticed some photographs set in ornately gilded frames in the cabinet. He recognized Grace Barnum, Tom Bell, Hilda Eacho and the Ratners among the pictures; he guessed one to be of Roy Carty, and another seemed to be Diane Roth as a teenager, standing next to a boy who was probably Norman Ratner. There were no pictures of Bill Wilson, none of Bill and Norma together, no honeymoon photographs, no wedding portraits. Next to the framed pictures were a few old-fashioned ceramic figurines and another vase—like the one on the coffee table, empty of flowers.

As Burnett looked around the room, he could see no evidence of a man's having lived here. An older woman lived here: cultured, sophisticated, wealthy. There were no "masculine" touches—nothing to say that the apartment was also Bill Wilson's home.

"A drink, Mr. Burnett?"

"No, thanks. But I'd like to take a look at the bedroom, if you don't mind."

"The bedroom?"

"I'd like to get some idea of what Norma left behind— clothes, jewelry, that kind of thing."

Wilson led him into a hallway and then into another large room, also thickly carpeted in white. A king-size bed was set in the far side of the room, covered with a powder blue and white quilted and laced comforter. Another feminine room. Burnett walked over to a closet filled with hundreds of dresses, skirts, blouses and coats. Above them on shelving, dozens of hat boxes sat in orderly rows. On the floor underneath the dresses, there were about thirty pairs of shoes—most of them with slim high heels. He studied the clothing closely. The dresses tended toward more formal evening wear; the labels read "Donald Brooks," "Christian Dior," and "Yves St. Laurent." Behind another louvered door was Norma Wilson's collection of fur coats and stoles: ermine, mink, fox, and others Burnett couldn't recognize. A small fortune in furs. And she had left it behind.

He crossed over to the bureau and opened the top two drawers; they contained Norma's lingerie—white silks mostly, but also some blacks and pinks, floral patterns and lace. The next drawer was filled with fluffy angora and cashmere sweaters.

Burnett closed the drawer, then reached for the purple satin-and-velour jewelry box on top of the bureau. He opened it, and the sound of tiny chimes filled the room, playing a tune Burnett didn't recognize. The box was neatly filled with diamond bracelets, pearl earrings, heavily ornate gemstone brooches, elaborate diamond-studded gold rings. Worth a pile, Burnett thought to himself as he closed the box; at least Bill Wilson hadn't tried to hock them. Yet.

Around the room were more photographs set in frames, but again, there were none of Bill Wilson. And there was nothing to indicate he slept here.

Burnett walked past Wilson, into the hallway. He noticed an opened door leading off into another room. "Another bedroom?" he asked.

"No. That's the . . . den. Where I do my writing." Wilson seemed uncomfortable, almost nervous.

Burnett walked into the room. Across the room, against the wall, were an old heavy desk and chair. Papers and books were scattered across its top. Along the wall to the left was a huge couch. Burnett strongly suspected it was a foldout. This was the room where Bill Wilson lived. This was his tiny corner of the apartment, where he was permitted merely to sleep and work. Beyond this room, he was trespassing in Norma Wilson's world of refined memories.

Burnett turned around slowly, the dead pipe still braced in his teeth. Wilson was looking down, studying his fingers.

"The bathroom?" Burnett asked.

"Norma's?"

Burnett nodded. The two men walked down the hallway a few feet and stopped. Wilson stood aside as Burnett walked in. Everything was pink: a fluffy pink rug covered the tile floor, pink drapes hung from the huge bath-shower, and the toilet seat was covered with pink-laced padding. Burnett opened one of the drawers of a small pink dresser; at least a hundred bottles were arranged in neat rows, many of them with prescription labels. Burnett sorted through them and found the bottle with the most recent prescription date—about two months before Norma Wilson had disappeared. Burnett didn't recognize the name of the medicine, but the instructions read: "One every other day until depleted"; the bottle was still half-filled. Burnett put the bottle into the side pocket of his gray flannel coat. He closed the drawer, then opened the mirrored medicine cabinet. Again, dozens of bottles, boxes, tubes and instruments stared out at him.

"Your wife seems to have left her toothbrush and toothpaste," Burnett said quietly.

"Hm? Oh, yes, Norma has one of those little folding toothbrushes she uses for travel. They come in a kit with a little tube of toothpaste."

Burnett nodded. He looked in the shower. A plastic bottle of shampoo stood on the side of the tub, a matching bottle of conditioner next to it. He looked back to the dresser and opened the second drawer. There was a hair dryer, small enough to take with her in a weekend case. But not worth taking on a two-day trip.

"Okay," Burnett said, turning to walk out.

Wilson followed him into the front room.

"Mr. Wilson, you have any idea what your wife's estate is worth?"

"Estate? Uh, I don't know. The lawyers are trying to put it together now."

"The lawyers?"

"Well, Norma's been gone for quite a while. I think we've got to assume something's happened. In any event, I've been advised to file a civil action with the courts. A 'missing persons estate,' or something like that."

"Will there be a trustee in charge of the estate, an executor?"

"Yes, well, I understand that I will be the executor, or whatever it's called. I mean, I'm her husband."

Burnett nodded. "By the way, who's Mrs. Wilson's dentist?"

"Her . . . dentist?"

"In case she's found and . . . well, for identification purposes."

"Oh, I see. Well, Dr. Bengstrom, Dr. Bert J. Bengstrom. I'm sure he has all of her X-rays and records, whatever you'd need."

"Tell me," Burnett added, puffing on the pipe, "did Mrs. Wilson leave a will?"

"Yes, of course."

"And if she dies, who gets the estate?"

"Well, I believe I do."

"When was the will drafted?"

"Let's see . . . it was in May, last year, I believe."

"No codicils or later wills?"

"No, not that I know of."

"Now, Mr. Wilson, can you give me a written statement, say tomorrow, laying out exactly where you were for the three weeks after Mrs. Wilson left L.A.?"

Wilson shrugged. "Of course, if it will help. Look, Mr. Burnett. I get the distinct feeling that I'm a suspect in this case."

"That's right. You are a suspect."

Wilson swallowed hard, then took a deep breath and looked up at the ceiling. Hell of an actor, Burnett thought; even his face was flushing. Wilson slowly let out the breath, then looked at Burnett.

"Do I need a lawyer?" he asked.

Burnett shrugged. "You've always got a right to one."

"Am I . . . I mean, am I under arrest?"

"No," he said, taking his pipe out of his mouth and studying it briefly. "You're just a suspect. We've got a half-dozen of them."

"I don't understand."

"Mr. Wilson, it's kind of tough to arrest someone when there hasn't even been a crime shown. It still stands as a missing persons case. But there is something you could do for us."

"Sure," Wilson muttered.

"Come downtown with me and take a lie detector test."

Wilson stared at Burnett in silence for a few seconds. Burnett continued studying him, searching his face. There was fear, yes, but that was a normal reaction to a polygraph confrontation. Burnett was looking for something else, some little sign, some tiny, subconscious twitch . . .

"All right," he said. "All right, when do you want to do it?"

"How about right now?" Burnett grinned and patted him on the back. "I'll give you a lift down to the office." And now, he thought, we'll find out what's happened to Norma Wilson.

Chapter 6

 INCONCLUSIVE," DECLARED KEN SCARCE, the D.A.'s polygraph examiner. He had hooked Wilson up to the machine in the lonely, barren interrogation room at the Hall of Justice. For two hours Scarce had fired questions at Wilson, slowly leading him into the critical area—the dozen or so "key" questions that Burnett had submitted in writing. Do you know where Norma Wilson is? Is she alive? Do you know if Norma Wilson has been murdered? Did you kill your wife?

Afterward, Scarce met the anxious investigator in the next room. "I don't think he's telling the truth about everything, but I don't think he knows about any murder." He looked down at the long roll of polygraph tape with its jagged lines and shook his head. "Inconclusive."

Back in his office, Burnett peeled off his gray flannel coat—musty smelling and soaked from a sudden cloudburst—and hooked it on the old clothes tree; it hung in a limp, soggy mess. Glancing at his desk as he poured himself a cup of lukewarm coffee, he noticed that the stack of files had grown; he could no longer see the green of the desk pad. Piled neatly on top of the files were the latest phone messages and mail.

Metegka was gone, but Cooper was busily working at his desk. Suddenly, Cooper looked up.

"Bill, you'd better call downtown. Stoner."

Stoner, Burnett thought; what would the Chief want with him? "Know what it's about?"

"Wilson thing, I think. I told you, Bill. Lay off that dumb-ass case. It's nothing but a lousy domestic hassle, and we got murders and robberies piling up here. Stoner's gonna want an explanation . . . And it better be good."

Burnett sat down heavily. He was cold, wet, tired, frustrated. And now Stoner. If only he could show something to him, convince him there was more to this Wilson case than a marital squabble. But how could he? There was no body, no physical evidence of a murder, no eyewitness, no confession. And, as of now, possibly no isolated suspect. In short, there was simply no crime.

But Norma Wilson had to surface sometime. Interpol had the police network of an entire continent searching for her, and Burnett himself had approached the State Department and requested the use of their diplomatic contacts. Airlines had been tipped; immigration and customs authorities were on the alert; banks and credit card companies had been notified . . . She had to be somewhere; even if she were dead, her body . . .

Within a few seconds he was on the phone with Norma Wilson's dentist, identifying himself and requesting all of her dental records. Burnett assured him that an official letter from the D.A.'s office would follow, confirming the request. Satisfied, Dr. Bengstrom told Burnett that besides records and X-rays, he had a plaster mold of her teeth and agreed to forward it along with the rest of the material. At least if any mutilated bodies turned up, they would be able either to identify or eliminate them as being Norma Wilson's. Before hanging up, he asked the dentist when her last appointment had been. October 13, 1968, he replied. She had made a subsequent appointment for December 11, but she'd neither kept the appointment nor called ahead to cancel.

Burnett hung up, then thought about the call to Chief Stoner. Stoner would just chew him out for wasting the Bureau's time and tell him to drop the Wilson case entirely. Burnett knew he had to call him today, but decided to put it off for a few hours. Maybe, he thought, maybe something will come up.

He shuffled through the telephone messages. Most of them involved other investigations; two were nasty messages from angry prosecutors demanding to know what was happening on their cases. And there were two messages from Chief Stoner: call "at once."

Burnett pushed the stack of messages aside, then opened the cannister of Amphora mild and began stuffing tobacco into the briar. He looked down at the pile of letters. What was it about this Wilson thing? Why couldn't he let go? Was it a personal vendetta? But he had never even met Norma Wilson. He pulled out her black-and-white photograph. Her smile was warm and her eyes sparkled with merriment. She seemed kind, open-hearted. And her friends and relatives—real nice people. But no one wanted to help old Mrs. Barnum, or gray-haired Hilda Eacho, or Norma's aging piano teacher, Ben Ratner. No one cared; everyone was passing the buck—no federal crime, no L.A. jurisdiction, too busy, wait in line, fill out form 27A-1 . . . But damn it, she was missing! Something was very wrong. Burnett could almost sense that the sharks had smelled her, then circled and struck.

Burnett rubbed his eyes wearily, then began shuffling through his mail. An envelope from the Sedro Woolley Police Chief caught his eye. Quickly, he tore it open.

Robert Jerry Forget. Male, Caucasian, 5'10", 170 pounds, brown hair and blue eyes. Born July 20, 1938, in Flint Michigan. [Flint? The Mounties said Montreal.] Washington State driver's license number H751092. Address: 1612 Eighth Street, Sedro Woolley, Washington. Telephone: (206) 855-2762. Forget has been a resident of Sedro Woolley since December of 1968, as has his new wife—reportedly, a topless dancer from Los Angeles. Forget has purchased four .22 caliber revolvers and automatics since November 22, 1967; a check on the serial numbers indicates no record of their criminal use. Upon Forget's return to Washington in December, he purchased a new Dodge pickup truck, a new motorcycle and requested a building permit to construct a new home. No local criminal record.

Burnett stared at the letter. Forget had been paid $4,000 to be a bodyguard; had he been permitted to keep all of it when he left Norma Wilson prematurely in Morocco? And apparently, Forget had only the maintenance job. Would even $4,000 be enough to support a new wife, buy a new truck and motorcycle, and begin building a new house? Or had Forget suddenly come into some really big money—maybe $137,000? Had Forget faked the illness and the return to the U.S.? Knowing Norma Wilson's itinerary, did he double back and meet her in Geneva after Devins had left?

Burnett's eye caught a return address on one of the other envelopes: Federal Bureau of Investigation. This one was a fact sheet on Thomas Devins.

Thomas Devins. FBI #142921D; CII #1-480-199. True name: Thomas Edward Utter, Jr. AKA: Thomas Duran. Male, Caucasian, 5'9", 140 pounds, brown hair, brown eyes. DOB: 7-20-40; Fordyce, Arkansas. Licensed real estate broker in the State of Washington and California. Father: Thomas Edward Utter; mother: Mamie Elizabeth Ford. Criminal record: burglary (juvenile); auto burglary; carrying a concealed weapon; various traffic warrants.

The crimes had all been committed in Los Angeles. Apparently, Burnett thought, R & I and C.I.I. had slipped up—probably because of the alias.

Burnett leaned back in his chair. Norma Wilson's trusted young business adviser had a heavy criminal record, and a couple of aliases. And the Washington real estate license was interesting; was it coincidence that Norma Wilson's other companion on the trip was from Washington?

So far it looked like the gentle Norma Wilson had been traveling around Europe with $137,000 cash, a mink coat, assorted diamonds and emeralds, *and* a convicted felon, a deported alien and a jilted boyfriend. And back home there was a husband who didn't particularly want to see her come back alive.

Chapter 7

BURNETT HAD DECIDED to check out Devins' handling of Norma Wilson's business affairs and had driven in the rain downtown to the County Recorder's office in the antiquated Hall of Records, across the street from the Hall of Justice. If he could dig up something here—anything to indicate Devins or Wilson or *someone* had a solid motive for doing away with the wealthy woman—then maybe he could convince Chief Stoner that this wasn't just a runaway wife. And if Stoner okayed it, he could fly up to Sedro Woolley and try to put the screws to Forget.

Burnett lit his pipe, the rain-dampened ashes spitting and sputtering in the flames. But even if he could convince Stoner there had been a killing, who was the murderer? What if Stoner threw the obvious at him: where is L.A.'s jurisdiction? What evidence did Burnett have that the murder—if there was one—was at least planned and partially executed within the borders of Los Angeles County?

The records clerk brought out two huge books bound in faded green cloth. Burnett thanked her and carried the heavy volumes to a wide table, setting them down with a loud thud. He now had the records of all conveyances relevant to two of Norma Wilson's properties: the Brentwood Convalescent Hospital at 11616 San Vicente Boulevard, and an office building at 1017 North La Cienega Boulevard.

The first volume contained the office building grants and

encumbrances. He found the deed granting ownership to Norma Wilson. After it, however, was a grant deed in favor of Thomas Devins, dated December 13, 1967. Apparently, Norma Wilson had conveyed the office building to Devins at least a year before she disappeared. Burnett scratched down some notes on the back of an envelope he had been carrying in his coat, then turned the page.

The next conveyance indicated that Devins had sold the property to a Joseph Zukin of Malibu on March 4, 1968. Then he noticed that the transaction had involved a trade of the La Cienega office building for a house and two parcels of land in Malibu—though Zukin appeared to be the current owner of the building. What was going on? Burnett walked hastily over to the counter and asked the clerk for the Malibu records. While she was retrieving them, Burnett checked out the second of the large green volumes. There was Norma Wilson's name as the owner of the hospital. But again, immediately following was a grant deed to Thomas Devins, filed on December 12, 1968—two weeks after Devins had last seen her, three to four weeks after she had last been heard from by relatives. The deed bore the notary stamp of Maurice Oberweger, November 9, New York, exactly like the copy Bill Wilson had brought into the office.

There was another grant deed: Devins had himself conveyed the hospital property to Samuel V. Abraham, the doctor who was leasing the hospital from Norma. Burnett noticed the date of the transaction: December 17, 1968—only five days after Norma had deeded the property to him, Devins had sold it. He noticed a promissory note, secured by a deed of trust, recorded against the property at the time of the transaction: the note was in the amount of $137,000, payable to Sandra Lynne Bell. Bell had been Norma's maiden name, Burnett recalled, and $137,000 was how much she was supposed to have received from the Biafrans.

Filed after the deed of trust was an "Assignment of Deed of Trust." Sandra Lynne Bell certainly had not kept the trust deed for very long. The very same day she had transferred the trust deed to "Okuma Aikba"; Aikba's address was listed as a post office box in Beverly Hills. Biafran? Again, Burnett added to the scrawled mess on the envelope.

Then, next to the assignment document, he saw a "Power of Attorney"—a document signed by Okuma Aikba designating Thomas Devins as his attorney and granting Devins the right to sign his name and conduct any transactions involving Aikba's property that Devins desired. The paper was dated January 13, 1969. Burnett jotted down the name of the notary public—Rochelle Rishe—and made a note to contact California's office of the Secretary of State to locate her. Rochelle Rishe had also been the notary on the assignment of the trust deed.

The clerk waved to Burnett: she had brought out the Malibu books—three more heavy green volumes. Burnett's little foray to the County recorder was taking longer than expected. He pulled off his wet gray flannel coat and threw it across the table. An elderly, well-dressed gentleman three chairs away looked up with irritation. Burnett winked at him as he relit his pipe. Then he sat down and opened the first book to the marker.

The entry indicated a conveyance of one of the Malibu lots from Joseph Zukin to a Joseph M. Mears on March 4, 1968—the date of the transfer of the office building from Devins to Zukin. On March 9, Mears transferred the property to a Mamie Elizabeth Utter. There followed a conveyance of the land on October 18, 1968, from Mamie Utter to Lois B. Glantz. Burnett turned the page and there, again, was the name Thomas Devins glaring up at him. What in God's name was all this about?

On January 8, 1969, Lois B. Glantz transferred the property to Thomas Devins and Adelle Devins, his wife. A quit-claim was filed two days later by Adelle Devins, ceding all interest in the property to—Tom Devins!

Burnett looked up from the grayness of the pages. His head was beginning to swim with numbers, dates, legalese. But one thing was becoming clear: Tom Devins was one hell of a wheeler-dealer. And maybe it was all even legitimate; maybe he had had permission from Norma Wilson. Maybe.

He turned to the second Malibu book. The records showed Zukin transferring a parcel of land directly to Devins on the day of the office building sale, presumably in partial payment. Then, on March 11, 1968, the property was transferred to Mamie Elizabeth Utter. Finally, on October 18, 1968—three weeks before Norma Wilson disappeared—the land was sold by Mamie Utter to the same Lois B. Glantz. Burnett checked back to his notes; both parcels had been transferred by Mamie Utter to Lois Glantz on October 18. He looked back to the book. There were no further entries after Glantz.

Burnett opened the third book, containing the records for a Malibu lot with a house on it. Again, a deed showed transfer of title from Zukin to Devins. And again, on March 11, 1968, Devins transferred title to Mamie Elizabeth Utter. He looked back to his notes. March 11—the same day Devins had conveyed one of the unimproved lots to her, and two days after James M. Mears had conveyed the other lot to her. The next instrument in the book showed a transfer by Mamie Utter to a Lawrence Kates on October 21, 1968; this was three days after Mamie Utter had conveyed the two lots to Lois Glantz.

Burnett leaned back in the chair, his pipe billowing smoke. There had been a lot of fancy footwork—a high-priced game of musical chairs. And it was Tom Devins' name that kept reappearing.

Burnett grabbed his limp gray coat and walked out into a clearing sky. As he drove across town on the Santa Monica Freeway, headed for Westwood and an appointment with Norma Wilson's lawyer, names kept popping up in his head. Okuma Aikba—Lois Glantz—Lawrence Kates—Rochelle Rishe—Joseph Zukin—Mamie Elizabeth Utter—of course!

Burnett, one hand on the steering wheel, began sorting frantically through the disorganized bundle of papers inside his briefcase. Finally, he found what he was looking for: the F.B.I. report. He held it up, his eyes darting back and forth between the road and the letter. Thomas Devins, true name Thomas Utter. Father: Thomas Edward Utter. Mother's maiden name: Mamie Elizabeth Ford. Her married name would be Mamie Elizabeth Utter.

Burnett almost swerved off the road as he let out a high-spirited, country-boy hoot.

Chapter 8

Horrigan's secretary ushered Burnett into a medium-sized office, lined with dark wood paneling and shelves of impressively bound law books. Along one wall was a collection of odd-sized diplomas, certificates and awards, each handsomely polished and framed. Burnett's shoes sank into the carpeting. Curtains hung opulently from the window, veiling the room in a muted darkness that gave Burnett the feeling of having entered a privileged inner sanctum.

A carved oak desk separated Burnett from the impeccably dressed gentleman extending his arm toward him. Burnett took the hand, feeling the firm grip, then accepted the offered seat. He took a closer look at Philip Horrigan, Norma Wilson's high-priced attorney. Maybe thirty-five, distinguished looking, conservatively dressed, he had the lean, sophisticated look of the new Westwood lawyers.

"I'm glad you were able to come, Mr. Burnett. I, too, am quite concerned about Norma's absence. And there are some things about her dealings with Mr. Devins that you definitely should know."

"Such as?"

"As I told you before, Norma asked me to assume her legal representation when her former attorney, J. Henry Schweitzer, died. Henry had been my associate. That was last year—the beginning of last year. In fact, the first matter I handled for her concerned Mr. Devins. The La Cienega property."

"The office building?"

"Exactly. Norma came in and showed me a signed agreement to exchange real property; T. Devins Company was printed across the top. She said Devins was her real estate agent and investment adviser or some such thing—at any rate, Devins was managing the property for her, and he had acquired an option to purchase some other property of greater value. The property was apparently near Mt. Sinai Hospital, and Norma and this Devins were planning to build a medical office building there. And so, under the written agreement, she was planning to convey the La Cienega property to him—to be used in trading for the new property near Mt. Sinai.

"Devins had laid out a plan for her. He was going to trade the La Cienega building for another property and then trade that to Atlantic-Richfield." Horrigan studied Burnett for a moment, hesitated, then went on. "The Atlantic-Richfield Oil Company. They owned the Mt. Sinai property. So it was to be a three-way deal." He shrugged. "And she wanted a legal opinion.

"Well, I reviewed it. And two, maybe three days later, I advised her that the agreement had substantial defects, and major changes should be made for her own protection. As it stood, you see, the agreement theoretically could have permitted Devins to pass valid title to a B.F.P."

"B.F.P.?"

"Bona Fide Purchaser. It's a legal term. Basically, a buyer of property legally gets that property if he buys it from someone he has good reason to believe owns it. Well, the agreement between Norma and Devins wasn't a recorded instrument, and so anyone buying the property from Devins—who would have the power to sell under the agreement—would obtain good title. And Norma could be left out entirely. Theoretically, of course.

"So Norma asked me to call Devins and have the agreement modified in accordance with my advice. Mr. Burnett, I called him a number of times and always failed to reach him. Nor would he return any of my messages. Finally—I believe it was in March—Norma told me she had discussed it with Devins, and he had agreed to meet with her here in my office. She said he was agreeable to any changes. Well, Norma appeared at the appointed time, but Devins did not."

Burnett nodded slowly.

"I finally reached him by phone on March 18, 1968." He looked at Burnett. "You see, I reviewed my time sheets this morning. They are quite accurate—I keep them for billing purposes. Four-thirty P.M., March 18. We had a long talk, and I advised the man of my objections to the agreement. Surprisingly, he didn't object to any of the proposed changes; he said he would be happy to meet with Norma and with me to change the agreement.

"Well, I inquired if there had been any action taken yet under the agreement, and he said yes, that he had traded the La Cienega property for a house and two parcels of real estate—all in Malibu."

"He told you about the Malibu deals?" Burnett asked.

"Yes. You know about them?"

Burnett nodded.

"Well, I was rather concerned. As I explained, this could leave Norma in a vulnerable position. I asked him in whose name the property was traded, and he said, 'Mine, of course!' And then he said he had traded this Malibu property, in turn, for a very desirable sixty-one acres of undeveloped land in San Bernardino County."

"San Bernardino?"

"Yes. I asked the man to send me copies of all the transactions, in detail. He said he would. Well, after that, it was just a long series of phone calls from me, unanswered. Norma managed to set up two meetings, but both times Devins failed to show. He did call Norma to apologize. He'd been called out of town on some big deal, he told her.

"Well," Horrigan continued, "I wrote him a letter on May 9, with a copy to Norma, demanding copies of all paperwork involved in the transaction. Devins never replied. And I continued calling. I was becoming quite concerned—and I advised Norma that she was in a very precarious position. I told her, quite frankly, that I felt her trusted business adviser was simply stalling me.

"It was June 25th, I recall Norma was in my office. She handed me a copy of a civil complaint that had been served on her by a Dr. Abraham. It was for failure to convey the title to another piece of property of hers—the Brentwood Convalescent Hospital, not far from here. Apparently, Devins had promised to sell the hospital to Dr. Abraham. Dr. Abraham was a tenant there—he ran the Convalescent Hospital, and had been trying to buy it from Norma for years. Be that as it may, Devins had a general power of attorney from Norma. But Norma had explained to him that she had given it for a limited purpose—to trade it for a large apartment complex in the San Fernando Valley, called 'E 'Questra Inn.' The power of attorney was to be used to complete this deal only if it came through while Norma was on one of her trips outside of the country. I read the document—it was dated sometime in mid-1967, and Devins had indeed signed an acknowledgment that his powers were so limited.

"I then advised Norma that I felt Devins was, well . . . dishonest. I told her that her property—both the La Cienega office building and the Convalescent Hospital— were in jeopardy. I suggested that, on the Abraham suit, we cross-complain against Devins. But she refused. She kept saying, 'I'm sure it can all be worked out.'" He shook his head. "This Devins had some kind of power over her, some kind of . . . influence. The facts were right there, staring both of us in the face. But she couldn't bring herself to do anything against Devins. She believed in him, I suppose.

"At any rate," he continued, "the next day, June 26, Norma came in to sign the answer I had drafted to the complaint. And she said she had arranged a meeting for June 28, two-thirty, at my office. Devins would be there. Well, my secretary received a call from Devins' answering service on the 28th. Something important had come up; Mr. Devins was sorry, but he couldn't attend. Please take notes and send them to him, and he will give them his immediate attention, or something to that effect. I called the service back, but they didn't know where he was. I left a rather testy message, threatening to sue him and all that.

"Norma, of course, was sure Devins had intended to show. She said she would try to set up another meeting and she did—for July 29 at my office, four o'clock. Well, just before four, Norma called. Devins had called her to apologize—he wouldn't be able to attend the meeting."

Horrigan shuffled through some notes and records on his desk, found one and studied it for a moment. "On August 8th, I called and told Norma it was absolutely imperative to get an assignment of Devins' interest in the La Cienega property until the status of the San Bernardino property could be established. You see, I had been unable to find any such conveyance recorded in the San Bernardino County Recorder's office. At last, she agreed and picked up the assignment on August 9th. I explained to her that we had to trace the conveyance and get Devins' signature on the assignment." He looked down at another sheet of paper on his desk. "August 15th. I called her, and she said she hadn't been able to get his signature.

"So finally, I called Devins' lawyer on the phone, Lawrence Kates. I told him I wanted copies of all documents to the sequence of property transfers—or else. Well, Kates told me he only—"

"Lawrence Kates?" Burnett interrupted. He pulled the scrawled envelope from his vest, searched the jungle of notes and found it. Lawrence Kates: the Malibu house had been conveyed by Mamie Elizabeth Utter, Devins' mother, to Lawrence Kates, Devins' lawyer.

"What's wrong?" Horrigan asked, puzzled.

"The Malibu house—Devins conveyed it, through his mother, to Kates."

Horrigan stared at Burnett for a moment, then seemed to sag.

"Mr. Horrigan, do any of these other names mean anything to you? James M. Mears?"

Horrigan shook his head very slowly.

"Lois B. Glantz?"

"No."

"Okuma Aikba?"

"No."

"Rochelle Rishe?"

Horrigan shook his head. "Conveyees?" he asked.

"Yes. Except for Rishe, who was the notary in a couple of deals."

Horrigan leaned over to the telephone and pressed the intercom. "Betty, call the Secretary of State's office, notary public. Find the location of a notary by the name of . . ."

"Rochelle Rishe," Burnett said. "L.A. County commission."

"Rochelle Rishe. Los Angeles County." He released the switch.

"So what happened with Kates?"

"Kates! He told me he only represented Devins in certain transactions. But he neglected to mention he was involved in the La Cienega deal up to his ears as a participant."

"Did you ever get to meet with Devins?"

"September 19, at about noon. I was walking out the door, toward the elevator, on my way to lunch. I had no appointment with either Norma or Devins that day. And I physically bumped into a man walking into my office. It turned out to be Devins, and Norma was with him. She introduced me to him and said something like, 'I know we're early for the meeting'—something like that." Horrigan smiled. "You see, Devins had told her he had set up this appointment, but obviously he was counting on my being out to lunch—so it would look like *I* was the one breaking the appointments. Well, be that as it may, we went into my office and talked for about forty-five minutes. I demanded a demonstration of legal title to the San Bernardino property, how it was being held, in what name, and so on. And I demanded that he return the $5,000 to Abraham—Abraham had already paid that amount out of escrow for the Convalescent Hospital.

"Well, Mr. Devins is a very smooth, very personable operator. Quite a charmer. He assured me there was no problem, he had been busy, he would get the documents, and of course he would return the $5,000, and so on. I demanded copies of all the documents involved in the transfers, and he agreed. But, of course, he never gave a thing to me.

"A few days later I called Norma into the office." Horrigan glanced at the papers again. "October 22, 1968. I told her there was no question in my mind: Devins was dishonest. I told her we had to take immediate legal action to protect her property. And I told her we had to contact the District Attorney's office. I had already warned Devins that I would do that if he didn't cooperate. But Norma had mixed emotions. She was concerned about the property, of course—she wanted the whole thing straightened out—but she simply didn't want anything done to Devins."

Horrigan suddenly slammed his palm down on the desk in an uncharacteristic outburst. "Can you believe it! This charlatan is stealing her blind, and she doesn't want to do anything to hurt him!" He shook his head in disbelief.

"You didn't go to the D.A.?"

"No. The next thing, she calls and tells me Devins says everything is proceeding well on the financing—on the Mt. Sinai office building. He had been up to Washington State to get money for the project and—"

"Washington?"

"Yes. Seattle, or somewhere like that."

"Any mention of a town called Sedro Woolley?"

"No. Seattle, I think. Then, on November first, Norma came in and told me she was going to Montreal in about a week. To get the financing for the medical building. She was just pleased as punch, sure that her wonderman financier had justified all of her faith in him. She said Devins had succeeded in getting someone who was going to give her enough money to construct the building. But she had to meet them in Montreal; the investors were from Africa, from Biafra, and they were having trouble getting U.S. visas."

Burnett looked directly at him. "Then this trip out of the country—and Norma's disappearance—took place right after you threatened Devins that you were going to the district attorney?"

Horrigan nodded his head slowly.

"What happened next?" Burnett asked.

"I advised her once again that she had no title in the Mt. Sinai land—only an option in Devins' name, and an unconfirmed one at that. And I told her everything was too vague—Biafra was a notoriously poor country: people wouldn't be coming from there with money to invest. But she was adamant: Devins said everything was fine and that was that."

Horrigan massaged his eyes with two fingers, then shook his head sadly as he again studied the records in front of him. "November 4th. I called her and again advised her that the whole thing was a bad idea. November 5th. I called her one more time and begged her at least to confirm the San Bernardino property. I told her I had had a title search made, and there was nothing in either Devins' or Norma's name recorded in San Bernardino County. But all she could say was that Devins assured her everything was all right."

Horrigan looked up at Burnett with genuine concern. "I never saw or heard from her again."

"Did you ever hear from Devins again?"

"Yes. Perhaps two months ago, in early January, I believe. Bill Wilson and Tom Bell, Norma's brother, advised me she was missing. I called Devins immediately. He said there was no reason to be concerned—he felt sure he knew exactly where she was. I asked him please to get in touch with her and tell her that her family and friends were very worried. He said that would be no difficulty."

"What about that Brentwood Hospital deal?"

"I ran a title check on the property. I discovered the conveyance to Devins, of course. And the reconveyance to Dr. Abraham. After the reconveyance, Dr. Abraham dropped the lawsuit."

"Did you ever find out what Abraham paid for it?"

"Yes, $734,161. I remember thinking how ridiculous that was. Norma bought it five years ago for $950,000 and refused ever to sell it for less than a million. And the original contract between Devins and Abraham was for

$810,000. Ridiculous. But Devins ended up selling it for even less than that. It made no sense at all."

"What about the La Cienega office building? What was that worth?"

"About $600,000. Although her equity in it was $219,000. But even with—"

The buzzer on Horrigan's telephone sounded. Horrigan pressed the lever.

"Yes?"

"Mr. Horrigan, on that notary public question. Rochelle Rishe is a licensed notary public, Los Angeles County. Her commission expires August 19, 1972."

"Anything else?"

Burnett listened quietly to the slightly garbled voice over the intercom. "Yes. Miss Rishe is employed by the law firm of David Rosen and Lawrence Kates."

The two men looked up at each other with a start.

Chapter 9

Y OU'RE UP THE CREEK, ol' buddy. Stoner's been screaming for your ass. Seems you were supposed to see him yesterday —that Wilson thing." Metegka shook his head. "Man, you aren't even near a pension yet. Why are you so anxious to get canned?"

Burnett sighed deeply. "When did he call?"

"You mean, how many times?"

Burnett reached for the phone. He felt a wave of relief when Stoner's secretary told him the Chief was not in. Burnett left his name, then dialed the Arizona number of Tom McSpadden. Burnett was keeping on this case no matter what. After the third ring, a man's voice answered— this time the elusive Mr. McSpadden was in. Burnett guessed from his voice that Norma Wilson's friend was perhaps in his fifties.

"Mr. McSpadden, when was the last time you saw Norma Wilson?"

"My God, it must have been . . . oh, many years ago."

"Had you called or written her?"

"Oh, Christmas cards—that sort of thing. Though I think the last card I received from Norma was in 1967—Christmas of 1967. We sent one to her, too."

"We?"

"Well, my wife and I."

"Mr. McSpadden, how would you characterize your relationship with Mrs. Wilson?"

"Our relationship? We're . . . friends. I mean, in the past, we were very good friends. But that was years ago. Since then, I've married, and all we do is send Christmas cards."

The man's voice sounded natural, open, sincere. "What do you do, Mr. McSpadden—what's your profession?"

"I'm with the Valley National Bank here in Phoenix. I'm the foreign trade representative."

"Foreign trade? Europe—that sort of thing?"

"Well, we're really more involved with Mexico and South America."

"Have you been to Switzerland or Sweden within the past six months?"

"Oh, my, no."

"Anywhere in Europe?"

"No. Mr. Burnett, I don't mean to . . . stick my nose into an official investigation, but I get the feeling you think Norma's more than just missing."

"We don't know yet, Mr. McSpadden. So far, it's just a missing persons report."

"I see. Well, of course, it's none of my business, but . . . I would certainly appreciate it if you would let me know if . . . something turns up."

"Of course. By the way, do you know a Tom Devins?"

"Well, now, the name sounds familiar, but I can't really . . . No, no—I don't think so."

"Mr. Devins is an associate of Mrs. Wilson's. He claims that you were supposed to meet Mrs. Wilson in Switzerland in November of last year."

"What!? I certainly don't know why this man Devins would say such a thing. I haven't even talked with Norma in years."

"And so you've been in Arizona for the past six months?"

"Well . . . no. I've been to Venezuela—on business."

"Venezuela?" Burnett bit on the pipe. "Can you—do you have anything to prove that?"

"Yes. It must be somewhere around here. Just a moment."

Burnett sat at the desk, his boots propped up on a stack of files. If McSpadden could prove he was in Venezuela for the whole time, it sure pointed a finger at Devins. Apparently,

Devins didn't realize that McSpadden would have a documented alibi; he couldn't have left Venezuela without having his passport stamped. And if Devins—

"Mr. Burnett?"

"Right here."

"Yes, it was on top of the desk. We just got back from Venezuela, you see. Now, let's see . . . Yes, the date on the visa is October 4, 1968. . . . Arrival at Caracas Airport on October 5, 1968. And we stayed there until . . . well, the exit stamp was just a few weeks ago."

Burnett was busily scribbling down the dates on one of the dozens of case files piled in front of him. "Mr. McSpadden, could you do me a big favor? Could you xerox your passport—and your wife's—including the page with the visa and the entry and exit stamps, and forward the copies to me?"

"Of course."

Burnett scribbled a note to the office secretary to write to the State Department for confirmation on the passport, visa and dates.

It was narrowing down: Tom Devins, AKA Tom Utter, AKA Tom Duran. But was Bill Wilson involved? Were the two men working together? Each had a lot to gain by Norma's death. And where did this Okuma Aikba fit in? A Biafran? How did Forget fit into the picture? He reached for the phone and dialed Devins' number. A girl's voice informed him that Devins was out but would return his call as soon as possible. Sure he would. This was the fifth time in two days that Burnett had unsuccessfully tried to reach him.

He dialed the next telephone number on the list in front of him. Within a minute he was talking with a Mr. Russo, the manager of the Westwood Village branch of the Bank of America. Horrigan had given him a list of banks in which Norma had accounts, including a loan with the Bank of America. The manager didn't even have to check the records; he remembered Norma Wilson well as a valued customer. Yes, she had an outstanding loan and had never even been late in making a payment—until November of 1968. It was very unlike her, Russo added.

Burnett thanked him. Then he began the laborious task of calling each of the banks having accounts in Norma Wilson's name. City National Bank; Equitable Savings and Loan; Home Savings and Loan; Provident Savings and Loan. At each, he got the same story: no activity in the account since October of last year.

Burnett noticed a large envelope on his desk from the Post Office Department. He opened it. It was from E. L. Jacobson, deputy postal inspector in charge of the San Francisco office. The letter advised that the attached Identification Laboratory Report was being submitted in reply to Burnett's earlier request. The two postcards from Norma to Bill Wilson were enclosed, together with a few large black-and-white blow-ups of the postmarks and an "Examination Report" from Simeon Wilson, director of the Identification Laboratory.

Findings: Card Q-1 bears an incomplete postmark and cancellation embodying the legend "BARCELONA Y —PONGAN DIST—CAVI-N," and fragmentary portions of a date which may be "11 NOV 68—." Q-1 was most probably canceled at Barcelona, Spain. The postmark, however, was not completely recorded and the missing portions cannot be restored to legibility.

Card Q-2 was postmarked "TANGER PPAL 15-11-1968" (with additional legend in Arabic) and appears to have been canceled at Tangiers, Morocco, on November 15, 1968.

Specialized macrophotographs with overlays showing what can be developed of the questioned indicia are enclosed.

Burnett put the report down. The handwriting on the cards had been proven to be Norma's. Now, the place of mailing was authenticated. As of November 15, 1968, Norma Wilson had still been alive in Tangiers.

Chapter 10

Burnett leaned against the side of the elevator as it ascended, a Manila file in his hand and the black briar in his mouth. One of those high-rise bank buildings, 9465 Wilshire Boulevard housed the city's more expensive lawyers, C.P.A.s and investment consultants. One of its tenants, or possibly a client, stood in the elevator with Burnett. An immaculately attired older gentleman, he glanced at the gray-flanneled man wearing cowboy boots. Then he stared steadily at the flashing numbers above the elevator doors, trying hard, Burnett supposed, to pretend he was alone.

The doors opened and Burnett stepped out. "You hang in there," he said with a smile to the older man. Then he turned and walked down the corridor until he found a door with a sign reading "Law Offices of Kates and Rosen."

An attractive young woman sat behind a reception desk. "May I help you?"

"Bill Burnett, miss. D.A.'s office."

"Oh, yes," she said with a professional smile. "We're expecting you." She pressed a button on the telephone and announced Burnett's arrival to Mr. Kates. "Mr. Kates will be with you in a moment. Coffee?"

Burnett shook his head. "No thanks, miss."

"It shouldn't be more than a few minutes."

"You wouldn't be Miss Rishe, would you? Rochelle Rishe?"

Her smile dropped slightly, and she looked at Burnett with new interest. "Yes . . . yes, I am."

"Well, I have a few questions for you, too."

"For me?" she asked, surprised.

"If you don't mind." Burnett grinned at her. She was maybe twenty-four, twenty-five, dark hair, a good figure draped in loose-fitting clothes expensively designed to look cheap. "Let's see, you're Mr. Rosen's and Mr. Kates' secretary, right?"

"Yes. I'm a legal secretary."

Burnett handed her a copy of the power of attorney executed by Okuma Aikba for Devins. "Miss Rishe, is that your signature and your stamp?"

The woman studied the document for a moment, then looked up without expression. "Yes. Yes it is."

"Do you recall when that paper was given to you?"

"Yes, I believe so. It was last year. Mr. Thomas Devins brought it to me."

"You know Mr. Devins?"

"He has a lot of business dealings with Mr. Kates and Mr. Rosen."

"Kates—he's an attorney, isn't he?"

"Mr. Burnett, you're going to have to speak with Mr. Kates about that. I'm afraid I—"

"Okay. About this power of attorney—did this Aikba show you any I.D. before he signed the paper?"

"Well, you see . . . Mr. Aikba wasn't really here. Mr. Devins just gave me the document and asked me to notarize it."

Burnett said nothing. Casually, he lit his pipe.

"Well," she said defensively, "Mr. Devins said that this gentleman, Aikba, had signed it. I had no reason to doubt his word."

"So you notarized Aikba's signature."

"Well, yes."

"Have you ever seen this guy Aikba?"

She shook her head, avoiding his gaze. "No."

A door suddenly opened and a man stepped into the reception area, smiling. "Mr. Burnett?" he asked.

"Yeah."

"May I help you?" It seemed more of a challenge than a question.

"You may. As I mentioned on the phone, I've got a couple of questions about one of your clients, Tom Devins."

"Why don't we go into my office."

Burnett walked through the opened door. It was a typically plush lawyer's office, complete with plaques and impressive shelves of unread law books. Kates was a slender dark-haired man in his early thirties, nattily dressed in suede shoes and a fashionably conservative suit. He appeared confident, almost cocky, a smooth talker used to manipulating people.

"Have a seat, please," Kates said.

Burnett sat in the ultra-modern chrome and leather chair in front of the desk.

"Now, what can I tell you?"

"I'm kind of curious about some business deals you and Mr. Devins were involved in."

"Yes?"

"The Malibu property—the lot you got from Mamie Elizabeth Utter on October 21st last year."

"Yes. What about it?"

"What did you pay her for it?"

"Well, actually, I didn't pay her anything. I received it as payment for my investment services."

"Services to Mrs. Utter?"

"Well, now, I can't really—"

"I know Mrs. Utter is Tom Devins' mother."

Kates studied Burnett for a moment. "That's correct," he said finally. "Yes. As you know, we represent Tom in some of his real estate transactions. The lot was conveyed to me in payment for my services to Mr. Devins."

"Why did Devins deed the lot to his mother before deeding it to you?"

"I really can't say, Mr. Burnett. That's something you'll have to take up with Tom."

"Mr. Kates, you're an attorney, aren't you?"

"I am, yes. I'm a member of the California Bar. But I

don't really practice law as such. This investment business takes up all of my time."

"Mr. Rosen's your partner?"

"Yes. David's also a member of the Bar."

"How long have you known Devins?"

"Oh, since about 1963."

"And what were the services you performed for Devins in exchange for the property?"

"Well, Tom was trying to sell the property. It was a house and two lots. He told me he was having trouble selling it and asked me if I could get a loan on the property. Apparently, his own credit wasn't sufficient to obtain a loan. So we made an arrangement where he transferred title to me, and I got a loan for $56,000 for him. I was to keep $5,000 and hold an additional $2,000 for payments on the house—five payments. If, after that time, Tom hadn't sold it or hadn't given me additional funds for payments, I would get the house."

"So in return for getting him this loan on the property, he gave you the house?"

"That's correct."

"And you gave him the money from the loan you got on the property originally?"

"Of course. It was about $50,000, give or take. I gave it to him in the form of five checks, about $10,000 each."

"Okay," Burnett said. "By the way, Mr. Kates, do you know a fellow by the name of James M. Mears?"

"I take it, Mr. Burnett, that you are conducting an official investigation?"

Burnett nodded slowly.

"All right. Yes, I believe Mr. Mears was an old friend of Tom's."

It was all beginning to fit. Devins trades Norma Wilson's La Cienega building to Joseph Zukin. In exchange, Zukin transfers a Malibu lot to Devins' buddy, who then transfers it to Devins' mother. Then it goes to Lois Glantz, and finally to Devins.

"And do you know a Lois Glantz?"

"I think my partner can tell you more about that." Kates'

charm was wearing thin, his irritation beginning to show. "Lois is . . . Glantz was her maiden name. Her present name is . . . Lois Rosen."

Lois Rosen . . . David Rosen.

"She's married to David," Kates added.

"Let me see if I get this straight. Zukin conveys the Malibu house to Devins, who then conveys it to his mother. Then his mother conveys the property to you . . . in payment of fees."

"That's right."

"And one of the adjoining lots Zukin conveys to Devins' mother, who then conveys it to your partner's wife?"

Kates nodded, his face blank.

"And the third Malibu property—another adjoining lot—Zukin conveys to a buddy of Devins'. The buddy then gives it to Devins' mother, who gives it to your partner's wife. She, in turn, conveys it to Devins and his wife. That about right?"

Kates shrugged.

"Do you know an Okuma Aikba?"

Kates shook his head.

"Mr. Kates, you ended up with a house, and your partner ended up with a lot, right?"

"That is correct."

"And this was all for getting a loan for Devins on the house?"

Kates nodded.

"I'm not too bright on all these real estate deals, Mr. Kates. Can you tell me why Devins couldn't have held the property in his own name and then just conveyed some of the property directly to you and Mr. Rosen as payment?"

Kates shrugged again. "David's more familiar with the transaction. You should probably talk with him, or with Tom. My understanding was that Tom was afraid of attachments, and so he wanted the property held in other people's names."

"Attachments?"

"Yes. He said that he was being sued, or he was going to be sued, or something. And he was afraid they'd attach the property to pay for a judgment. This way, nobody would know he held the property."

"Why use Mr. Rosen's wife? Why not Mr. Rosen himself?"

"Well, we represented Tom. We were attorneys of record for Tom in some lawsuits. So David's name would be associated with Tom's."

"See, there I go again. I just don't understand these deals. *You* used your own name, didn't you?"

"Yes!" Kates said impatiently. "The house was the payment, for getting the loan. The lot, well, we were really just holding it for Tom . . . in trust, more or less. He could have had it whenever he wanted."

Kates suddenly stood up. "Mr. Burnett, of course I'd be happy to cooperate in any way I can with the District Attorney's office. But you'll have to understand, I'm very busy right now and—"

Burnett stood, smiling and holding up his hand. "Sure, sure. I understand. You're a busy man."

"If you have any other questions . . ."

"Right. I'll give you a call." He looked directly at Kates with his vaguely annoying grin. "I'll be seeing you."

Chapter 11

IT WAS NOT one of the city's showcases. 524 North Spring Street was an ancient, dilapidated brick building that had been home for the old County Farm Bureau—back when L.A. still had farms. A block to the south of the old building was the Mexican tourist trap of Olvera Street and the old Spanish mission; two blocks to the east was Chinatown, while two blocks to the west stood the Hall of Justice, home to L.A.'s central criminal courts and the District Attorney's office. The area immediately around the dirty three-story gray building was filled with empty parking lots, crumbling buildings and sleeping winos.

Burnett walked into the building, the Norma Wilson file under his arm. A desk was set up across the corridor just inside the door, blocking his way. Next to the desk stood two men, one holding a cup of coffee; each wore a shoulder holster with the butt of a gun sticking out. They looked up at him.

"That's Burnett," the younger of the two men said to the other.

The older one studied Burnett for a moment, then nodded at a door down the corridor. "He's waiting for you," he said.

Burnett walked past the desk and down the corridor. The dirty linoleum floors were peeling at the edges, and the faded green paint on the walls was cracking. On the ceiling bare bulbs offered harsh light, blocked in places by exposed pipes covered with years of solidified dust and grime.

Outside the door Burnett stopped for a moment. This was the office of George R. Stoner, chief of the D.A.'s Bureau of Investigations. The building was the headquarters for the Bureau; the first floor housed, besides Stoner's office, the S.I.D. unit—the elite Special Investigations Division. At one time it had been designated the A.O.M. unit—Alleged Official Misconduct—but the highly secret organization now handled all "sensitive" matters for the D.A.'s office, including the Sirhan Sirhan investigation. The upper two floors housed the bulk of the Bureau's more routine operations.

Burnett looked back down the corridor at the two men. The added security was because of the Sirhan trial going on at the Hall of Justice; ever since Robert Kennedy's assassination, the Bureau had been plagued with threats and reported conspiracies. He looked at the innocuous-looking door halfway down the corridor, the small numbers "113" painted on it. The mysterious room 113: only four men in the world had keys to it; only four men knew what went on behind its closed door.

Burnett knocked at the Chief's door.

"Come in." It was more a growled order than an invitation.

Stoner's was a small office. The black wall was lined with bookcases. Along another wall was a worn-out couch; the wall itself was covered with crudely aligned plaques and awards. Across the room from the couch was a door, slightly ajar, revealing a small toilet. The office had one window, offering a view of the old federal courthouse two blocks away. In the middle of the room was a plain desk, covered with paperwork and three telephones. A cigarette lay burning in a dirty metal ashtray, filled to overflowing with ashes and butts.

A heavy-set man sat behind the desk, scowling at Burnett. He looked like the cliché Irish cop: big, broad, bulky. Heavy muscles layered with fat. A thick, bulldog head mounted on an oversize fireplug body. Before he opened his mouth, you knew it was going to be a snarl. The conservative business suit he wore looked out of place on him, but the belt-mounted, snub-nosed Smith and Wesson .38 seemed a part of the man.

Chief George Stoner was in his forties, a veteran of more than twenty years with the L.A. Police Department. But Stoner hadn't been just an ordinary cop: he had been a member of the notorious "Hat Squad." The Hat Squad—so-called because the plainclothes detectives in the group always wore hats in a hatless city—consisted of the biggest, toughest, meanest detectives on the force. Assigned to the robbery-homicide detail in the "old days" before the concept of constitutional rights came into vogue, the Squad specialized in quick "field justice." One example was a rash of liquor store robberies that was plaguing L.A. in the late forties. The Squad staked out the back rooms of a few liquor stores; when an armed man would come in, they quickly gunned him down and then yelled, "Halt, police!" The epidemic of robberies came to an abrupt end.

The men of the old Hat Squad were a relic of the past—a group of tough, hard-drinking, no-nonsense gunmen with badges. One of the few survivors of the Squad, Stoner still had difficulty adjusting to the modern world of search and seizure, "Miranda" rights, and community relations.

"Get your ass in here, Burnett," he growled. "Now what's this bullshit about crapping away all your time on some old broad?"

Burnett set the file down on the desk in front of Stoner. "It's all in there, Chief."

"I don't give a goddamn where it is! It's a missing persons case, and what the fuck are you doing on it?"

"Murder."

"What?"

"Murder, Chief. Not a missing person. First degree murder."

Stoner sat back and studied the man standing in front of him. He looked to Stoner like nothing more than a lanky hayseed. "How long you been in the Bureau, Burnett?"

"Three years."

Stoner pointed down at Burnett's cowboy boots. "I heard about those shit-waders. What you wear 'em for?"

"I like them."

"All right, cowboy. What's going on?"

Burnett told him the whole story: an aging millionairess, married to a young gigolo, goes to Montreal for a three-day business trip with her handsome young business adviser and a bodyguard to meet a Biafran investor. She makes a sudden detour to Europe and never returns. The not-very-grieving husband wants her declared dead. The bodyguard starts throwing big money around after his return from Europe. The Biafran is a big unknown. But the primary suspect is the adviser: he appears to have swindled her out of a million dollars in real estate; he is also the last known person to see her alive.

Stoner leaned back, glaring at Burnett. "Now let me get all this straight! There's no body, right? And no witnesses?"

"Not yet, Chief."

"No body! But you say it's a murder!"

"That's right."

"And what if the old broad comes waltzing through that door right now?" he yelled, jabbing a finger at the door behind Burnett.

"She won't be walking through any doors, Chief."

Stoner studied Burnett in silence for a moment. Finally, he said, "You ever hear about a little thing called jurisdiction, Burnett?"

"Yes, sir."

"Okay, goddamn it! Tell me where this swell 'murder one' of yours happened! Geneva? Spain?"

Burnett shrugged. "Don't know yet."

"You don't fucking know," Stoner repeated quietly, his eyes still locked on Burnett. "Well, Burnett, let me educate you. The Swiss take a very dim view of us Americans barging in on their affairs. And the D.A. here, he takes an even dimmer view of us running all over the goddamn world solving everybody else's crimes. See, he's got this crazy feeling we got enough problems right here in L.A.— know what I mean?"

Burnett nodded.

"What the fuck you always grinning for, Burnett?" Stoner asked, "You look like a goddamn idiot!"

Burnett laughed, shrugging his shoulders.

"So you got no body, no weapon, no eyeball witness, no cop-out . . . nothing, right? And on top of that pile of shit, you tell me it happened over in Europe. That about it?"

"That's about it, Chief. But I think I can prove the murder was planned here. The body—well, it'll turn up; Interpol's on it."

"Interpol," Stoner repeated, as if it were a joke. He looked down at some papers on his desk. He thought for a moment in silence, as Burnett shifted the weight on his feet.

"It's the biggest crock I ever heard of," Stoner finally said. "But somebody thinks you got something." He looked up at the suddenly puzzled investigator. "You know Jerome Weber?"

Burnett nodded. Weber was one of the slickest, highest-priced lawyers on the West Coast. He handled only the biggest criminal cases.

"Well," Stoner continued, "the son of a bitch calls me. Seems your ol' buddy—what's his name? The old broad's adviser?"

"Devins. Tom Devins."

"Yeah. Seems Devins has hired Weber to represent him."

Burnett stared at Stoner. I'll be go to hell, he thought; he'd flushed himself a bird.

"Yeah," Stoner continued. "Weber says there's some smart-ass investigator from my office snooping around into his client's business. Some hillbilly in a cheap gray flannel suit. Says you're invading his client's privacy, and he wants us to put up or shut up: file murder charges, or leave him alone." Stoner suddenly grinned. "You must be on to something big, Burnett. Weber don't come cheap." He wrote something on a piece of paper. "I'm transferring you downtown. Clean up in Santa Monica, then report to S.I.D. Your new partner'll be George Murphy.

"Find her, Burnett. And bring me the son of a bitch that did it."

Part II

THE HUNT

Chapter 12

THE SANTA ANAS were early. The bone-dry winds were whipping down through the valleys, then accelerating through the narrow passes into shrieking crescendos. A fine, siltlike dust came with the winds, covering everything, and the heat dried the area into a wasteland of crackling brown. The brittle, scraggly chaparral that covered so much of the Southern California landscape would be blown loose and go rolling through the fields and cities like bands of aimless nomads.

The burning winds baked the earth, drying the L.A. basin into a huge pile of tinder. Then it would be only a matter of time before the fires would strike once again, feeding on the dryness and carried along on the back of the scorching Santa Anas. The Santa Monica Mountains, the Malibu coastline, the San Gabriels, the Hollywood Hills, Bel Air, the San Fernando Valley—there were few communities that could not be hit by the fires. Then, after the vegetation had been burnt off, there would be little to hold the soil when the winter rains came. Mountains would begin sliding across highways; homes would be drowned in seas of mud.

Yet, there was a strange quality, a silent sun-baked beauty to the dry and dusty winds, the scrub-covered peaks and canyons that rolled in endless waves from the high deserts into the coolness of the Pacific. The earth gave off a warm, musty smell that lulled the senses and carried the mind far back into hazy memories of childhood. One could remember lying in sprawling fields of sweet hay, or sitting by a favorite swimming hole, feet dangling in the cool water.

Burnett's mind was in just such a place as he inched along in the early morning traffic of the Hollywood Freeway. A horn honked behind him, and he jerked the car forward a few more feet. He loosened his collar, then lifted his arms to get air into his sticky shirt.

He thought of Cooper, heading about now for the Santa Monica branch office. Cooper looked at the Santa Anas differently. He'd hear the first hot winds, feel the dry electric charge in the air, and say, "Aw, shit—the Santanas again." Cooper had a theory that the "devil winds" did something to people—rubbed at something deep inside. He swore that the homicide rate skyrocketed when the hot winds were blowing. They seemed, he said, to trigger a looney switch in "the funny people"—like the full moon does to the werewolf. He claimed he had statistics from the crime reports to prove it. Burnett grinned. Well, maybe he did.

A half-hour later Burnett pulled his car into the dingy parking lot on Spring Street. He walked past a dozing wino and into the crumbling old building that housed the Bureau of Investigations, past the reception desk and down the hallway to the squad room. He hesitated for a moment, then opened the door and walked into his new home.

The room, designed originally for a conference area, was large. Like the building itself, it was old and worn out. The floor was covered with a threadbare olive green carpet, worn through to the wood in spots. On the grimy beige walls there were calendars, photos, and office memos hanging randomly; only one window let in the light.

The large room had been converted into two areas by a six-foot-high wood and glass partition. As you walked in, the right third of the room held four or five desks belonging to the investigators and deputy D.A.s in the Organized Crime Unit. The left section consisted of seven desks belonging to the detectives of the Special Investigations Division, with a small area at the back set off by another glass and wood partition. This was the office of George Murphy, lieutenant in charge of S.I.D.'s detectives. The only other door leading out of the room was a back door into the offices of John Howard, the deputy D.A. in charge of S.I.D. But the word around the office was that there would soon be a new boss; Howard was too busy prosecuting Sirhan Sirhan.

Half of the desks were empty. Burnett started toward the back office, nodding toward the four tough-looking older men at their desks. Joe Medina shrugged and went back to his papers. Medina had put in twenty years with the Los Angeles Police Department, then retired as a burglary investigator. Next to him, Al Kalkawitz simply ignored Burnett. Another L.A.P.D. detective, Kalkawitz had been signed on after retiring from the frauds section. "Chops" Lawrence, the only black cop in the section, leaned back and studied Burnett as he walked by. Tall, lanky and fiftyish, Lawrence was an ex-Bakersfield deputy sheriff. Jim Economine's desk was empty; he was another L.A.P.D. draftee, retired as a detective lieutenant. The empty desk in the far corner was Burnett's new niche. Next to it was the vacant desk of Orville Davis, the retired chief of the El Monte Police Department. The final desk, sitting next to Murphy's partitioned office, belonged to Bud Schottmiller, a retired L.A.P.D. bunko detective.

Burnett had been occupying his new desk for a week now, but he still sensed a coolness in the air, a vague resentment. Every one of these men was proud to be a part of the D.A.'s elite S.I.D. unit, and every one had at least twenty years of hard street experience behind him. There was a deep mutual respect in the unit, a feeling born of toughness, wisdom and memories. They had all been through the city's wars; they had served their time.

And now a young kid from the "country club" branch out in Santa Monica had been transferred in. A kid with no experience pounding a beat or taking down a bookie joint, a rookie wet behind the ears—in S.I.D. What strings had he pulled? Who did he know? Whose ass was he kissing?

The difference between Burnett and the others was even officially recognized. As an investigator, Burnett was civil service. The men in S.I.D. were not "investigators," but "detectives." They thought of themselves as freelance guns, hired by the D.A. because of their experience and reputation. But Burnett was just a civil servant.

"Hey." It was Schottmiller.

Burnett walked over to his desk.

"The name comes back to me now," Schottmiller said.

"The name?"

"Yeah. Devins. That case you're working."

Burnett nodded.

"Yeah," Schottmiller continued. "Adelle Devins. Know her?"

"Sure. She's the suspect's wife."

"Right. Anyway, I knew that name meant something to me. The Eddie Wein case."

Burnett looked blankly at him.

"Jesus." Schottmiller looked disgusted. "The Eddie Wein case, for chrissake! The Hollywood Rapist!"

Burnett vaguely recalled something about a front-page investigation a few years ago. Some guy who'd answer classified ads in the Hollywood papers, placed by people who were selling their clothes and personal belongings. Beautiful, starry-eyed young hopefuls from Topeka and Norfolk would come to Hollywood, strike out, and then realize that it took money to eat. And to a shark like Eddie Wein, the tersely worded ads were like a faint tinge of blood in the water, a faraway scent, across L.A.'s sea of humanity, of a damaged, helpless creature. Wein would answer an ad, gaining access to the young girl's apartment to view her pitiful merchandise. Then he would brutally rape and beat his latest victim.

"That was my case," Schottmiller said. "Anyway, this Adelle Devins—she was one of the witnesses, one of his marks."

"Adelle Devins was hit by the Hollywood Rapist?"

"Yeah. She'd won some beauty contests up in Seattle and

had a contract or something lined up in the movies. And it all falls apart when she gets here, of course—you know the story. So she puts an ad in the paper, and Eddie Wein hits her."

"I'll be damned."

"Yeah. Kind of ironic, huh? I mean, what with you tryin' to put her husband in the slammer. Eddie's up in Folsom right now." He grinned broadly. "Hell, they could end up cell mates!"

Burnett walked toward Murphy's partition. Through the glass he could see the big man sitting behind his desk. About six foot two and 240, George Murphy was, like Stoner, the gruff Irish cop. And like Stoner, Murphy had been on the Hat Squad and had become part of the legend before retiring from L.A.P.D.'s ranks. Three years ago, he'd accepted an offer from the D.A.'s office to head their S.I.D. investigations. As the head, he answered only to Stoner, chief of all investigations, and to John Howard, the prosecutor in charge of S.I.D.

Murphy looked up. "Hey, c'mon in, Bill," he yelled. "What the hell's on your alleged mind?" He grinned, flashing a set of yellowing teeth.

"I got word from Sedro Woolley," Burnett replied as he stepped into the cubicle. "From the chief of police up there—a guy named Tom Jackson."

"Yeah?"

"He's got Forget staked out. At his home, outside of town. He'll haul him in for questioning anytime we say."

"Okay," Murphy said slowly. "Guess we better go on up. See what Monsieur Forget has to say."

"I'll call the airlines."

"Naw, hold on." He jerked his head toward a pile of papers on his desk. "I got some things to clear up first. I'll let you know in a couple of days. No hurry; this guy Jackson's got him on a string. You still got the tail on Devins?"

"Him and Wilson, too." Burnett had arranged for a round-the-clock surveillance. Somehow, somewhere, Devins would make a move—and Burnett wanted to be there. So there was now one investigator in a car, keeping an eye on Devins at all times. And Burnett made sure they weren't the cars usually supplied by the D.A. that stood out like black-and-whites: tan, blue or green businessmen's coupes with blackwalls and no chrome trim—complete with a spotlight and an oversized radio antenna to alert anyone slow enough not to recognize the car otherwise.

Bill Wilson wasn't off the hook yet, either. He could still be behind his wife's disappearance, alone or in league with Devins. So he rated a tail, too.

"Anything else?" Burnett asked.

"Naw."

Burnett returned to his desk and began sifting through the piles. They had already grown as unwieldy as the ones on his old desk in Santa Monica. He'd been transferred, but he'd kept many of his old cases and been assigned new ones. The Norma Wilson investigation was only one of twenty or so cases that Burnett was responsible for, and each demanded time—time away from the road to Norma's killer. If there was a killer. If she was dead. The possibilities kept nagging at him, as they had from the beginning.

He brushed aside a memorandum he had dictated on Jean Marie Wilson, Bill Wilson's former wife. Burnett had found her living in the fiberglass world of yachts and singles bars in Marina del Rey. Reluctantly, she told Burnett that she had met Bill Wilson in Washington, D.C., in 1949 or 1950, at an Arthur Murray Dance Studio where he was teaching. They were married, and he then served three years in the Army. Following his discharge, the couple moved to Los Angeles, where they both enrolled at L.A. City College and obtained parttime jobs. In 1955 the marriage broke under the strain of Southern California's easy living, and the couple separated. It was not until 1960 that Jean Marie went to a sleazy lawyer in a shack passing for a law office in Tijuana; within a few weeks, she had a decree of divorce from the Mexican courts in Juarez. She had not seen Wilson since.

Burnett shuffled through the telephone messages, then placed them under the pinkish clay mold of Norma Wilson's teeth, sent obligingly by Norma's dentist. It had been sitting on Burnett's desk for three days now, drawing sarcastic comments from some of the detectives.

As for Devins, three times now he had agreed to meet with Burnett at the D.A.'s office to discuss Norma Wilson's disappearance. And three times he had failed to show. It was the same stall he had given to Horrigan before Norma had flown off into oblivion.

A letter on his desk caught his eye. It was from the law firm of Hess, Segall, Popkin, Guterman, Pelz and Steiner on Park Avenue in New York City.

Dear Sir:

I have your letter of June 11, which I will attempt to answer, at least in part.

    (a) To my knowledge, Sophia Loren has never undertaken cosmetic surgery in any country.

    (b) To my knowledge, Sophia Loren does not have a doctor in Sweden.

    (c) The name and address of Sophia Loren's gynecologist in Geneva, Switzerland, is Prof. Hubert de Watteville, Hôpital Cantonal, "La Maternité," Geneva, Switzerland.

Miss Loren's husband, Carlo Ponti, will be in my office in about a fortnight. If you wish, I could obtain from him an affidavit setting forth the above facts. Furthermore, if you wish to speak to him, that can also be arranged, and I would be delighted to put him in contact with you on the telephone. He will be staying at the Sherry Netherlands Hotel, and if you cannot reach him there, you can, of course, reach him through my office.

In the meantime and just out of curiosity, I would appreciate your sending me a newspaper account of the Wilson case. The one thing I cannot understand is how there can be a murder charge without a body, but I guess this is your problem, not mine. Obviously, anything that my office or Miss Loren or Mr. Ponti can do in order to assist you is at your disposal.

Yours sincerely,
Lee N. Steiner

So much for Devins' Sophia Loren story. Then he reread the lawyer's closing paragraph: "The one thing I cannot understand is how there can be a murder charge without a body . . ."

"Hey, Burnett!" Schottmiller yelled. "Line three. For you. That Devins guy."

Burnett froze. "Tom Devins?"

"Yeah. Says he wants to talk to you."

Burnett looked across at Murphy, pointing to the telephone on Murphy's desk. Murphy nodded, then put his hand carefully on the receiver; both men lifted their receivers simultaneously.

"Burnett, S.I.D."

"Is this Bill Burnett?" It was Tom Devins all right.

"Sure is. Who's this?"

"Tom Devins, Bill."

"Oh. Mr. Devins. Thanks for returning my call."

"Yes, well . . . I'm sorry about the delay, Bill. Been real busy. . . . Deals everywhere."

"I understand, Mr. Devins."

"Hey—Tom. Just call me Tom, okay?"

"Tom."

"Now, what can I do for you, Bill?"

"Well, Tom, I guess you know we're still involved in the Norma Wilson investigation. I was wondering if you could come into the office, give us a statement, something like that."

"A statement?"

"What you know about Mrs. Wilson's disappearance."

"Well, now, Bill . . . I'm still a suspect, aren't I?"

"One of many," Burnett answered. "But so far, there hasn't been any crime shown."

"Right. Well . . . Hey, Bill, straight-out: is this being taped?"

"What?"

"Taped. You got a tape recorder going? I mean, hooked up to the phone?"

Burnett looked across at Murphy listening on his receiver. "No, Tom. No tape. But my partner is listening on an extension."

There was a pause. "Why's that, Bill?" Devins asked finally.

"Saves time," Burnett answered. "I don't have to repeat everything to him later."

There was a pause again. "Right," Devins said slowly. "Okay. Look Bill, I'd like to help you. I'd also like to get this thing off my back, you understand? But, look, I just don't have the time. I mean, I'm running my ass off, one deal after another. It's crazy."

Burnett waited for a moment. "Well, can you give us what you know over the phone, now?"

There was silence again. "Sure. Sure, Bill. Be happy to. What d'ya want to know?"

"Well, for one—have you heard anything new on Mrs. Wilson's disappearance since the last time I talked with you?"

"No," Devins replied slowly. "But I tell you what, Bill. I changed my mind about the whole thing."

"Oh?"

"I mean, I think something's happened to her. It's just been too long. How many months now? And she's still gone? She's not the type to just drop out like that—she wouldn't just disappear and leave all her business affairs in the air. That's not like her. I tell you, Bill, I think maybe you guys are right. I think maybe something's happened to her."

"What do you think happened, Tom?"

"Hell, I don't know, Bill. I'm just a real estate guy. But like I told you before, I'd sure take a hard look at her husband."

"Bill Wilson?"

"Right. And I'll tell you why. Wilson didn't wait too long to hire a lawyer and get control of Norma's money."

"What do you mean?"

"I mean I was down at probate court a couple of days ago. Wilson's lawyers were trying to get control of the estate for him, trying to get him appointed trustee of the estate until she's legally declared dead, in seven years or something like that. Anyway, I opposed the whole thing in court."

"You opposed it?"

"Right. I filed papers, and I testified in court. I told the judge that Bill Wilson's valuation of her estate was a fraud. I mean, Jesus, Bill, he had her assets down as only a *tenth* of what they really are! He's trying to rip her off, rip off the estate! Anyway, I told the judge that, and I told him I personally knew of over a hundred grand in oil stocks she owned, which Wilson never listed for the court. Kareston Oil Company and Sawyer Petroleum. And I can prove it. Shoot, the son of a bitch probably sold it already! I mean, the guy's got to be living on something, right? He's sure as hell not working."

"So what happened at the hearing?"

"I don't know. I left. I think the judge made him trustee." He laughed. "There goes the estate. Anyway, take a good look at her husband, Bill. I mean, you know about the new will. And about him beating her up all the time. Hell, Norma's relatives will confirm that for you real quick."

"They already have, Tom."

"I'll tell you, Bill. This guy is a real fruitcake, you understand? I mean, besides marrying a woman old enough to be his mother, and then beating her up all the time . . . well, the guy has a real sex problem, from what Norma tells me."

"Sex problem?"

"Yeah. You know that room where he supposedly does all his writing? Sometimes he covers the walls with photographs of nude women. You know, from magazines. And not just regular nudes. Crotch shots—lots of crotch shots.

Real porno stuff. Norma'd get real angry, and they'd argue and all, but he'd just say the photos inspired him in his writing. Inspired him, that's what he'd say."

There was a pause. "Anything else you can help us with, Tom?" Burnett asked.

"Well, like I said, the guy doesn't work. He doesn't even write. Dead broke. I know Norma gave him $12,000 to pay some back taxes he owed—in 1963, I think. And . . . oh, yeah. Norma told me his first wife had been killed in a car crash. Right. A car crash. I don't know if there was any big insurance or anything like that, but . . . I mean, a pattern starts forming, you know?"

"Yeah."

"Other weird things, too. You see, Norma confided in me a lot. She was pretty lonely, I guess, what with no real husband to speak of. She told me once that Wilson had spent some time studying to be a priest, but he gave it up because he realized he was becoming homosexual." There was a pause. "Stuff like that. Real weird."

"Tom, what about this Swiss bank account?"

"Oh, that. Well, my understanding was that Norma planned to divorce Bill Wilson. Cut him off cold. So she was running around selling off her property. Liquidating. And then she wanted to dump it all in a secret foreign account so when the divorce came, he wouldn't get anything. I remember she kept telling me that I wasn't supposed to mention to him anything about these deals."

"I thought Norma was trying to finance a new construction in L.A."

"She was. But that was going to be handled carefully, you understand? Meantime, everything gets liquidated and the money goes to Switzerland."

"Tom, did you ever see Norma with any money in Europe?"

"Hell, yes. I personally handed over $133,000 to her in Montreal. For the Brentwood Convalescent deal."

"Bob Forget was with you two at the time?"

"Yeah," Devins replied quickly. "Bob was hired as a

bodyguard and interpreter. Norma wanted a bodyguard—she asked me to get one. I mean, that's a lot of money to be carrying around."

"Can you tell us exactly what happened on the trip, Tom?"

"Sure. But we've already been over all this before, haven't we, Bill? I mean, the last time we talked on the phone?"

"Yeah, but I don't always get it all down."

"Okay. Well, like I said before, we went to New York; we got the deed notarized. Then we flew to Madrid. Norma visited some relatives there—I don't know who. Then we went on to Malaga. Same thing: she visited a friend. Then we took the ferry to Tangiers—that was where Bob took sick. He had to fly back home. Well, then we flew to Zurich—"

"Anything happen in Tangiers?"

"Just a lot of sightseeing, that kind of thing."

"Okay."

"Anyway, Zurich . . . She went into a bank, I forget the name of it. Understand, I didn't actually see her do it, but I assume she dumped all the money in an account there. And the next day we rented a car and drove on to Geneva."

"Who'd you rent the car from, Tom?"

"I don't remember, to tell you the truth. Avis, Hertz—one of those big ones."

"You two drove straight to Geneva?"

"Right. And she checked in at the, uh, the Intercontinental Hotel there in Geneva. I checked in at another hotel, I forget the name right now. It'll come to me."

"Did you and Norma always stay in separate hotels?"

"No. We usually stayed in the same one—in different rooms, of course. But in Geneva, I checked into another one because . . . well, she was supposed to meet her boyfriend there. This Tom McSpadden guy, you see? So I figured I'd make myself scarce. Anyway, about four hours after checking in, I called Norma at the Intercontinental. She didn't answer. Later, I went to the hotel, but she wasn't in. So I figured they were alone somewhere, Norma and

McSpadden, and they didn't need me. Anyway, my job was finished. So I flew home the next day."

"What day was that, Tom?"

"Uh . . . November 23rd, 24th—around there."

"What airline?"

"Oh, damn, I don't recall. One of those foreign ones. Swissair maybe."

"And then you came back to the U.S.?"

"Yeah. But I went back a month ago."

"You went back to Europe?"

"Right. To look for Norma. I gotta tell you, that phone call I got from you began to worry me. Anyway, I flew over there. I went to the Intercontinental; I talked to the employees there. I checked with the airlines, taxis, train depots— everything. I even ran ads in the newspapers, offered a reward for information about her. Nothing. I called the bank, but they wouldn't give me anything. I tried to check some health spas, plastic surgeons—I think I told you about that? Her going to a spa for a face-lift? Well, anyway, I got nothing. So, finally, I flew home."

"Tom, did you contact Forget after you—"

"Aw, jeez! Bill?"

"Yeah?"

"My secretary just handed me a note. Something's come up. Real urgent, you understand?"

"Sure."

"Look, I'll call you again. As soon as I get a second free. Things are a mess here, Bill. They really are."

"Sure."

"Okay. That's a promise. First chance I get. Gotta go now, Bill. Pleasure talking to you."

Yeah, Burnett thought. A real pleasure.

Chapter 13

SEDRO WOOLLEY IS a small town of around 6,000, sprawling almost randomly about eighty miles north of Seattle and thirty miles south of the Canadian border. The inhabitants either work in the nearby steel mill or struggle to keep small, one-horse farms from reverting to the local bank. The few buildings in the business section of the town are in various stages of collapse, the weather-worn paint barely concealing the rotting timber underneath. Fully half of the structures with any signs of life are beer taverns and cocktail lounges.

Burnett braked the car outside the Sedro Woolley Police Department; the rental car slid to a halt in the mud. Burnett and Murphy buttoned their overcoats and stepped out into the blackness of a thunderstorm. Rain poured down heavily on the two men as they ran up the steps and into the building.

Inside, Burnett and Murphy shook themselves and pulled off their coats. A man in a policeman's uniform walked over to them.

"Anything I can do for you gentlemen?"

"Chief Jackson," Burnett replied, pulling out his wallet with the silver-and-gold badge inside. "He's expecting us."

The officer studied the badge for a moment, more interested in its novelty than in its authenticity. "So you're the guys from L.A." He grinned. "Sure. Chief's expectin' ya. Last door on your right."

Burnett and Murphy walked down the hall, still shaking the water from their bare heads and their clothes.

"Jesus fucking Christ," Murphy said. "Like tryin' to swim out there."

Burnett stopped at the open door. Inside sat a man behind a desk with a "Chief of Police" sign on it. The man looked up, smiled and walked around the desk with his right hand outstretched.

"You'll be the boys from L.A., right?"

Burnett nodded, shaking his hand. "Bill Burnett. My partner's George Murphy."

"Tom Jackson." Jackson was big, the lanky logger type, with huge hands that wrapped around even husky George Murphy's grip. He had a friendly manner that thinly masked the look of the toughest man in town. It occurred to Burnett that in a backwoods town of steel mill workers, the law had to come up with more than just a badge.

"Sit down, sit down," Jackson said, leading the men into his office. "You want Forget?"

Burnett nodded. "Like to have a few words with him."

"No problem. Had him under our eye since you called," he said to Burnett as he dialed the telephone. "The patrol unit cruises his house regularly—even drops in once in a while. He knows he's on the hook, and I sort of let him know I'd take it poorly if he were to leave town without—Bob? . . . Right . . . Get on down here. . . . No, goddamn it, I mean now. Haul your ass, y'understand?"

He hung up, smiled at the two men again. "He'll be here in ten minutes, lives just the other side of town."

"Chief, what's your picture of Forget?"

Jackson shrugged. "He's an asshole."

Murphy laughed. "Anything specific?"

"He's just a smart-ass young punk. Runs around with a bunch of hoods. I know he's into something around here up to his ears, but I haven't tagged him with anything yet."

"Like what?" Burnett asked.

"Guns," Jackson replied. "The son of a bitch buys guns all over the state, but he never seems to have more than two or three at his house. And he gets a steady stream of late-night visitors, all hours. I figure he's running guns into

Canada and then to . . ." He shrugged. "Asia, Africa—who knows?"

Burnett pulled out two photographs, one of Devins, the other of Bill Wilson. He put them on the desk in front of Jackson. "Ever see either of these men?"

Jackson shook his head slowly, studying the photos. "Nope."

"Okay. Chief, do you happen to have a quiet room where we can talk to Mr. Forget without being disturbed?"

"You bet. Down in the basement. Can't hear a thing from outside." His teeth flashed. "We use it for interrogation."

Burnett started the tape recorder hidden in his briefcase, then closed the cover and set it carefully on the table in the damp subterranean room. Murphy sat across the table from Burnett, leaving the chair at the head of the table empty.

The door opened and a darkly good-looking young man in his early twenties walked in. He was about five feet ten, solidly built, with bushy brown hair and blue-green eyes. Marring the rugged features were a broken nose and a scar running across his jaw. "You Burnett?" he asked in a low voice.

"Naw," Murphy said. "Come on in, close the door, grab that chair. That's Burnett. I'm Murphy."

Forget pulled off a soaking wet tanker's jacket. Underneath he wore only a dirty white T-shirt, stretched tightly over a muscular physique. Levi jeans were equally tight and hardly required the broad black leather belt he also wore. Muddy working boots completed the picture.

"Sit down," Burnett said quietly as he began lighting his pipe. "Aren't you a little cold in that T-shirt?"

Forget shrugged. Murphy kicked the door shut, and for a split second panic flashed in Forget's eyes.

"We're from the District Attorney's office in L.A.," Burnett said.

"Yeah," Forget said, "I heard you guys was coming up." He grinned slightly. "I been expecting you."

Burnett blinked, glancing quickly at Murphy. How the hell had Forget known they were coming up? He knew

Jackson hadn't told him. And there couldn't be more than a half-dozen men, all in S.I.D., who knew of the trip. Was Forget bluffing?

"How's that?" Burnett asked casually.

"I heard."

"When?"

He shrugged again. "Week ago."

"Who told you?"

Forget grinned, shaking his head. A real smart-ass, Burnett thought. If he had really known, he would have done better not to have tipped the two men off to the fact. Give himself an edge. But he just had to flaunt his one ace in a bad hand.

"Bob," Burnett said, "before we go any further, I'd like to advise you of your constitutional rights. You have the right to remain silent. Anything that—"

"Sounds like the movies," Forget interrupted.

"Anything you say can and will be used against you in a court of law. You have a right to an attorney, and if you don't have one, we'll try to get one for you. You understand these rights?"

"Yeah."

"You still want to talk to us?"

"Sure. I got nothing to hide," Forget replied with a slight suggestion of a French accent. "Go ahead; I'll play ball."

"Okay. Do you know Tom Devins?"

"Sure. I known Tom since about 1960 or so. Just before I went back to Canada and got a permanent resident visa."

"And do you know Bill Wilson?"

"That's Norma Wilson's husband, right? Naw, I only know his name."

"You know Norma Wilson then?"

"Sure. Real good. Way back, I started working for her, in her building, right? I did odd jobs—carpentry, painting, like that. So I'd run into her all the time. A nice lady."

"When did you start working for her?"

"I guess 1965 or somewhere around there."

"Who first introduced you to her?"

"Tom."

113

"What was the relationship between Tom Devins and Norma Wilson, if you know?"

"Well, Tom's a schemer, you know? One of those real estate guys—big deals and all. All the time, wheelin' and dealin'. Anyway, she's worth a pile of money. Tom told me she was worth ten million bucks. Hell, she looked pretty impressive to me—always wearing furs and diamonds and all. Anyway, the relationship is, well, she's a rich lady with a lot of money to put into real estate, and he's a wheeler-dealer, and she thinks he's real smart." He grinned. "I think she kind of dug Tom, being young and all, and good-looking, you know? But, I mean, it was still business, all business. She had a lot of faith in him."

"Were you aware of the relationship between Norma Wilson and her husband, Bill Wilson?"

"Well, only what I heard from Tom. She'd tell everything to Tom. He was kind of her . . ."

"Confidant."

"Right. Anyway, they were pretty close. And he says she was always cryin', you know? Her old man, Bill Wilson, he was beating her up all the time. And he was a whole lot younger than her, but he'd really beat the crap outa her over and over. So, anyway, one time she's cryin', and she tells Tom that she's leaving her husband. And Tom tells me the guy's a phony. He was supposed to have money when he married her, but he didn't have a dime. He was a hustler, is all. And he was always bad-mouthing me and Tom to her, running us down, you know? So, anyway, she says she's going to divorce him. So I guess he's the guy you should be lookin' at real hard."

"Looking at for what?"

"Well, investigating."

"For what?" Burnett persisted.

"Norma. She's gone, right?"

"Who told you Norma Wilson was missing?"

Forget shrugged.

"Okay, when was the last time you saw Norma Wilson?"

"The last time I saw her, Tom and I—no, I was getting on the plane out of Tangiers, and Tom and Norma were there, seeing me off. See, I was hired—I mean, Tom and Norma hired me—as a bodyguard. Mainly because I speak French. I was born and raised in Montreal. And I can speak some Spanish. So I was the interpreter, too."

"Why did she need a bodyguard?"

"I don't know. Some big real estate deal in Europe. They didn't tell me anything about it, but I guess she was carrying a whole lot of money. Anyway, Tom calls me up and asks me do I want to make five grand, and I says, hell yes. I figure some remodeling on a building, and I need the money, things are slow, but he says we're going to Europe."

"When was this?"

"Oh, last year. October, November. Something like that."

"You were living here?"

"Right. He calls me up here. And he says to get my passport and get on down to L.A. right away 'cause we leave in a couple days. And I figure five grand's a lot of money just to go with her on a trip to Europe, bodyguard or no. But I want something up front, so Tom wires me a thousand bucks, just like that! So I paid off some bills and told my wife I'd be back in a few days and flew on down to L.A."

"What did Devins tell you there?"

"He says we'll be gone a couple of weeks, and we got to fly up to Montreal today, right away, and Norma's gonna meet us there. See, I don't even have a passport then, and I gotta get one in Ottawa. So we fly to Montreal, get a car and drive to Ottawa, and I get a passport. Then we drive back. And we meet Norma at the hotel at the Dorval Airport in Montreal. Next day, we all fly to New York."

"What happened in New York?" Forget was a nonstop talker, Burnett was thinking. But he was beginning to realize that there was a lot of fear behind the bravado flow of words.

"Well, I don't know. They signed some papers, some real estate shit. They found a—whattya call 'em—a notary public. In one of the drugstores at the airport. And, anyway, then we get a plane for Madrid. And so then we're in Madrid. And we're going around, sightseeing and all, and I'm impressing her with my translating, and when people come around, I look tough and all so I look like a body-guard, and all. Playing the part, you know? So, anyway, from there to Tangiers, and the same shit all over again. Telephone calls, sightseeing, shopping, and me speaking French and looking tough.

"Well, about this time I'm beginning to wonder what the hell's going on, you know? I mean, I didn't like it over there; I wanted to come home. There was an awful lot of money they were talking about, and I'm thinking maybe I'm in it deeper than I know."

"Did you get paid any more than the thousand?"

"Yeah. Norma gave me $1500 more in Montreal, at the airport. Anyway, I finally decided, screw it, I don't need all this—and I kinda felt funny about the whole thing anyway. Besides, I ate the goddamn shish kebob over there and got some kind of stomach poisoning, and I got sicker than hell. And the place makes me nervous, you know? I mean, over there, everything's so communist. The way people talk, and the way they think. And they're all down on Americans. So I told Tom and Norma, I told them my wife's sick and so I said, listen, I wanna go home.

"And so anyway, they said they didn't need me anymore. So they took me to the airport, and I took the plane to Paris, and walked around Paris for a while, and then flew back home. See, I wanted to get home, but I also wanted to see Paris. So I spent a couple of days there, one night in a bar, and got clipped for a couple of hundred bucks there by these broads, and I didn't even get laid. So I said, fuck it, and I flew home. Well, to L.A., then home.

"And I even got in trouble in L.A., at customs. I had on this antelope suede jacket and a Rolex watch and shit, they wanted me to prove where I got it, and I didn't declare it and all. And a gold ring. And so, anyway, it ends up costing me $233.44 taxes and penalties. And then they really searched my luggage. And they found some seeds in my jacket, the suede jacket. It was from some green fruit I had in Morocco, I don't know, and some of the seeds ended up in my jacket pocket. So the customs guy looks at the seeds, and he says, 'Oh, you've been to Morocco,' and he says, 'Did you bring any hash in with you?' And, hell, I didn't, so I say no. Anyway, I finally got out of there, and I stayed overnight in L.A., went to a couple of topless bars, then took a plane back to Seattle. And, uh . . ." Forget shrugged. "That's about it."

A gold mine, Burnett was thinking; if he was going to break the case, it would be through Forget. A big ego, a lady's man, but a cheap punk with no brains. And he was scared. Scared to death. The weak link in the chain. Forget would crack, given time.

"How did you know we were coming up, Bob?" Burnett puffed on the pipe. "Did Devins tell you?"

Forget looked down at his hands. "Yeah, Tom called me last week. No big deal. Says you guys were gonna come up and ask me questions. He says Norma's missing, you know, and you guys think he's a suspect, or some shit like that. But then after a while I started thinking. I mean, Tom wouldn't never kill Norma. But all this stuff about the trip kinda ties me in, you know? Makes me look kinda bad. 'Cause I was over there with her, before she disappeared, right? And she was, well, coming on to me all the time, you know?"

"Coming on to you?"

"Well, shit, Norma's . . . she's pretty healthy, know what I mean? And she's always giving me the eye, and coming on, and all. But, hell, I never did nothing with her. I mean, she's a good-looking lady, pretty good body and all, but rich old broads aren't my style, I guess."

"Bob, our records show that you and Norma Wilson were registered in the same room at the Rif Hotel in Tangiers."

"What?" Forget shook his head. "Naw, that's not my style. Your records are wrong. I never slept with her. You can't pin that on me. No way. But she was looking, all over the place. Me, Tom, other young guys. Hell, it's like she was in heat half the time. So I figure she's probably over there with some young cat, you know, some young guy, screwin' her brains out someplace and doesn't want nobody to know where she's at.

"Hey, look, no matter what you think, I'm clean. 'Cause I got one thing that saves me. I got a passport. And I got dates on that passport. And they show when I left Tangiers and when I got back to L.A. And there were plenty of people around the airport that saw Norma alive the day I left. Plenty of people. And they'll remember. She stood out like a sore thumb—mink coat, and diamonds and all. They'll remember."

Forget's eyes were darting nervously back and forth between Burnett and Murphy.

"Okay, Bob," Burnett said quietly. "What airline did you fly to Montreal?"

"Huh?" Forget looked up, almost startled. "Uh, United. Yeah, United."

"Who bought the tickets?"

"Tom did."

"What kind of a car did you rent in Montreal?"

"Mustang."

"From who?"

"Avis. Or Hertz. I forget. Avis or Hertz."

"Who bought the tickets in Montreal?"

"Tom."

"For all three of you?"

"Yeah."

"Round trip to Madrid?"

"I guess so. I don't know, really."

"What's the name of the notary public in New York?"

"Oh, shit, I don't know. But I tell you, that's when I first started coming apart, know what I mean? I mean, I'm standing around acting like a bodyguard, 'cause I'm supposed to be a bodyguard! Nobody's telling me nothing, and I'm nervous, you know? I mean, maybe there's a pile of money, and somebody's going to tap me on the head."

"Did you recognize the papers they were signing in New York?"

"Naw, I didn't know what they were. All that real estate shit. I don't understand any of it. See, I'm just thinking five grand's a lot of money, and why're they paying me, 'cause I'm not really a bodyguard, you know? And I'm—"

"How long were you in Tangiers?"

"A couple of days, I think. We rented a car. Norma

wanted to drive up the coast to Marrakesh or something. But the winds got real strong, and the sand and all, and we had to go back. I mean, it was—"

"How did you get to Tangiers from Madrid?"

"Flew. Yeah, we flew."

"What airline?"

"Airline? Oh, some Spanish airline. Mickey Mouse outfit, you know. Wait a minute, I forgot—we flew down to Malaga. We looked around Malaga, that's right, and then we took a ferry over to Tangiers. Shit, I was getting worried about what I was doing there. Once, I asked Tom right out, what am I doing? And he says, 'Don't worry about it. Nothing to worry about. It's just good to have you around.'"

"What did you do in Tangiers?"

"The same thing as Malaga and Madrid. Sightseeing, shopping, that kind of shit. Visited the Casbah, and all that."

"What about the rest of your five grand?"

"She paid me. Norma paid me, in Tangiers. Gave me $2500. Five grand total."

"And you didn't have to finish the job."

Forget shrugged. "They both said they didn't need me anymore."

"Did you take a gun to Europe, Bob?"

Forget glanced quickly at Burnett, then at Murphy. "Yeah. Sure I did. I was a bodyguard."

"What kind?"

".380 Star automatic."

"No trouble at customs?"

Forget shook his head. "Naw. Tom said there wouldn't be no trouble, and there wasn't. Then when—"

"Where is it?"

"Huh?"

"Where's the gun now?"

"Uh, I don't have it. I don't know where it is. See, I had it, but then I lost it. In Malaga. It was stolen from my room."

"When's the next time you heard from Devins after returning to the States?"

"I guess it was . . . well, he called me from Switzerland about five days after I left. Just wanted to see if I got home okay and everything and if I'm over my sickness, 'cause I told them I was sick in Tangiers. And he said he'd be back in a day or two, and he'd give me a call when he got back, you know?

"Anyway, next time I talk to him was a couple of months later. See, he'd offered me a loan, to build my house with. Five grand. So I called him and asked for the loan, and he says sure, so I flew down. And we went to his bank, Charter Bank of London, or something like that, and he gave me the five grand."

He'd been rehearsed well, Burnett thought. All the tracks covered, all the possible signs explained away.

"Do you have the note?"

"The note?"

"The paper you signed for the loan. Do you have a copy?"

"Sure. It's at home."

"What were the terms? The interest rate, payments, due date?"

"It was . . . seven percent, something like that. I'm not real good at figures. There wasn't any due date. I mean, it was all pretty friendly, and he just wanted the money back when I got the house built and then sold it for a profit."

"Everything you've told us so far is true, isn't it, Bob?" Burnett began relighting his pipe again, his eyes playing on Forget.

"Sure, of course it is."

"So you're willing to take a polygraph exam?"

"Polygraph. What's that?"

"A lie detector."

"Lie detector. Well, see, I was told not to fool around with that stuff because that could be unreliable, right? Could turn out one way, could turn out another. This is one point where I'd really like to talk to a lawyer. Because I don't know. I really don't. I never been involved in heavy stuff like this, you know? I mean, I don't got a fucking thing to worry about. But I seen movies, and I'm a nervous guy sometimes; I don't like to be questioned. See, tell you the truth, I'm nervous right now. The reason I'm talking to you guys now is 'cause I want to get this shit off my back, you know. And—"

"Did Tom tell you what he and Norma did after you left them in Europe?"

"He said she stayed. He came back and she stayed. I think he said they went to Switzerland. Look, I know you guys think he's up to something, but I don't think so. He told me that Bill Wilson gave you that idea. And Tom, he was really pissed when he heard that. He was trying to figure some way he could sue Wilson for coming up with shit like that. He says—"

"Devins ever mention Biafra?"

Forget stared at Burnett for a moment, then down at the ring on his hand.

"You know where Biafra is?" Burnett asked.

Forget nodded. "It's someplace in Africa. You guys know about that, huh? Yeah, well, that was a little deal I was supposed to go on with Tom, some stupid fucking mission, you know? I mean, after he got back from Europe, a few weeks later, he lays this crazy idea out. But Tom, he's a hustler, you know? I mean, he can make it sound real reasonable, you know? I mean, he wants to do this mercenary shit, hired gun and all.

"Anyway, I guess there's a lot of oil over there, in Biafra. And Tom knows some people at Richfield in L.A. And I guess when the new government took over in Biafra, they kicked out the American oil companies. Anyway, this is what Tom tells me. They just kicked 'em out. So Tom wants to get into Biafra, make some connections, make a deal with the oil companies to get them back in. I don't really understand the whole deal. Something about knocking off a president over there, some shit like that. But I said no way."

"You ever meet anybody from Biafra?" Murphy asked.

"No."

"The name Okuma Aikba—does it mean anything to you?"

Forget shook his head.

"Did you ever go out on a private yacht with Norma while you were in Spain?"

"Shit no. Only that ferryboat."

Murphy stared at him. "How many guns do you own, Forget?"

"Right now? Four. Two rifles, two pistols. Two twenty-twos, two forty-four magnums."

Murphy pressed him. "How many guns have you bought in the past year?"

Forget shrugged. "I don't know . . . maybe a few. What's that got to do with anything?"

Burnett looked into his pipe bowl, playing with the cinders. "What do you think happened to Norma, Bob?"

"What do you mean what do I think happened to her? Shit, I told you—I don't know! She's probably shacked up with some young stud someplace over in Europe."

Murphy leaned toward him. "You were with Norma constantly until you left Tangiers?"

"Pretty much, I guess. Yeah, most of the time."

"And you never saw Norma Wilson or Tom Devins meet anyone in Montreal or in Europe?"

Forget shook his head. "Nope. Of course, she could have—I wasn't with her *all* the time. But I never saw her meet anyone."

Burnett pushed his chair back and slowly rose to his feet. "Anything else you want to tell us, Bob?"

"Naw, except that nothing happened. You guys are making a big deal out of it, and I know why. I know what you guys are thinking, but nothing happened; it was no big deal."

"What are we thinking, Bob?" Burnett asked.

"That I was fucking hired to kill Norma, something like that."

"Devins tell you that?"

"No, but it's pretty obvious, isn't it? I mean, me with a gun, and getting a lot of money, and her disappearing and all."

"What did Devins tell you?"

"He said you guys had a writ of probable murder, or some shit like that."

Burnett smiled. "We're just trying to find Norma, Bob."

"Yeah, well, and I'm trying to help. That's why I'm sitting here, talking to you. Tom told me not to sweat it. He said just to tell the truth. Tell you guys the truth, everything that happened. So that's what I'm doing."

"Okay," Burnett said. He opened the briefcase, switched off the recorder.

"What the fuck's that?"

"Tape recorder, Bob."

Forget shook his head. "Shit, man."

Burnett picked up the briefcase and started walking toward the door. He hesitated for a moment, then turned around. "Bob, have you ever heard of the little green room?"

"The what?"

"The little green room. You've been lying to me, Bob. Just about everything you've told me is a lie."

"Hey, man, wait a minute—"

"Norma Wilson's dead. Murdered. And I think you're in it up to your ass." He pulled out his pipe, tamped studiously at the ashes. "The little green room is in San Quentin. It's where they strap you in and drop the gas pellets, Bob. And I'm going to do everything I can to put you there."

Chapter 14

IT WAS TIME to meet Tom Devins.

Through his sources at the telephone company, Burnett had located Devins' home in the hills above Encino. Situated in the wealthy area of secluded corrals and tennis courts, it was a large, rambling ranch-style house nestled in an acre of trees and dense shrubbery. It was set well off the meandering country road that rose into the hills above the bustle of the Valley and approachable only by a long winding gravel driveway. Most of the house was hidden by thick vegetation, and the entire grounds were surrounded by a chain link fence. From behind the house, on a bluff a few hundred yards above, some surveillance could be conducted with binoculars. The swimming pool was visible next to the patio, but the windows and sliding glass door leading into the house were invariably covered with drapes or curtains.

Burnett had wanted the house staked out. He wanted Devins' movements traced, wanted to know who he was meeting, when and where. He wanted to establish patterns for the man, then note deviations from those patterns. If there was a clandestine meeting, a big bank withdrawal, a visit to a travel agent, he wanted to know immediately. And if Devins caught onto the surveillance, there was value in that, too: the constant pressure might just cause the young wheeler-dealer to crack.

So Burnett had gotten authorization for a surveillance team to be assigned to him. Ron Moss and John Goche, investigators from the D.A.'s Organized Crime Intelligence Division, were now trading watches on the house. These men were the D.A.'s experts in surveillance work. They drove special cars with racing engines and heavy-duty suspension, and carried sensitive taping equipment, electronic monitoring units, telephoto cameras and night binoculars. If Devins moved, Burnett would immediately know by radio.

But it wasn't enough. Burnett wanted to meet the man in person. He wanted to get inside the house, see where he lived, study the world in which he operated. And inside the house, there might be a clue—some indication of Devins' guilt. But a search warrant would be impossible to justify; there was simply not enough evidence yet to show Devins was involved in a crime, or even that a crime had taken place.

Then Burnett remembered that Devins was having a room addition constructed, extending from the back of the house out onto the patio. So he dropped by the Valley office of the L.A. City Building Department. Was there a building permit on file for a Thomas Devins? The clerk sorted through the massive paperwork and finally located the card: yes, an application for a private dwelling annex.

Then he corraled one of the building inspectors. He identified himself, showed the man the building permit, and asked if the project had been inspected yet. The inspector checked some more files, then informed Burnett that an inspection was due to be made in the next few days. Burnett had then pulled him aside and had a short talk.

Now he sat parked on Ventura Boulevard, wearing slacks, a sport shirt, and an L.A. city building inspector's I.D. He checked in the rearview mirror, then saw the plain white Rambler he was waiting for pull up behind him. Burnett quickly walked over to the passenger's side and got in. "How's it going?" he said with a grin to the man behind the wheel.

The building inspector was a middle-aged, heavyset man, with a long-sleeved white shirt and a plain green tie. He swallowed, then looked nervously in his side mirror. "Fine,

Mr. Burnett. Just fine." Tiny beads of sweat had formed on his forehead.

The two men drove out on Ventura Boulevard, then turned up on White Oak. Within minutes they had left the snarling traffic of the Valley's floor and were in the tree-lined roads of the foothills.

The building inspector pointed to a gravel road up ahead. "That's the one. The Devins house."

Burnett nodded. "Like I say, I'll just tag along, quietlike. You just tell Mr. Devins that I'm a new inspector, a trainee. Get him out in the backyard for a couple of minutes, out by the addition." He looked over at the man and winked. "I'll take care of the rest."

"You, uh, you sure this is . . . legal?"

"Absolutely," Burnett replied. If it blew up, he thought, the fall would be his own. Best to keep the poor guy in the dark for his own protection.

The car pulled to a crunching stop outside the garage. The two men got out and walked to the door. A woman in white slacks and a yellow print blouse stood behind the screen door. She was about thirty, slender, with sun-bleached hair and brown eyes. She was pretty, in a fresh all-American way, a prettiness that was reenforced by a trim athletic figure. But there was a strange kind of sadness in her eyes, a look of fatigue. The honey-colored hair was dull and slightly disarranged, strands falling across her face as if she no longer cared. Burnett had seen her picture before. He recognized the hesitant smile of the former beauty queen from Seattle. This was the woman who had fallen victim to the rapist, Eddie Wein.

"Yes?" she asked.

The inspector looked back at Burnett for a second. "Uh, building and safety, ma'am. Here to inspect the addition."

"Oh, sure," she said, opening the screen door. "Come on in."

The two men stepped into the darkness of the house. All of the windows were covered with curtains, and drapes sealed off what appeared to be the sliding glass door leading to the patio. It was like stepping from the brightness of the noonday sun into the depths of a cave. Burnett blinked, waiting for his eyes to adjust to the darkness.

A voice yelled out, "Who is it?"

"Building inspector, Tom," she yelled back.

A figure stepped from out of the darkness, walking slowly toward the two men. Burnett felt his heart beating faster; he realized that he was now meeting Norma Wilson's murderer for the first time.

"Tom Devins," he said softly to Burnett.

Burnett accepted the handshake, introducing himself as Frank Haltmeyer. As the inspector began writing on his clipboard and talking about the room addition, Burnett studied the man more closely, Yes, he thought, this was a different man from the one who lived in his mind. Physically, he was the same: medium height, trim physique, an impish grin, laughing eyes, boyishly handsome—with a pipe in his mouth, he would have been a dead ringer for Hugh Hefner, the *Playboy* kingpin. And yet he radiated an almost overpowering intelligence.

Devins stood a few feet from Burnett, perfectly relaxed, talking with the building inspector. A cocktail glass was in his hand, scotch on ice, or perhaps bourbon. He was wearing bright green slacks, Italian-looking cordovan shoes, and a loud green, white, and gold Hawaiian sport shirt unbuttoned down his chest. His hair was medium length and immaculately combed, his finely angular jaw clean shaven. His eyes gave the effect of intensity, of deep concentration and confidence.

Burnett glanced around the room, noticed magazines lying on the floor, an empty glass, an encrusted fork, a pair of socks. Somehow, the neglected condition of the living room didn't fit the perfectly groomed and composed figure of the man who stood before him.

Burnett thanked Devins for an offer of a drink but declined. Controlled. Devins seemed controlled, and in control of all around him. Suddenly, Burnett could see how Norma Wilson could have continued believing in him even after Horrigan's harsh warnings. This man had an aura about him, a charm. He exuded a sense of . . . what? Trust? Goodness? No, it was more like innocence, but with a dynamic quality—a strange mixture of dynamic masculinity and the mischievous little boy. That was a powerful combination to many women.

Burnett realized he was staring at Devins. And Devins was looking back, smiling.

"Beautiful place," Burnett said quickly, as he began lighting his pipe. "Uh, excuse me, mind if I smoke?"

"Sure, feel free," Devins answered. "So you're a little new at it, huh?"

"New?"

"Inspections."

"Oh, yeah. Finishing up my training period. Next week, I go out on my own."

Devins nodded; his eyes, still on Burnett, reflected a vague uncertainty. "Well," he said, "I don't want to keep you guys too long. It's out here." He turned and walked toward the sliding glass door in the rear.

Adelle and the building inspector followed him. Devins pulled back the drapes, slid the glass open, then looked back at Burnett still standing in the room. Burnett was pretending to look up at the beams in the ceiling.

"You coming?" Devins asked.

"Hey, this is really nice work," Burnett answered. "Who built this?"

"Stahl Brothers," Devins answered.

Burnett nodded approvingly. "Mind if I look around the house? They just don't build them like this anymore."

Devins said nothing for a moment, then shrugged. "Sure, be my guest." Then he turned and walked out to the patio, joining his wife and the inspector.

Burnett knew he had two minutes, maybe three at the outside. He looked around the living room. In the dimness, he could barely see disheveled clothing lying across the expensive furniture marred with food stains and glass rings. Papers lay sprawled across a coffee table and on the floor;

they appeared to be contracts and various forms for real estate deals. He glanced at the bookcase, with its jumble of cheap paperbacks and record albums, then walked quickly into the hallway.

The first room on the right was closed. Softly, he opened it. A guest bedroom, apparently unused. He walked down the hallway to an open doorway. The master bedroom. The bed was unmade, and clothing was strewn about the floor. Adelle was not a fastidious housekeeper. He walked to the window, peering out onto the patio. Devins was pointing toward the addition, discussing something with the inspector. The inspector was nervously glancing back at the house. Adelle was standing dutifully by, seemingly bored.

Burnett stepped back, then walked over to a painting on the wall and looked behind it. No wall safe there.

He stepped out into the hallway. At least, there didn't appear to be any luggage packed. But where was the den? Burnett was looking for something—anything—that might give him a clue to Norma's disappearance: papers indicating a Swiss bank account, phone books, telephone recording equipment, jewelry, a mink coat, photographs, a passport . . .

He stepped through the door at the end of the hall. Devins' den. More real estate papers were scattered across a desk and on a small sofa. Quietly, Burnett tried the top drawer. Locked. He checked behind a wall-mounted diploma, then behind a framed photograph. No wall safes. A small bookcase against the wall. Nothing. Then a bright object among the papers on the desk caught his eye.

There were three unused bullets lying on the desk. He looked quickly around again. No gun. Then he picked up one of the cartridges. Nine millimeter. The only popular use for the short nine millimeter load was the Luger or the Browning automatic pistol. Burnett put the cartridge down carefully.

Time was up. Quickly, he walked out of the den, down the hallway and out into the living room. He glanced into the kitchen. Expensive tile, wood and stainless steel. Modern built-ins. With two or three days of dirty dishes in the sink and on the stove. And, again, the darkness of shuttered windows.

He stepped out the front door, then walked around the side of the house and into the backyard. Devins would conclude he had been studying the outside structures of the building.

"Beautiful work," Burnett said, nodding toward the house.

"Thanks," Devins replied.

The building inspector took a deep breath and looked over at Burnett. "Well, it looks pretty good to me. I guess we might as well get going."

Burnett could feel Tom Devins' burning gaze following him all the way back to the car.

Chapter 15

"CHIEF WANTS TO see you," Murphy said, taking a sip of coffee from the white ceramic mug. "Pronto."

Burnett closed the glass door behind him, took off his gray flannel coat and threw it across an empty wood chair standing alone in the corner. "Know what for?"

Murphy shook his head. "But he ain't happy, Bill."

Burnett shrugged, then walked over to his desk. Two envelopes caught his eye. The first bore a return address in Madrid. It was from Margaret Corcoran. Inside was a letter addressed to Mrs. Corcoran from the American Embassy in Madrid.

Dear Mrs. Corcoran:

We have checked with the Spanish police to see if any information was available on Mrs. Norma Bell Wilson. We also checked under the name of Norma Carty concerning her stay in Spain, and we checked on Mr. Thomas Devins as well.

I regret that the Spanish police had no information that either of those people had stayed in Spanish hotels under any of these three names. We also checked personally with the Hilton Hotel with equally unsatisfactory results. Neither person had been registered at the Hilton, according to the records.

At this point there seems nothing more that we can do unless you can provide us with some fresh information on the case. I would be glad to discuss this case with you by phone should you think this is necessary.

Burnett felt a surge of anger. Some junior staff member at the Embassy, he thought. His whole job was dictating form letters, soothing ruffled feelings, sweeping things under the rug, keeping the Embassy from being bothered with petty problems like missing older women. Had the Embassy really contacted the Spanish police? Doubtful. He had certainly never "checked personally" with the Hilton Hotel. Interpol had quickly confirmed the stay of Norma, Devins and Forget at the Hilton, registered under their true names. And the Spanish police were aware of the situation.

"Hey, the ol' man's serious," Murphy said. "He wants your ass standing tall . . . now!"

Burnett nodded vaguely. He reached for the other piece of mail—an expensive white linen envelope with "Mrs. W. Carlton Eacho" embossed on it. Mrs. Eacho. His mind flashed back to the meeting in the living room filled with silver, lace and polished mahogany. He ripped the fine paper open, then read the ornate handwriting.

Dear Mr. Burnett:

It was very kind of you to meet with us at my sister's home. We appreciate your kind interest in our problem, and had hoped we would have received some positive information by this time.

Thank you very much for what you have done so far. It is a comfort to know that someone in an official capacity is aware of our feeling of frustration and sorrow, and is giving attention to the cause.

Sincerely yours,
Hilda B. Eacho

"Hey!" Murphy said, walking with mug in hand toward Burnett. "This ain't no shit. The old man's really uptight about something. I'd get my butt in there if I was you."

Burnett pulled the briar out, tamped down the thin top

layer of ashes, then relit the pipe. He looked at his partner with his eyes sparkling playfully, and winked.

Murphy shook his head in disbelief as he turned away.

Slowly, Burnett tucked his shirt in under his belt, centered the brass buckle with the bucking bronco on it, adjusted the small gun holster. Then he walked out the door and down the hall to the Chief's office. He paused, then knocked.

"Yeah," the gruff voice bellowed from inside.

There was something wrong, something very wrong. Burnett looked around the small, scroungy office. The Chief was sitting behind the desk, a cigarette clenched between his lips. To his right, standing next to the paper-littered desk, was Dick Hecht, the deputy D.A. in charge of the Organized Crime Section. Hecht looked at Burnett, nodding in recognition.

Seated on the couch next to the wall were two men. One was short, in his early thirties, and wore a blue serge vested suit. His mild, ordinary face was dominated by a large pair of glasses. A lawyer, Burnett thought; he had the bland, nondescript, conservatively inoffensive look of the lawyer. The other was maybe forty years old. A slightly dark complexion, fine features, balding dark hair and dark eyes marked him as Italian or possibly Spanish. There was no expression on his face, only a cold, withdrawn impassivity. But the eyes were riveted on Burnett, sizing him up as if he were an opponent. A pistol grip stuck out slightly from under his blue blazer, a belt-mounted cross-draw like Burnett's. A cop. But Burnett couldn't place him.

"Chief," Burnett said.

Stoner grunted, then gestured toward an empty chair. There was an awkward silence. The man with the glasses coughed, covering his mouth with his hand. He looked down at his knees, began picking at the fabric.

"Burnett," Stoner said suddenly, "this here's Mr. Huffman." He waved toward the seated figure wearing the glasses. "He's a deputy A.G."

A deputy A.G., Burnett thought as he nodded back to the

man. A prosecutor from the State Attorney General's office. What the hell did the A.G. want with him?

"And this is Mr. Sana," Stoner continued quickly. "Special agent, A.G.'s office. And you know Hecht."

Hecht looked uncomfortably across the room at Burnett, then down at his own shoes.

"What's up, Chief?" Burnett asked.

Stoner studied Burnett closely before answering, as if trying to make a decision. "Burnett . . ." He looked down at his hands for a moment, then over at Huffman. "It's your goddamn show," he said to the lawyer.

The young man coughed again, clearing his throat. "Well, Mr. Burnett, uh, certain matters have come to the attention of the Attorney General's office—matters concerning a Mr. Thomas Devins."

Devins, Burnett said to himself. Now what the hell . . .

"Mr. Devins recently came to our office with a complaint. He claims you're trying to extort $35,000 from him. And he has proof."

Burnett stared at Huffman. "You want to run that by again, slower?"

"In return for a payment of $35,000," Huffman continued, "he was promised that an investigation which you have been conducting would be dropped."

"Go on."

Huffman shrugged, looking at Stoner. "That's all I'm prepared to divulge at this time."

Burnett continued studying him. "You said he had proof."

"Mr. Devins is about to give a statement. Under oath."

Burnett grinned. "That's it? That's your proof? Devins' word?"

Stoner breathed in deeply. "He says he has a tape. Devins was wired and got a conversation on tape that lays it all out." He looked up at Huffman, glaring at him darkly. "That's what he says."

A tape—extortion—$35,000—A.G.'s office—Devins—proof—everything was flying through Burnett's mind, making no sense. "You said Devins is about to give a sworn statement?"

"He's waiting in a room down the hall," Huffman replied. "Is there anything you'd like to say, Mr. Burnett? Anything before we take his statement? Of course," he looked down at his knee again, "you don't have to talk. You have a right to remain silent."

Burnett nodded, then pulled out his matches and began lighting his pipe. "I'd like to be there," Burnett answered quietly, "when Devins gives his statement."

Huffman looked at Sana, then at Stoner. "No objections," he said, shrugging.

Stoner took a deep breath. "Okay. Hecht'll represent our office. Huffman, both you and Sana will be present, is that right? And Burnett. And Jennie will take it all down." He looked around the room at the stony faces. "Any questions?"

"Where is he?" Hecht asked.

Stoner looked directly at Burnett. "One thirteen," he replied slowly.

Burnett suddenly felt cold.

Chapter 16

ROOM 113. SMALL, plain, cold, stark, empty of any sign of human warmth. A battered old conference table stood squarely in the center of the room, surrounded by four metal folding chairs. A steel safe squatted in one corner, two filing cabinets lined up next to it. A large, badly worn couch sat against one wall. Oddly, a small portable refrigerator sat alone in a corner. There were no windows in the cell-like room. Only one door let in or out.

Room 113 was a very unusual place. Located in the hallway outside of the S.I.D. squad room, it was strictly off-limits to all but eight men. Very few ever knew what went on in that room, and there was hushed speculation as to its purpose. Only one key existed for the ordinary-looking door, and only a handful of men knew where it was kept.

The room was used for highly confidential meetings and high-powered interrogation. The safe and files contained top secret documents, sensitive information and confidential evidence. Prosecutors John Howard and Dave Fitz had virtually lived in this room during the preliminary investigation into the killing of Robert Kennedy.

Burnett sat at one end of the old couch. He pulled out the box of wooden matches and once again lit the charred tobacco. At the table sat Tom Devins. A slight triumphant smile told Burnett he had just been recognized as the impostor building inspector. Christ, Burnett thought, if he says anything about that, Stoner will really have my ass. But Devins said nothing. He thinks it's all a game, Burnett decided. That big ego of his would never allow him to admit he's been tricked.

"All right," Hecht said finally, rising to his feet. "Mr. Devins, may I swear you in?"

Devins stood and raised his right hand.

"Do you solemnly swear that the statement you are about to give shall be the truth, the whole truth, and nothing but the truth, so help you God?"

"I do."

"Have a seat, please," Hecht said as he sat down. "Would you state your full name again for the record."

"Thomas Devins."

"And for the record, this statement is being taken in room 113, 524 North Spring Street, in Los Angeles, California. The date is August 15, 1969, time 3:00 P.M. My name is Richard Hecht, deputy district attorney, County of Los Angeles. Present are Richard Huffman, deputy attorney general, State of California, Leroy Sana, special agent for the Attorney General; and . . ." Hecht looked over at Burnett, ". . . William Burnett, investigator, Office of the District Attorney. Mr. Devins, this is a free and voluntary statement on your part, is that correct?"

"That's correct."

"You understand that at any time you can terminate the conversation. You are currently under investigation as a possible suspect in a possible murder case, and you are free to leave at any time. You can refuse to answer any questions. You understand?"

"I do."

"All right. It has come to our attention, Mr. Devins, that as a result of the investigation I mentioned, you had occasion to visit a Mr. Jerry Weber, an attorney. Is that correct?"

"It is."

"When was this?"

"Sometime in the second or third week in March."

"Of this year?"

"Yes, 1969."

"And who referred you to Mr. Weber?"

"Larry Kates. My real estate attorney."

"All right. And you went to his offices, to Mr. Weber's offices in Beverly Hills, is that correct?"

"Right."

"Now, I don't want to intrude upon the attorney-client privilege. The privilege is yours, and you can exercise it or not. Bearing this in mind, tell us, if you will, of your first contact with Mr. Weber."

"Well, actually, my first contact was by telephone. You see, I told him about this investigation by the D.A. and that I was a suspect. And he said, 'You should come over right now.' So I did. It was late in the afternoon. Anyway, I went to his office, and the first thing he said was, 'You know I'm expensive?' I said yes, I realized that. And then he said before he could talk to me he'd have to have a retainer—$2500 to be applied at the rate of $100 an hour for his time. So I paid him."

Devins glanced at Burnett, then looked back at Hecht. The guy was a charmer, Burnett thought. Calm, cool, respectful, convincing.

"Then I explained to him briefly my relationship to Mrs. Wilson, and filled him in on our business dealings and the trip to Canada and Europe. And then I told him about Mr. Burnett. Well, he said, 'Burnett—Burnett—I don't know any Burnett. Where is he?' And I told him I thought he was in the Santa Monica office. So he said, 'Okay. The first thing I'm going to do to show you that I'm earning your money is to get Burnett off the case.' I said, 'Fine.' And he said to come in the next day at nine in the morning and to bring everything—files—everything."

Devins paused. "The next day I went in. And we talked. He canceled everything else, and we talked for three days. At a hundred dollars an hour. And he told me, 'By the way, I told you I was going to get Burnett off the case. Well, unfortunately, Burnett's on it, but I did get the case transferred downtown, and that's where my control is.'"

"He told you he had control in the D.A.'s office downtown?" Hecht repeated.

"Right. That's what he said. Then he asked for another $1500."

"That's $4,000."

"Right. Well, he impressed me. I mean, he seemed to know—you know—the ins and outs. He seemed to have connections. And he had a big reputation. The best in town. Anyway, then he said, 'You know, it would cost a great deal of money for a defense for any of this. Frankly, I don't think they have anything. But the point is you don't want to be indicted because it's very expensive, a long process, and who cares if you win? And even if you do win, you've been indicted, and you lose your business.' So, yes, I agreed.

"Anyway, then he said, 'This Burnett is out to get you. That's for sure. He's got you labeled as a con artist, and he's convinced you murdered that Wilson lady.' And then he explained that there were problems with jurisdiction and Europe and all, but that there was a lot of circumstantial evidence, and people get hung every day on circumstantial evidence."

Devins looked directly at Hecht. "Then he said he had a lot of connections. He said he could get me a policy."

"A policy," Hecht repeated.

"A policy. And I asked him, 'A policy for what?' And he said, 'Well, this is how it works. Now, I don't know if it's possible in this case, but I'm going to put some feelers out. I'm going to talk to some friends.' He said it involved getting Burnett off the case and somebody else on. Getting *his* people on the case, he said. And then just sitting on it until the statute of limitations ran out.

"Well, I said I didn't think there was a statute of limitations on murder. But he said not to worry about the murder, that they had no case, never would. The thing to worry about is the fraud, the embezzlement and all that. Anyway, to get Burnett off and his people on and get the investigation killed, it was going to cost a lot of money.

"I asked him how much. I mean, he impressed me. And I

was scared. I figured I was being framed, railroaded. I figured I was being set up by Mr. Burnett. And Weber impressed me. I mean, he got Mr. Burnett transferred downtown where he had control. The man was very influential. So I asked how much. And he said, 'Maybe six or seven thousand, but that's a hell of a lot less than paying for a defense.'"

"He told you he had Burnett transferred downtown?"

"That's correct. He told me he was going to, and then he told me he did."

"I see," Hecht said. "Did he tell you what influence he had in the D.A.'s office—who his contacts were?"

"No. Not right off. He just said he had control in the downtown office. And he said not to worry about Mr. Burnett. He had him under control."

"He told you specifically that Burnett was under his control?"

"Correct."

"Did he say he was paying Burnett?"

Devins looked calmly at Burnett. "No, he just said he had him under control."

"All right. What happened next?"

"Well, he said it was up to me. If I was interested, he'd send out feelers. And so I said yes, I was interested.

"A few days later, we were in his office again. He showed me a report. It was from the D.A.'s office, prepared by Mr. Burnett. A confidential report. And it was all about the investigation. Well, I was pretty impressed—I mean, that Weber could get the report. It was very confidential, and it laid everything right out. And I knew it was authentic—there were phrases used in the report that I'd heard Mr. Burnett use before on the phone.

"Anyway, Weber said he was still working on arranging a policy for me. And he was paying visits to his contacts in the D.A.'s office. I was paying him a hundred bucks an hour for the trips."

"Let me get this straight," Hecht interrupted. "Weber was charging you for the time he spent in the D.A.'s office trying to get the case fixed?"

"Correct. Anyway, then I got nervous. It was maybe ten days later. And I asked him, 'What happens if I don't want the policy? I mean, you know, I'm not guilty. What if I don't want the policy? Will these people in the D.A.'s office lean on me?' And Weber said, 'Don't worry. There won't be any more heat; these are friends of mine. I've done this a thousand times. They understand. If I say you're not interested, then that's that.'"

"He told you these contacts in the D.A.'s office were friends of his?"

"That's right."

"And that he'd fixed cases before?"

"'A thousand times,' he said."

Hecht nodded. "Go on."

"Well, then, one Sunday he calls me to his home, says it's important. I go over there, and he's sitting out by the pool, with a cigar and a drink. And he tells me Mr. Burnett is really out to get me. Then he tells me Mr. Burnett has located Forget, and he's going up to Washington to talk with him. And he asks me if there's anything Forget can say to hurt me, and I tell him there isn't. I mean, I didn't commit any crime, so what could he say? Anyway, Weber says to call Forget and warn him that Burnett is coming up. And then he says he's arranged to have Murphy go with him."

Burnett's slight smile was locked rigidly in place, his eyes riveted to Devins. There was something about the story that had the ring of truth to it. How the hell *had* Forget known he was coming up?

"Wait a minute," Hecht said. "He told you that he, Weber, had arranged to have—"

"Yes. In fact, he said he'd arranged to have Burnett wait until Murphy was free to go with him."

"Was this the first time Murphy's name came up?"

"Yes. I asked, 'Who's Murphy?' And he said, 'Don't worry, I've got him under control.'"

"He said he had Murphy under control?"

"Correct. And he said to just call Forget and tell him Burnett's coming up, and that Burnett's going to lie and try to scare him and maybe offer him a deal. He said to warn

Forget that Burnett's a bad character, and he—Burnett—was going to try to put the screws to him.

"And then he said, 'That's what Murphy's going along for. Murphy's going to keep him in line.'"

Hecht glanced at Burnett, then back at Devins. "Weber told you he'd arranged to have Murphy accompany Burnett to keep him in line?"

Devins nodded.

"You'll have to answer out loud," Hecht said, "for the reporter."

"Yes. That's what he told me. He said to tell Forget that if Mr. Burnett gets out of line—you know, if he tries to get rough with him—Murphy will keep him in line."

Burnett sat quietly, studying the man he'd been investigating for so long. There was something about the story—Devins was holding back a lot, changing things here and there. But if it were fabricated, why didn't Devins just finger his longtime antagonist? Basically, Devins was giving Burnett a relatively clean bill—and burning Murphy.

"So I called Forget and told him not to talk, like Weber said. Then, about a week later, Weber meets with me. And he knows about what happened up in Washington, all about the conversation with Forget. And he's angry that Forget talked at all with Mr. Burnett. He called Forget an idiot—said he was hanging me. And then he tells me that the policy's available."

"Did he tell you who he contacted to get the policy?" Hecht asked.

"No. So I asked how much, and he said, 'Thirty-five big ones—35,000.' I said, 'That's a lot of money,' and he said, 'It's doing a lot of work; you don't realize what they have to do.'"

"They?"

Devins shrugged. "I don't know who. Anyway, he says he can get the case killed for thirty-five grand. Twenty-five grand for his contact and ten grand for himself. And I don't know what to do. I mean, I'm not guilty. I didn't do anything wrong. But Mr. Burnett's tightening the rope around my neck. I'm innocent, but that doesn't mean much if I hang. So I didn't know what to do.

"Weber says, 'Look, Tom, you're in business. You're young, you're doing all right, you got a good clientele and you can't afford to be indicted. You're going to be ruined. You have to sit in jail, you have to pay bail and pay a lot of money for a lawyer.' Well, I told him I wasn't worried about the murder. What I was worried about was being harassed and railroaded. And meantime, nobody's trying to find Norma Wilson, because they're all concentrating on me. I mean, I want them to find Norma Wilson and clear me."

Devins took a deep breath. "Anyway, Weber wanted an answer: Do I want the policy? So I told him I'd let him know the next day. And I thought about it long and hard that night. I decided against it, finally. I just didn't want to get involved in bribery, not when I hadn't done anything wrong.

"Next day, I told Weber I didn't have the money. And he said, 'You've got the bread—my contacts know all about it.' I mean he knew all about my finances—my bank accounts, everything. Well, I told him it would take time to get it together, and he asked me how long. I said a month, and he said okay, he'd expect the money in thirty days."

"This was when?"

"May, first part of May. Anyway, a month passed, and Weber was pressing me. I didn't know what to do. I didn't want to get involved in bribery, but I didn't want Mr. Burnett getting me gassed in San Quentin either. So I stalled him: I told him it would take a few days to get the money from the banks. I told him I knew Burnett was watching my accounts, and if I pulled out a pile of money all of a sudden, he'd think I was leaving the country.

"So he says, 'Okay, as long as you'll have it in a few days.' And then he makes a telephone call from his desk. We were in his office together. And it was the D.A.'s office that answered. You see, I'm listening because he's got one of those speakers on his phone. Anyway, some guy finally came on the line. And Weber says, 'You got a deal,' and this guy says, 'Great.' And Weber says again, 'Understand? Devins and I've got a deal,' and the guy says 'Fine.' Then Weber says, 'All right, now call off the dogs.'"

Hecht interrupted. "Could you recognize the man's voice?"

"No. But Weber called him 'Stony.'"

Hecht's head jerked up suddenly. "Stony?"

"That's what he called him. 'Stony,' he said, 'you got a deal.'"

Burnett continued studying Devins. Stony. The nickname Chief Stoner's old cronies had given him years ago. Stony. Chief of Investigators George Stoner. First Murphy, the lieutenant in charge of S.I.D.'s detectives. Now Stoner. Devins was going after the top men in the office.

"You're sure," Hecht repeated with a forced calm, "Weber called him by the name Stony."

"I'm sure. Stony."

Hecht nodded. "Go on."

"Well, so we had the policy. But I didn't really want it. And then I started getting scared. I mean, getting involved in . . . well, bribery. And it would make it look even more like I was guilty of something. So I kept stalling Weber, putting him off from day to day. And I didn't know what to do.

"Then I started worrying that this was all a con. Maybe he didn't really have Murphy and this guy Stony in his pocket. So I called up the D.A.'s office. I asked for Murphy, and when I got him, I told him I was going to come down the next day and give a statement and I hung up. Then later in the day, I went to Weber's office. And first thing he says, he says, 'What in hell is this, you're going to give a statement to the D.A.?'"

"This was a few hours after you'd talked with Murphy?" Hecht asked.

"Right. Anyway, then I figured the policy was on the level and I was really in it up to my ears. I told Weber I wasn't going to give a statement. I'd just gotten panicky. And he started pressing me for the money. I told him I'd have it in two hours. And, well, at that point, I still didn't know whether to go along—to put up the thirty-five grand or not.

"I mean, Weber obviously had connections. I'd seen that, with Murphy. And I figured maybe he owns Mr. Burnett, and Mr. Burnett was just playing the heavy to keep the pressure on me. But, on the other hand, I was digging myself into a hole. And I couldn't see any way out.

"Then it occurred to me. The way out. I'd tape-record my conversations with Weber and turn the tapes over to the authorities."

Huffman leaned back, still concentrating on the ceiling. Sana hadn't moved; his expression hadn't changed.

"So I got this little tape recorder. I made an appointment with Weber to meet him at Diamond Jim's. Then I got there early and set up the recorder behind a curtain next to our booth. And Weber got there right on time. He asks if I've got the money, and I explain I don't, yet. He says, 'You've been stalling us too long; things are beginning to look like maybe you're trying to con me.' And then he says he could put more heat on me." Devins looked at Burnett. "He says he could have Mr. Burnett put heat on me."

"Did he explain what he meant?" Hecht asked.

Devins shook his head. "He just said he'd done it before. He'd put heat on me before through Mr. Burnett. He said he wanted me to understand that he had the power, the control to put heat on me, or take it off. So I agreed to bring the money the next morning to his home."

Hecht nodded. "So Weber's statements about Burnett—you've got them on tape?"

Devins shook his head. "After he left, I opened up the recorder. The tape was still in the starting position—it hadn't worked."

Hecht glanced at Burnett. "All right, Mr. Devins. What happened at Weber's the next morning?"

"I didn't go. That's when I decided to go to the authorities. I mean, I couldn't stall Weber any more. And I knew he could have his contacts arrest me for murder, and there wouldn't be any bail. Then it'd be too late.

"Well, I couldn't go to the D.A. So I called the attorney general. I ended up talking with a Mr. Rubin, and I explained I couldn't come down to the State Building because I might be followed. But we discussed the whole situation over the phone, and he suggested that I be provided with a special recording unit on my body.

"Anyway, Mr. Rubin had Mr. Sana meet me at the Red Roulette Room at the Continental Hotel on Sunset. We talked about everything, and then he fitted me with a recording unit and showed me how to operate it.

"Then I called Weber and told him I'd slept late and wanted to meet with him. So he agreed to meet me at the Friars Club."

"You did meet him at the Friars Club?" Hecht asked.

"Oh, yes. We met. We talked for a long time. He asked for the money, and I explained I'd been stalling because I hadn't decided, but that now I'd decided and I'd get the money for him. And I agreed to go get the money and meet him over at his house in an hour.

"So I left and went home. Mr. Sana was waiting for me there. We took the recorder off, and I gave it to him."

"Where is the tape?" Hecht asked.

Sana coughed. "There is none," the investigator said quietly. "I had the recorder checked by Sac Electronics, out on Jefferson, and there was a malfunction in the unit. It was a brand new unit, and the tension mounts on the batteries weren't working."

Burnett's grin widened slightly as he studied the slightly embarrassed agent.

"All right," Hecht said. "What happened next?"

"Well, I knew I couldn't go see Weber again. I mean, how many times could I stall him? So I went down to the Attorney General's office and gave them a statement, just like I'm giving you now.

"Then the gentlemen at the Attorney General's decided to give it one more try. So they wired me again, with a different recorder, and I called Weber and we met again at the Friars Club. And I took along $6,000—a bunch of hundreds wrapped around some ones. He thought it was $35,000. And we talked about the policy."

"This is on tape?"

"We have it," Huffman said, still gazing at the ceiling.

"Anyway," Devins continued, "then we went over to his office. And he made another phone call. To the D.A.'s office. The same voice finally came on the line: Stony—only this time Weber called him 'George.' And they talked for a minute, and Weber explained that the policy was on. And the guy—George—said the case wouldn't get any further. And that was it."

"All this is on tape?" Hecht asked again.

Huffman nodded.

"And do you know who Weber's contact is?" he asked the prosecutor.

"Haven't ID'd the voice yet," Huffman said. "And there's no reason to believe there's just one contact."

"Well," Devins continued, "then we met again a few days later, Weber and I, in his office. I was wired again. This was going to be the last time, to get the names of his contacts on tape. And so I told him I wanted the policy. And he looked at me kind of strange, and he said real innocent, 'Policy? I don't know what you're talking about, Tom.'"

Devins took another deep breath. "Well, I insisted. And he played dumb—said he didn't know about any policy. Never even mentioned the missing cash from the last time. His advice to me was to go down to the D.A. and cooperate, give a statement and try to get immunity.

"And then I realized he was on to us. He knew. Somehow, he'd found out I was taping him. So I got out of the office." Devins looked at Hecht, shrugged. "That's about it."

Huffman sat upright. "Do you need anything else from our witness?" he asked Hecht.

Devins coughed. "Uh, I'd like to add something."

"Okay," Hecht said.

"I don't know who it is in the D.A.'s office who's working with Weber. But I do know this. Someone's trying to frame me."

The room was silent for a long moment.

"Someone's trying to frame me," Devins repeated. "And I think I know who's behind it. For the record, I want it clear that I'm concerned that information regarding me is getting to other people. I'm concerned that Mr. Weber, a very powerful man, will sure as hell not take this lightly. And I'm concerned that members of the D.A.'s office, and maybe someone in this very room, will try to silence me.

"Like I said, I want this on record." He looked again at Burnett. "In case anything suddenly happens to me."

Burnett returned his look. But Burnett's mind was back in Sedro Woolley. He was remembering how surprised he had been to discover Forget had been tipped to their visit. And he was thinking of the three or four men in the office who had known of the trip. One of them was dirty. Maybe more than one.

"If there are no further questions," Huffman said, rising from his seat. Sana rose with him.

Hecht shook his head. "End of statement," he said quietly to the stenographer, who quickly picked up the steno machine and walked out of the room.

"There'll be indictments," Huffman announced. "You can count on it."

Chapter 17

Burnett leaned back in his chair, propping his cowboy boots up on the file-covered desk, and once again studied the list of numbers on the sheet of paper with "General Telephone" printed at the top. He had obtained the list from a personal contact in the telephone company's central billing unit. Every week now for the past two months he received a similar list in the mail, a detailed catalogue of every toll call made from either Devins' home phone or his office phone.

Burnett's attention had been attracted to the New York number. He'd had the number traced to a steamship line. Then, he'd called Paul Vitrano again in the D.A.'s office in Queens. Vitrano had checked it out and called back: yes, a Thomas Devins was on the passenger list for the S.S. *Rafaello,* sailing in a few weeks for Algeciras, Spain, and Genoa, Italy; also on the list for the same cabin was an Adelle Devins.

Why was Devins going to Europe? If he was going to skip, he wouldn't take a slow steamship. And anyway, there hadn't been any activity on Devins' bank accounts or on the Encino house. If Devins had attempted to list his house on the market or withdraw any large sums from his accounts, Burnett would have been instantly alerted by the bank managers or brokers he'd carefully cultivated.

No, Devins was probably just trying to get away from the shadow of the investigation. Maybe the pressure was finally getting to him. Maybe. But somehow, Burnett thought, Devins seemed too cool, too much in control, to be running away for a breather. It wasn't like him; it didn't fit the image of the calm, calculating manipulator.

"Burnett."

He looked up with a start. Stoner was standing next to the desk; a man in a three-piece pinstripe suit was standing next to him.

"Burnett, this is Sid Cherniss."

Burnett slowly pulled his feet off the desk, brought the chair back level and stood up.

"Mr. Cherniss'll be taking over as head deputy of the S.I.D., effective immediately." Stoner coughed.

Burnett shook the man's hand. He was tall, slightly overweight and pushing fifty. He had carefully groomed, thinning brown hair, and wore dark, thick-framed glasses. A polished brown Dublin-style pipe jutted from between a row of small white teeth. He looked the typical corporate lawyer: quiet, restrained, proper. Yet, somewhere in the back of his mind, Burnett remembered hearing the name Cherniss. Some big murder case. Cherniss, he thought. Vaguely, he remembered him as one of Younger's high-powered trial deputies. Not a desk man. Ex-Navy pilot in World War II and Korea. Sid Cherniss.

The lawyer smiled back at Burnett, his soft eyes carefully studying the lanky investigator as if he were on a lab slide. "I'm looking forward to working with you, Bill."

Burnett nodded. "Thanks, Mr. Cherniss. I guess—"

He was cut off by the telephone's ringing.

"We won't keep you," Cherniss said, holding his hand up in farewell. The two men began walking toward the next desk as Burnett picked up the receiver.

"Burnett," he said.

"Mr. Burnett? This is Jack Plaia." There was a moment of silence. Then Burnett remembered. Jack Plaia, the operations officer at the Charter Bank of London, down on Sixth Street in the financial center. Burnett had discovered three accounts there in the names of Thomas Devins and Robert

Forget. Burnett couldn't get a subpoena for the records on the accounts since there were no charges pending. So he had simply obtained blanks from the court clerk's office, typed up his own subpoenas and served them on the bank. Legally, of course, they had no effect, but the bank personnel didn't realize that; the subpoenas looked very official and intimidating. It turned out that one of Devins' accounts held $40,000.

"Yeah, right. Sorry, Jack. Slipped my mind for a second. What've you got?"

"Uh, well, you remember you said I should call if there were any large deposits or withdrawals from, uh, any of the accounts in question?"

"Right."

"Well, we just received a phone call from Mr. Devins."

"Oh?"

"He asked us to have $26,000 ready for him by three-thirty this afternoon. On account number 2-01798R."

Burnett held the receiver in silence for a moment. Twenty-six thousand dollars. Was he really running? But he had more than $26,000 in the account. And what about the other accounts?

"Mr. Burnett?"

"Yeah, sorry, Jack. Uh, fine. Many thanks for the information."

"Certainly. If I hear of anything else, I'll be sure to call you."

Burnett waited a few seconds, then called Organized Crime's Intelligence Division. Within minutes, he had arranged for a surveillance team to be sitting in a modified car outside the Charter Bank of London.

Burnett was coming back from a late lunch at one of his favorite greasy taco stands in East L.A. when the call came over the radio.

"Wildflower, Wildflower. This is Daisy Two. Over."

Burnett picked up the mike. "Daisy Two, this is Wildflower. Over."

"Wildflower, we are now on Hollywood Freeway west-bound. Rabbit has picked up the package and we are on his tail. Over."

"Rabbit" was the name the surveillance boys always gave to their subjects. Devins had collected the twenty-six grand and was heading back to the Valley.

"Ten-four, Daisy Two," Burnett said. "Maintain contact with Rabbit, report any activity. Out." He replaced the mike in the cradle, then whipped the Ford station wagon around and accelerated toward the Union Station on-ramp to the San Bernardino Freeway westbound. Within minutes, he had merged onto the Hollywood Freeway and was weaving his way through the traffic toward the Valley.

Twenty minutes later, as Burnett was nearing the pass, the radio again crackled with his call name.

"Wildflower, Wildflower, this is Daisy Two. Over."

Burnett grabbed the mike. "Daisy Two, this is Wildflow-er. Whattya got? Over."

"Wildflower, we are eastbound on Ventura Boulevard near Reseda. Rabbit has just exited from a Security Pacific Bank on Ventura and is now in our sight heading eastbound. Over."

"Daisy Two, wasn't the bank closed?" It was almost 4:30.

"Affirmative, Wildflower. But the bank opened the doors for him right away. Looked like Rabbit had made earlier arrangements. Over."

"Daisy Two, was he carrying any packages, briefcase—anything? Over."

"Negative."

If he'd yanked more money, Burnett thought, he had it in cashier's checks or in cash in his pockets.

"Maintain contact, Daisy Two. Report every fifteen min-utes."

"Ten-four."

"This is Wildflower out." Burnett hung the mike in the cradle. He drove the station wagon down the pass into Studio City and eased it off the first off-ramp. Then he drove three blocks to a coffee shop across the street from Universal Studios. This would be a good place to maintain control. He could hear the radio from the coffee shop, and he was at the juncture of the Hollywood, Ventura and Golden State freeways. This gave him quick access to the Valley and central L.A., with the San Diego Freeway near enough to give him the west side—including the airport.

It was nearing midnight, and Burnett was sprawled half-asleep in the back of the station wagon. He had received seven or eight calls from the surveillance team that had picked up Devins, and two or three from the second surveillance unit that Burnett had pulled in from Devins' house. Both cars were now tailing Devins.

After leaving Security Pacific, Devins had driven out to Valerio Street in Van Nuys. He owned a residential unit there which he was renting to a young couple. There appeared to be some kind of a party going on in the house, and a number of people came and left during the following hours. Burnett had called off the first unit, meeting them at a Mexican restaurant about a mile from the house; from now on, Daisy One and Two would alternate their watch on Devins.

The radio in the station wagon crackled to life. Burnett's head jerked awake. "Wildflower, this is Daisy One. Do you read?"

Burnett grabbed at the mike. "Daisy One, this is Wildflower. I read you. Over."

"Wildflower, we are southbound on Valerio. Rabbit is moving. Over."

"Ten-four, Daisy One. Maintain contact. Out." Burnett started to replace the mike.

"Hold it, Wildflower . . ."

Burnett held the mike, listening to the static emptiness of the radio. Then the voice returned.

"Wildflower, Rabbit has reversed his route, laying rubber. Has made surveillance. Repeat, Rabbit has made us."

"Maintain contact, Daisy One. Keep lines open, advise of locations." Burnett started the ignition, slammed the accelerator down, racing the engine, then popped it into gear. "Daisy Two and I will join you. Do you read? Over."

"Ten-four, Wildflower. He is heading north on Valerio, accelerating. Over."

"Ten-four, Daisy One. Daisy Two, do you read?"

A different voice came over the speaker. "This is Daisy Two. We are right behind you, Wildflower." Burnett looked quickly over his shoulder. Two men were on his bumper. He looked back in time to swerve sharply to avoid a dog walking across the street.

"Wildflower, this is Daisy One. In pursuit of Rabbit, estimate speed at eighty, westbound on Channel."

"Shit," Burnett muttered to himself. The station wagon wouldn't be able to keep up, and he was just holding Daisy Two back. He grabbed the mike. "Daisy Two, this is Wildflower. Over."

"Wildflower, Daisy Two here."

"Daisy Two, do not wait for me. Repeat, do not wait. Get on Rabbit."

"Ten-four, buddy."

Burnett had barely replaced the mike when he heard the shrill screeching of tires and the deep roar of the big engine as the surveillance car/hot rod tore around him, belching black smoke.

Burnett kept the accelerator down, dodging late night traffic and running red lights. The big station wagon drove like a yacht: slow, cumbersome, sluggish. Yet, the speedometer read eighty. Burnett grabbed the mike again. "Daisy One, this is Wildflower. Gimme a reading. Over."

"Wildflower, we are still in contact. Southbound on Sepulveda, nearing Victory, estimate ninety miles per hour. Oh, shit . . . Passed Victory. Over."

Sepulveda and Victory, Burnett thought. "Ten-four, Daisy One. Out." Ninety miles an hour. He could hear the squealing of tires over Daisy One's mike. Devins must want to lose them pretty bad. Why? What was up? Sepulveda and Victory, eight or ten blocks away, heading in his direction, cut over to Sepulveda, may intersect. Was it worth it? There wasn't much traffic this late at night, but at those speeds . . .

"Wildflower, this is Daisy Two. Over."

Burnett grabbed the mike again. "Go, Daisy Two."

"Have contact with Rabbit and Daisy One, and will . . . Hold it, Wildflower. He's heading east off Sepulveda onto Vanowen. Estimate ninety, ninety-five."

Jesus Christ. What was Devins driving? Ninety-five miles and climbing. There'd be a wreck, sure. Some tipsy old lady coming home from a bingo game. No, it wasn't worth it. "Daisy One and Daisy Two, do you read?"

"Daisy Two, affirmative. Over."

"Daisy One, we read you, Wildflower."

Burnett could hear the screaming sounds of rubber on asphalt against the static backdrop of the radio. "Heat him up good, then back off. Repeat, heat Rabbit up, then back off. Do you read?"

There was silence for a moment. Burnett knew they wouldn't like it. These guys enjoyed a good chase. Almost made up for the long, lonely hours of sitting slouched in a dark car with a hamburger on stakeout. But it was getting too risky. A civilian could get hurt. And how the hell could he justify it? He couldn't even prove there had *been* a murder yet, much less that Devins was the murderer. But he'd damn well put the fear of God into him before calling off the chase.

"Ten-four, Wildflower. This is Daisy One. We will chase for a few blocks, then fall off. Over."

Burnett talked softly into the mike. "You got it. Daisy Two?"

"Affirmative, Wildflower."

"What is your ten-twenty, Daisy One and Two?"

"Southbound Woodman, estimate ninety-five, coming up on Magnolia."

Magnolia! Burnett was on Magnolia eastbound, and Woodman was just ahead. He pushed the accelerator harder, watching the red plastic needle climb up past the "80." He slammed on the brakes, laid smoking rubber across the black asphalt as he spun the wheels into a four-wheel drifting turn, then threw the steering wheel back, countering the drift. The Ford wagon lurched violently, began rocking almost uncontrollably, then started a rocking oscillation, swerving to the left and then to the right. "C'mon, mama,"

Burnett whispered. Slowly, the swerving and rocking dampened out as the car straightened out, made the turn. Burnett grinned. "Good ol' girl," he said. Within seconds, the needle had again climbed to seventy, seventy-five.

They should be coming up on him, he thought, as he looked in the rearview mirror, his foot pressing hard to the floor. Then he saw it. A large white mass quickly gaining size in the mirror, looming larger and larger until he could hear the shrill roar of the engine and the screaming of the tires. Burnett watched it as it ran up to his tail, then swerved to pass. He looked out the rearview mirror as the car pulled alongside him in passing.

It was a brand new Cadillac El Dorado. White over white, with white wheel covers and white upholstery, and gleaming like it had just been polished. The dropout from Arkansas wanted the world to know he was no longer parking cars at Frascatti's.

Behind the wheel was Tom Devins, alone, his eyes on the rearview mirror. As he passed the station wagon, he glanced over at Burnett. The two men's eyes met for only an instant, but in that instant there was a flash of startled recognition in Devins' eyes.

Burnett grinned, the pipe sticking out between clenched teeth, and waved to him. In a second, Devins was past him and pulling away. Then Daisy Two shot by him, quickly followed by Moss and Cocke in Daisy One.

Suddenly, Burnett heard a shrill, deafening scream of tires ahead. He let off on the accelerator, eased down on the brakes. Just ahead, maybe two blocks, he could make out a cloud of smoke in the middle of the street. As he neared the smoke, he saw the rear ends of the two surveillance cars disappearing down the street. But directly ahead of him was the white El Dorado, sitting sideways in the middle of Woodman Boulevard, smoke still rising from the wheel wells, a trail of black tire marks laid out for two hundred yards down the pavement. And about fifty yards from the Cadillac was an L.A.P.D. black-and-white.

The patrol unit was parked alongside the street, and one of the two officers was apparently writing a traffic citation on a Ford Mustang parked just in front of it. But right now the officer was looking up, still startled, at the smoking Cadillac which had just passed him sideways and come to a screeching stop.

Devins leaped out of the El Dorado, ran toward the squad car. He was pointing frantically down the street at the two rapidly disappearing surveillance cars.

Burnett drove by the scene slowly. Devins was still pointing and flailing his arms, and the cop was running back to his car. Suddenly, Devins looked up and saw Burnett driving by. He stared at the Ford wagon for a moment, stared at the man with the pipe behind the wheel. Then he ran to the squad car, pointing at the station wagon.

Oh, Christ, Burnett thought to himself. He didn't need this. He floored the wagon again, then nearly rolled the old car in a sharp turn onto a side street. He grabbed at the mike.

"Daisy One, Daisy Two, this is Wildflower."

"Daisy Two here, Wildflower."

"Daisy One," another voice answered.

"Daisy One, Daisy Two, take elusive action. Then meet in five minutes at Bob's Grill on Vanowen. Do you read?"

"Affirmative, Wildflower."

"Ten-four. Out."

Those guys could lose a whole fleet of black-and-whites, Burnett thought. And there may be a whole fleet of them before the night was out. But could the old station wagon lose them? He could just imagine how it looked to the cops and what Devins was telling them. Jesus, he thought, he could be in a helluva lot of trouble, using three D.A. units in a high-speed chase on a wealthy, respected real estate broker because some old lady was having a romantic fling somewhere in Europe.

Ten minutes later, Burnett was sitting in a coffee shop with the four surveillance men, eating a taco and listening to the sirens wailing up and down the streets.

Chapter 18

BURNETT WALKED ALONG Broadway, past Temple, a five-inch-thick Manila file tucked under his arm. It was hot under the afternoon sun, so he loosened his tie and threw the wilted gray flannel coat from his right arm to his left. He walked past the gray granite Hall of Justice, housing the central criminal courts and the D.A.'s main office. Up the street, Burnett could see the County Administration building, a huge honeycomb of bureaucrats and nightmarish red tape. He'd heard stories that people went into the County building on business and were never seen again; suffering from an aversion to government bureaucracy himself, Burnett could almost believe them.

He walked on along Broadway, past the County Courts building. The twin to the County Administration structure, it was home to the civil courts of the central district; there, lawsuits sat and languished for five or six years until the parties either died or forgot what they were suing or being sued for.

On the corner of Second Street, a tall, black-coated man, his face deeply bronzed and wrinkled, was waving a frayed Bible in the air and yelling out to passersby a warning of the coming judgment day. His eyes were light blue, almost colorless, rheumy with age. But in those eyes, opened wide with fervor, there was clearly the image of a ravished and destroyed Gomorrah.

Farther along Spring was the familiar tower of City Hall. No doubt there were as many useless and parasitic civil servants working for the city as for the county or the feds, but Burnett had a particular fondness for the tall, elegant old building, a fondness he did not have for the rest of the maze of officialdom that was loosely referred to as the Civic Center. The City Hall seemed to rise above the sunbaked grayness around it, carrying itself above the mean, petty business of government. More than anything, the old tower was a symbol to Burnett, a memory of what Los Angeles was in an earlier and better day. Los Angeles in the thirties had been vibrant, gaudy, innocent—a virgin land, peopled with children. And like children, they stuffed themselves with candy and did whatever felt good today, for tomorrow was only a hazy picture of yesterday.

Burnett reached his destination: the tall State building, containing yet another layer of administrative fat. He wondered if it was possible for a government to die of hardening of the arteries. On the other side of the street was the old L.A. *Times* building, scene of the labor riots and bombings that caused headlines right up to the time the defendant's lawyer, Clarence Darrow, was indicted for jury tampering.

Burnett walked up the steps into the State building. He pressed the ornate brass elevator button and waited. The lobby was surrounded by marbled granite and brass sculpture, a holdover from a time when buildings were considered more than people containers.

He checked the file again. Everything he had accumulated on the Norma Wilson case was in it, as Stoner had ordered. He had received the call from Stoner that morning at nine-thirty, and the message had been simple: "Be at your desk at one-thirty." Then, at one-thirty, a second call: "Go to the A.G.'s office. Take everything on the Wilson case." Nothing more—no explanation, no further instructions. Just be at the Attorney General's office, standing tall, with the Wilson file.

Burnett got into the elevator. What did the A.G. want now? Was it Huffman and Sana again? Why was he going alone, with no instructions? Was he being fed to the wolves? Burnett had a sudden heavy feeling in his stomach, a coldness. It must be from the elevator, he told himself.

Minutes later, Burnett found himself in a room much like room 113: stark, plain, with a large conference table in the center and seven or eight chairs around it. Present were some familiar faces: Leroy Sana, Richard Huffman, George Stoner. To Burnett's right sat Lynn "Buck" Compton. Jesus, Burnett thought with a start, what the hell's Compton doing here? Compton was the chief deputy D.A., Evelle Younger's right-hand man. The top dog in the office. Big and burly, with a square bulldog face, Compton had features dominated by the remnants of a nose that had been smashed all over his face in the course of innumerable football games and barroom brawls. At one time a star fullback for U.S.C., he was still remembered as the hero of a Rose Bowl victory over Michigan State. Two decades later, with a dozen years in L.A.P.D. and a reputation for cleaning out bars singlehandedly, "Buck" Compton was a feared and respected fighter in the courtroom.

Burnett nodded toward Compton, who did nothing, said nothing. Burnett had seen him before only from a distance, and had never really noticed the scars and smashed bones that incongruously set off the quick, alert, intelligent eyes.

Huffman coughed. "Well, gentlemen. Let's begin." He signaled to the shorthand reporter, who sat at a separate table behind George Stoner. "We are in the offices of the Attorney General of California. Present are . . ."

Burnett could feel the tension in the room, the hostility. The two sides were pitted against each other, waiting only for the first shot—Huffman and Sana wearing the Attorney General's colors, Compton and Stoner the D.A.'s. And Burnett had the distinctly uncomfortable feeling that it was his body they were warring over.

". . . Mr. Burnett," Huffman continued, "if you'll please stand."

Burnett rose slowly to his feet.

"Do you solemnly swear to tell the truth, the whole truth, and nothing but the truth, so help you God?"

"I do."

Huffman nodded toward Burnett's chair, and they both sat down. "Now, Mr. Burnett, I am required to advise you of certain constitutional rights. You have the right to remain—"

"Cut the crap, Huffman!" It was Compton. Burnett looked across at him, saw the restrained anger in his face. Buck Compton was one man he would not want to anger.

Huffman looked calmly down at his fingernails. "Do I take that to be a waiver, Mr. Compton?"

"Get on with it," Compton snarled.

Huffman shrugged. "Very well. Now, Mr. Burnett. I assume you know Mr. Compton? He will act as your adviser and attorney during this . . . interview. If at any time you feel you want to consult with him before answering any question, please feel free to do so. We are here today because Mr. Devins has made further allegations. Allegations that, in view of circumstances . . . ," he looked quickly at Compton, then again back at Burnett, ". . . we must investigate."

"The son of a bitch says you've been trying to kill him," Compton growled.

"Ah . . . yes," Huffman continued. "Mr. Devins has made allegations that you have been involved in attempts to . . . murder him."

Murder, Burnett repeated silently to himself. Murder. First, bribery. Now, attempted murder. What the hell?

"Specifically, Mr. Devins has alleged that you, together with certain other members of the district attorney's staff under your orders, planned to isolate him in his car and execute him. He alleges that three nights ago, in furtherance of this conspiracy, you and certain others from the D.A.'s office, in three separate vehicles, brandishing guns, tried to run him off a road near Van Nuys. This was a little past midnight."

Jesus H. Christ, Burnett thought. The little bastard . . .

"You and your associates, he says, then engaged him in a high-speed chase through residential areas, reaching speeds in excess of a hundred miles per hour. You and your associates repeatedly attempted to ram him and run him off the road and, on one occasion, attempted to trap him in a deserted cul-de-sac in the hills above Encino. Mr. Devins alleges that he had done nothing wrong, had broken no laws, that your only purpose was to kill him, and that, had you managed to run him off the road or corner him, you would have done exatly that.

"Now, ah, Mr. Burnett, what type of county car do you normally drive in the field?"

Burnett looked to Compton for a signal. Compton nodded slightly. "A '68 Ford station wagon," Burnett said.

"Mr. Burnett, do you deny the incident three nights ago?"

Burnett shrugged. "Hell, no. I mean, no. I was there, in the station wagon."

"And who was with you? Who were the others from the D.A.'s office?"

"I'd rather not say right now, if you don't mind."

Huffman wrote something on a note pad in front of him. "Why don't you just give us your version of what happened?"

"Well, sir," Burnett began. "Mr. Devins got some of it right. I *was* tailing him, with two other units. But it was strictly a tail—we sure as hell had no plans to kill him." He grinned broadly. "At least not right away. Anyway," Burnett continued, "at about midnight he took off like a bat out of hell. So I ordered the units to make contact. For a while. They got up there all right, but damn, I don't think they ever got to a hundred."

"Mr. Burnett," Huffman interrupted. "I should warn you that Mr. Devins' story is not unverified. We have reliable witnesses, officers of the Los Angeles Police Department . . ."

"Like I said," Burnett continued, "they never got up to a hundred. Anyway, there wasn't any traffic, but I figured there was just too much risk involved. So I told them to drop off, let him go."

"Mr. Burnett, the police officers—"

"And that was about the time Mr. Devins laid rubber in front of the L.A.P.D. unit."

Huffman nodded slowly. "And what was the reason for this high-speed chase, Mr. Burnett? Had he just committed a crime? Were you trying to arrest him?"

"Tom Devins is a suspect in a murder case, sir. He's been

under surveillance. A few hours earlier, I'd received reliable information that he'd just yanked out twenty-six grand from one bank and an unknown amount from another." Burnett pulled his pipe out and once again began the ritual of relighting it. "I felt that he may be making contact with another party for the purpose of a payoff, or possibly, he may be trying to skip the country."

"Was there any indication," Huffman said, "that Mr. Devins wasn't simply engaged in a real estate deal?"

"As I said, sir, the circumstances suggested a possible skip or payoff. Maybe I was wrong, but it was a possibility that had to be checked out."

"Mr. Burnett," Huffman continued, "why didn't you simply—"

"Oh, bullshit!" Compton growled. "I've heard enough." He rose quickly to his feet.

"Are you terminating this interview?" Huffman asked indifferently.

"You're goddamned right! I've had enough of this." He looked at Burnett. "Burnett, get back to work."

Burnett grinned widely as he stood. He motioned to the Wilson file on the desk in front of him.

"Yeah," Compton said. "Take that with you."

Chapter 19

STONER THREW THE newspaper across Burnett's desk. The headline read:

POLICE HARASS ENCINO BROKER

"In the last 45 days there have been two attempts on my life and my house has been burglarized three times," Thomas Devins, 29, has claimed. "Jerome Weber and two top investigators in the District Attorney's office sold me a license to commit first degree murder for $35,000. I feel like I'm living on borrowed time.

"Now that Jerome Weber is being investigated, the D.A.'s only defense will be to discredit me and my statements by attacking my integrity. To do that he'll have to change my status from that of a citizen to that of an accused criminal awaiting trial for some major crime," Devins added.

Devins has been accused of murdering Norma Wilson, 62, on a trip to Europe. Mrs. Wilson vanished from her Geneva hotel November 24, and a few months later the Santa Monica branch of the D.A.'s office began an investigation.

"The D.A.'s man on the case has simply been trying to prove I'm a murderer," Devins said. "I needed an attorney and someone suggested Jerome Weber.

"Weber told me, 'I'm going to have your case transferred downtown where I have more control.' He got the case moved downtown and then offered to sell me a policy for $35,000. I declined and the next day an investigator named Burnett called to threaten me with an indictment. At that point I took the case to the Attorney General's office.

"The Attorney General's office equipped me with a tape recorder. We set a trap to catch Weber and the two D.A. contacts he worked with—George Murphy of Special Investigations and George Stoner, chief of the Bureau of Investigations. $10,000 was to go to Weber for his fee and $25,000 was for Stoner and Murphy to quash the investigation. I got it all on tape, how I bought the policy from Weber in marked bills and lots more."

District Attorney Evelle Younger said there was no evidence that any member of his staff is involved in the payoff to quash investigation of Mrs. Wilson's disappearance, but the tapes show numerous contacts between Weber, Stoner and Murphy during the critical period. The grand jury instructed the Attorney General to continue investigating the matter. Devins turned over his copies of the tapes to Pete Miller, George Putnam's news partner on Channel 11.

Since he set the trap for the D.A.'s men, Devins says he has experienced police harassment. The Encino realtor has some resources to fight with and has managed to pit the different police agencies against each other.

Burnett laid the newspaper on the desk. "Hell, Chief, it was bound to hit the papers sooner or later."

"That was yesterday's. This just made the stands." It was the L.A. *Times.*

WITNESS SAYS LAWYER CLAIMED HE COULD CONTROL D.A. INQUIRY

Beverly Hills attorney Jerome Weber claimed—according to a witness before the grand jury which indicted the lawyer on charges of soliciting a bribe—that he . . .

Burnett looked up quickly.

Stoner nodded. "They came back with an indictment this morning." He picked up a smoldering cigarette from the ashtray, and drew deeply on it. Calmly, too calmly, he added, "Word is, they're continuing to investigate other suspects."

Burnett watched his chief for a moment, letting it all sink in. Then he returned to the paper.

. . . indicted the lawyer on charges of soliciting a bribe— that he:

—Had such "influence" in the District Attorney's office that he could quash a murder case if the suspect paid him $10,000, and two D.A.'s investigators $25,000.

—Could "control" the investigation of the suspect, Thomas Devins, by getting the investigator transferred from Santa Monica to the downtown office.

—Obtained advance information about plans to question a key witness in the State of Washington and got an immediate report on the result of that interview.

—Arranged to "control" the interview of the out-of-state witness by sending along with the primary investigator a senior investigator who would "protect" the suspect.

Burnett looked up. "How the hell did the *Times* get this from the grand jury so fast?"

Stoner shrugged. "I figure Devins had something to do with it."

Burnett returned to the article. It went into detail about Burnett's trip to Sedro Woolley and the $35,000 shakedown by Weber. Then the article turned to Murphy.

Murphy, who also was quizzed by the grand jury, testified he had accompanied Burnett to Washington to question Forget and admitted he had talked with Weber after his return.

But how had they gotten Murphy's testimony? Devins couldn't have been present.

> Asked how long after his return, Murphy said: "Shortly after I returned."
>
> Q: "It would be the next day?"
>
> A: "Could have been."
>
> Q: "What did you tell Mr. Weber, if anything, about the trip?"
>
> A: "I think essentially that we talked to Forget and didn't find out anything."
>
> Devins said Weber "instructed" him to tip off Forget and tell him Mr. Murphy was there to protect his interests.
>
> Later, Devins testified Weber "began repeating for me what had taken place in Sedro Woolley"—that Forget "blabbed for hours."
>
> Murphy, it is understood, admitted frequent telephone conversations with Weber during the months following Devins' employment of the attorney.
>
> George Stoner, chief of the D.A.'s Bureau of Investigation and another witness before the grand jury, testified he had instructed . . .

Burnett again looked up at Stoner. So the Chief had been called in to testify before the grand jury. It was the first Burnett had heard of it, but he suspected it. The whole thing had been so hush-hush. He remembered Huffman's calling him a few days ago, telling him to appear before the grand jury. The matter was confidential; he was not to advise anyone in the D.A.'s office of his appearance.

He'd been admitted to a huge room, what appeared to be a modified courtroom. Where the judge's bench was normally found, an elevated platform stood with a chair on it; this would be the witness box. Next to it sat one man, who rose as Burnett walked forward; Burnett guessed this to be the grand jury foreman. Directly in front of the witness stand was a long counsel table. Only one man sat at the long table: Richard Huffman. Behind him, where the audience would normally be accommodated, were the men and women of the grand jury. They were all staring at him, tight-mouthed and narrow-eyed. Everything else in the room looked like any of the dozens of old courtrooms Burnett had testified in before: the ornate oak woodwork, the royal purple drapes, the deep glossiness of the floor and furnishings, the tall silken flags of California and the United States. But no windows. No judge. No bailiff. No defense attorney. Only Huffman, a reporter, and the grand jurors.

Burnett had taken the stand, been sworn in by the foreman and then undergone the detailed questioning by Huffman that was to last for hours. Why had he been transferred to the downtown branch? By whom? To whom did he turn in his reports? Occasionally, a grand juror would hand a note to Huffman; he would read it, then ask a question from it. When had he first met George Murphy? Had Burnett ever been with the Los Angeles Police Department? Was he receiving any pressure from anyone in the office to ease off Devins? Had he been denied any assistance during the investigation by Stoner or Murphy? And on it had gone, waves of questions . . .

The newspaper story continued:

> Stoner said he had instructed Murphy to accompany Burnett to Washington.
>
> He did so, he explained for three reasons:
>
> —If evidence was developed that would be admissible at a trial, it would be necessary to introduce it through a backup investigator if the first were unavailable.
>
> —Murphy was acquainted with law enforcement officials in the area.
>
> —The advisability of sending an experienced man with a younger on an interview "which we consider to be very important."
>
> Devins named Stoner, as well as Murphy, as Weber contacts in the D.A.'s Bureau of Investigation. Both deny

leaking any information about any phase of the investigation and claim he never was shown Burnett's March 18 progress report.

Burnett looked up slowly. Stoner studied him for a few seconds and then said, "Burnett, I figure I owe you an explanation. Weber and me, well, there's no way around it. We've known each other a long time now. We go way back, back to when I was pounding a beat downtown. Weber had a bar he ran then, he and some other guy. This was before he got to be a lawyer. Anyway, a lot of us guys in the department would go there, get drunk, and that's where Weber got to meet a lot of us, made friends." He looked directly at Burnett. "Those contacts never hurt him in later years, when he got to be a big-shot criminal lawyer. Hell, I liked the son of a bitch. And,"—he shrugged, "Murph, he goes back, too. He knew Weber back then. You gotta understand, it was different then, it was a small world, a friendly world. We could be on opposite sides but still be buddies. There wasn't none of this 'conflict of interests' crap."

Burnett started to get up. "Chief, I—"

"Naw." Stoner waved his arm down at Burnett. "Sit down. You gotta right to hear this. Anyway, so I know Weber. We're buddies. And we talk. We talk about the Wilson case and about you. Hell, you're a novelty here, Burnett—all shiny new and all. Anyway, we shoot the shit. But I never . . ." Stoner leaned toward Burnett, looking him directly in the eye. "I never passed on any information to him. I never told him about the trip up to Washington. I never let him see any reports. And I sure as shit never talked about any fucking policy."

Stoner sat there for a minute, staring at Burnett. Then, slowly, he eased back into his chair. "Now, Weber's indicted. Okay. And maybe Murph next. Okay. But . . ." He suddenly jabbed his stubby finger at the skinny figure in gray flannel and caribou. "You're still on the case. No matter what the fuck happens, you're still on that son of a bitch Devins. And you don't stop goin' after him till I tell you! Got that?"

"Got it, Chief."

"Now, it's true that I told Murph to go up to Washington with you. You're green, Burnett. And it was an important interview. I didn't want you fucking it up. Anyway . . ." Stoner waved his hand aimlessly in the air. "Maybe you're not so green," he said, almost under his breath. "At least, you got some common sense.

"Now," Stoner continued, "like I said, you keep on as if nothing's happening with the grand jury. You're on Devins. Fuck the A.G. But you should know a few things. We know that asshole, what's his name—Sana, Leroy Sana—we know he's got Devins holed up somewhere. He's fucking dead sure we're a bunch of crooks over here, and we're all doin' our damndest to snuff out poor little Tom Devins before he can testify at the Weber trial." Stoner suddenly slammed his fist down on the desk. "All right," he continued. "So you gotta do without Devins. You gotta nail him independent, understand?"

"Got it."

"Fact of life number two," Stoner continued. "As you may know, Mr. Younger has announced his candidacy for the vacated position of attorney general."

Burnett nodded. It was big news all around the office.

"What you may not know," Stoner went on, "is that Charles O'Brien has also announced. So it's O'Brien versus Younger for the job."

Burnett looked blankly at Stoner.

"Jesus!" Stoner growled. "You poor dumb hillbilly! Don't you know who Charles O'Brien is? The number two man in the A.G.'s office right now. He's the head of their criminal section, and," Stoner pounded the desk again, "he's the son of a bitch who's sicking Huffman and Sana on us!" Stoner glared at Burnett. "Getting the picture?"

Burnett was beginning to.

"Let me spell it out, Burnett," Stoner continued. "There is absolutely nothing in this whole fucking world that

O'Brien would like more at this point than to publicly embarrass his political opponent with charges of corruption in office."

It was making sense.

"If O'Brien can get a conviction—hell, if he can even just get an indictment on one of us alleging corruption in the D.A.'s office, you know what that would mean at the polls come election time? Huh? Evelle Younger might just as well pack it up!

"So, okay," he said quietly. "Fact of life number three. It's gonna look real bad, I mean real bad, if after all this happy horseshit we can't even come up with charges on Devins. Understand?" He continued studying the spiraling smoke. "In other words, cowboy," he continued in a forced calm, "you have got yourself a tiger by the fucking tail. You got to nail Señor Devins with that murder rap. You got to get enough evidence together to justify an arrest. And then you gotta make it stick. And," he added almost in a whisper, "you don't even have a fucking body."

Burnett grinned. "Other than that, though, everything looks pretty good, huh?"

"Yeah, right . . . By the way, I got a call from Miller Levy."

Burnett nodded. J. Miller Levy was probably the D.A.'s top trial man.

"Yeah," Stoner continued. "He got a call from Adelle Devins. It seems Levy prosecuted Eddie Wein in that rape case back a while. Adelle was his witness and, well, she was pretty shaken up; she leaned on him pretty heavy—father figure, I guess. Anyway, she called him up, wanted to know why the D.A.'s office was investigating her husband. She told him it was putting a lot of pressure on her. Devins was getting real uptight, taking it out on her—you know, beating her up and all. She asked Levy to look into it, call off the investigation if there was nothing to it. Otherwise, she was afraid Devins would . . ." He shrugged. "Anyway, I promised Levy we'd let him know if the case wasn't going to make it. Okay?"

"Sure."

"Oh, and one other thing. Word is, someone in the office here's been assigned to keep an eye on us, just in case. You, me, Murph. I don't know who. So . . ." He shrugged. "You're being watched." He shook his head slowly for a moment, then looked back up. "Now, let's get down to it. What kinda help you need?"

"Well," Burnett said, looking intently into his pipe bowl, "I could use some legal talent." But the words were still burning into his mind: "You're being watched."

"You want a deputy?"

Burnett nodded. It was getting time to bring in the lawyers. There were too many complex legal issues popping up: jurisdiction, establishing a corpus delicti, getting search warrants, establishing probable cause for an arrest warrant . . . And, anyway, the sooner a trial deputy got into the investigation, the better prepared he'd be to try the case.

"Got anybody in mind?"

Burnett nodded again. "Steve Trott," he replied.

Stoner knew of Trott. A bright young deputy, Harvard Law School, tough, competent. "Any reason?" he asked.

Burnett shrugged. "We were on some cases together in Santa Monica. He's good. We get along."

Stoner pondered the matter for a moment. "Okay," he said finally. "I'll take care of it. Anything else?"

"Yeah, Chief." Burnett relit the pipe. "How about a vacation in Europe?"

Stoner just stared at him.

"Well," Burnett continued. "Without Norma Wilson's body, we don't have much of a murder case, right? And I figure she's gotta be last seen in Switzerland. We're pretty sure she made it as far as Spain. After that . . ." He shrugged again. "I figure we gotta go there. We gotta find her body."

Stoner took in a deep breath. "Europe . . . Jesus." He picked up a pen and began jotting something down on the note pad. "Okay," he mumbled. "You got it."

Burnett rose to his feet.

"Burnett!" Stoner growled. "You got *carte blanche* on this

case. *Carte* fucking *blanche.*" He jabbed his pudgy finger at the grinning investigator. "But I want this asshole. I want him real bad, you understand?"

Burnett nodded.

"You find her, cowboy." He glared directly into Burnett's eyes. "And then you give me Devins."

Chapter **20**

Dᴀɪᴠɪɴɢ ᴡɪᴛʜ Sᴛᴇᴠᴇ Tʀᴏᴛᴛ through the dry, dusty streets outside of Madrid, Burnett remembered another time, another place. His mind drifted back to the heat of Ethiopia, to stiff-necked uniforms, shy, dark-eyed women, wide-open barroom brawls . . . and to Ann Elizabeth. Her face, softer and more serene than it had ever been in reality, drifted before his half-closed eyes. With time, of course, the problems had sunk from memory, the troubles erased; only the laughing and the lazy days were left. Ann Elizabeth. And then the baby who had given a fresh purpose to his life, and then suddenly was gone.

"Let's check with the Embassy first, before we see Nieto."

The voice startled Burnett, brought him with a jerk back into the reality of the taxi.

"The Embassy," Trott repeated. "Let's check with them first."

"Sure," Burnett replied. He looked at his watch, trying to strengthen his grip on the present. Eight-thirty in the morning. Plenty of time to visit the Embassy, then Nieto. After that, they'd get a hotel room and maybe call on the Corcorans. He doubted if they would find any leads to Norma Wilson's whereabouts, but he wanted to confirm that she had, in fact, left Madrid alive and headed south. The postcards could have been written at gunpoint in Madrid; with Devins, any convoluted plan was possible.

Half an hour passed, during which Burnett looked out at

the passing panorama of Spanish city life. Everything seemed cleaner, faster, more efficient than he had expected—modern, yet with a gracious quality from another age. Somehow, he had expected Spain to be exactly like the Mexican border towns he had known so well when stationed in San Diego: filthy, run down, foul smelling. But Madrid was no giant Tijuana. It was a city of culture, sophistication, beauty and pride.

The taxi pulled up at the steps of the American Embassy. Trott paid the driver, leaving a fifty-peseta tip. Then the two men walked up the steps and into the impressive, elegant facade that housed America's diplomatic corps. A Marine sentry, in the stiff-necked dress-blue uniform of the embassy guard, eyed them. Looking at the young sergeant, Burnett fought back the wave of memories that were again surging forward from a distant darkness.

In rapid Spanish, Trott asked the crisply efficient receptionist for directions to the office of the legal attaché. She pointed down a hallway, explaining the route. As she described the way, Burnett looked at Trott, thinking that he had made a good choice. Trott was not only smart, tough, and as honest as they come, he could also speak fluent Spanish and French, and had a workable knowledge of Italian and Portuguese. One smart son of a bitch, Burnett thought admiringly.

Steve Trott was about the same age as Burnett—thirty years old; tall, dark and baby-faced, he always wore immaculately neat and traditional Brooks Brothers clothing—whether an ivy green suit or a button-down Madras sport shirt. A sparse moustache and dark Ivy League haircut, complete with cowlick, added to the total impression of a college sophomore on a fraternity outing from Princeton. In fact, Trott had graduated from Harvard.

He was known for a quick sense of humor and for being very "square" and old-fashioned. His relaxed, casual manner seemed strangely out of place with the dark, alert eyes that grasped everything. But his abilities in the courtroom were becoming known, and the baby-faced Ivy Leaguer's reputation was rising quickly in the D.A.'s office. More than one defense attorney had been caught off guard and bloodied in court by the seemingly naive, easy-going college kid.

Trott's abilities were not limited to the legal world. He was rated as a master magician and often performed professionally at Hollywood's Magic Castle. An expert guitarist as well, Trott had formed a small group of buddies into a singing group during undergraduate days. They called themselves "The Highwaymen," and eventually interested a recording company in cutting a disk they were to become famous for: "Michael Row the Boat Ashore." The royalties from the gold record put the young singer through law school.

Trott was a very sharp, talented prosecutor. But the main reason Burnett had asked for him was that the two men had worked together in the past. There was a mutual respect between them, a respect that had grown into friendship. Burnett had eventually introduced the deputy D.A. into his very private world of Baja and motorcycles. Trott loved it, of course, and the two were off to the beautiful desolation of the Mexican deserts whenever there was time.

Trott thanked the receptionist, then turned and began walking down the hallway with Burnett. They finally found the office of legal affairs and went inside. A massively built man in his fifties rose from behind a desk and held out a meaty paw. He was tall, dark complected, with a large jaw and sad eyes. He wore a poorly fitting black suit which hung limply from large muscles layered with fat. This was Modesto Mestanzas, the ex-chief of police of Madrid. Now retired, he worked for the Embassy's legal attaché, and proved invaluable in smoothing over legal problems visiting Americans found themselves in with the local authorities. Burnett had called from Los Angeles, advising him of their arrival and the purpose of the investigation. Mestanzas had told him that he would arrange a meeting with Nieto, the current head of Spain's Interpol branch.

Burnett shook his hand, then introduced him to Trott. "Anything come up?" he asked the big man.

Mestanzas shook his head sadly. "No, Señor Burnett. I find nothing. The files, they show nothing. No bodies of women of the age you seek, nowhere in Spain. But, then this is good, is it not?"

Burnett shrugged. "I guess so."

"Well," he continued. "Nothing. And the hotel. The Castellana Hotel. This, we must check with Señor Nieto. The *policía*, they have very good records in the hotel control department. You see, hotel control will have the cards from all hotels in Madrid, the original registration cards. All the hotels must give hotel control the card, to show who is staying in the hotel, the passport number, the dates, the signature. It must have been filled out by the señora if she stayed there, and hotel control will have the record."

Burnett nodded. The records kept on transients in Europe were much more efficient than those kept in the States. The police were not hampered by considerations of privacy or civil rights, and the hotels realized that incomplete or inaccurate records could mean a license revocation or worse.

"And the Corcorans?" Burnett asked.

"Yes. Señor Laurence Corcoran," Mestanzas said. He opened a drawer and pulled out a Manila file. It was labeled: *Thomas Devins y Norma Carty Wilson: Legajo Expediente #33.* It had been an outside shot, but Burnett had thought he had better check out Corcoran.

"Calle Rey Francisco Numero Ocho," Mestanzas said, reading Corcoran's address in the file. "Margaret Corcoran, the sister of Señora Wilson by marriage. Señor Corcoran arrived in Madrid many years ago. He is very wealthy, a producer of the cinema in Hollywood, in the years after the last war. He comes then to Madrid, to escape from the American taxes. Very much money. And after some time, he becomes, ah . . . He wants something to do. And he buys a store where he sells very expensive furniture." He looked up from the file. "Señor Corcoran is, ah, very respected. An old man, very much money, much respect in Madrid. A gentleman of . . . dignity. I do not think he is a man to be doing terrible things."

Burnett nodded again. "Figured. Just had to check it out. You talk with them?"

"Yes. I talk with both. Señor Corcoran tells me that in early November, last year, Señora Wilson comes to the store, the store of furniture. She does not write first, so it is a surprise. She tells him she is in Europe to make a big business deal. She is to meet some people from another country and is to get very much money. She says she is traveling with two men; one is a bodyguard, one is an adviser."

"Were they with her?" Trott asked.

"No. She tells him no; they are in the Hotel Castellana. She tells him that she is to go south with the two men to get the money. She talks about a boat, a very large boat that she is to go in. It is in the Mediterranean, and there are government officials on it, from another country."

"Biafra?" Burnett asked.

Mestanzas shook his head ponderously. "She does not say. She says she is unhappy with the idea of the boat. She does not want to make the deal this way. She says she only wants to get the money and go back to America."

Jesus Christ, Burnett thought. If she went out on some boat, and they tied a weight to her . . .

"She asks Señor and Señora Corcoran about the Swiss bank accounts. But they did not talk of this much."

"What did she ask about the accounts?" Trott interjected.

"She asks what is the way to open one, to begin one. How this is done. But they do not talk of this much." Mestanzas shrugged his huge shoulders. "This is all. Señora Wilson leaves, and they do not see her again, ever."

Trott nodded slowly.

"Well, señores," the big man said. "You have some questions of Señor Nieto?"

Trott stared at the white card closely, then back at the sheet of paper. He looked up at Burnett. "Looks good," he said. The card was the registration form filled out by Norma Wilson at the Castellana. He was comparing it to one of the exemplars the two men had brought with them; the sheet of paper was the last page of her will, given to Burnett by Philip Horrigan. The signature on the card appeared identical to the signature on the bottom of the will. Of course, it was not an expert comparison.

In Spanish, Trott asked the man seated behind the large desk, "Señor Nieto, may we take these cards with us? We wish to have our experts compare them for authenticity."

"Of course, of course," Nieto replied. "Whatever we can do to be of assistance."

Mestanzas stood next to the desk, to the side of Burnett and Trott. He had driven the two tall Americans across the city to police headquarters. He had parked the car directly in front of the entrance, then escorted them inside, past the saluting guard and the reception desk, down a series of corridors and into a large office. There, they had met Nieto, Madrid's Interpol connection. Congenially efficient, Nieto had the hotel cards brought into his office from hotel control.

The cards signed by Forget and Devins showed their destination as "Lisbon"; there was no destination written on Norma Wilson's card. Their correct home addresses were listed, as well as their passport numbers. All three signatures appeared authentic.

As of November 12, 1968, Norma Wilson appeared to have been alive in Madrid.

"Señor Nieto," Burnett said, "you got any way of telling where Forget, Devins and Norma Wilson went after they left the Castellana? Does this hotel control work for the whole country?"

Trott rapidly translated Burnett's question into Spanish for the Interpol branch chief.

Nieto listened to Trott, then smiled. "No," he answered, "we do not have the records here for all of the hotels of Spain. That would be very difficult, you see. But Señor Mestanzas explained your problem to me yesterday, and I made some inquiries of the different provinces." He looked briefly through a pile of papers on his desk, located what appeared to be a telephone message. "Yes, here it is. Malaga. The two Americans and the Canadian stayed at the Malaga Palacio Hotel on the evening of November 13."

"That checks with what Forget told us," Burnett said. "Malaga. He said they stopped there on the way to Tangiers, then took the ferry."

"That will be simple to see," Mestanzas said. "You go to Malaga?"

Burnett looked at Trott, then said, "Yeah, reckon we are."

Mestanzas mumbled something to Nieto, who smiled and said, "Gentlemen, it will give me great pleasure to call Señor Barranco personally. He will arrange for an inspection of the hotel records, of the Limadet passenger manifest, and of anything you wish."

"Señor Barranco," Mestanzas added, "is the chief of police of Malaga."

"Thank you very much, Señor Nieto," Trott said in Spanish. "We greatly appreciate your kind cooperation."

"It is my pleasure," Nieto replied. "Is there anything more I can do? My facilities are at your disposal."

"No, you've been very helpful," Trott said.

"Well, I wish you well," Nieto said, rising to his feet. "In the meantime, I will make certain further inquiries. Please let me know where you are in Spain, and I will forward the information."

"I expect the Palacio Hotel in Malaga is our next stop," Trott replied, "then the Rif Hotel in Tangiers. But we'll let you know."

Burnett nodded at the file in Mestanzas' hand. "Mind if I copy down that address on the Corcorans, señor?"

"Of course, of course," the big man said. He opened the folder and read the address out loud. *Calle Rey Francisco Numero . . .* number eight."

"Got it," Burnett said, writing on a piece of scratch paper.

Mestanzas began to close the file, then stopped and pulled

out an envelope. "Ah," he said apologetically, "I forget to give you this." He handed the envelope to Burnett. "Señora Corcoran wishes you to have this. I tell her you are coming soon, and she asks me to give you this. And to tell you she gets it in the mail a few days earlier. She says it is very important."

Burnett tore open the envelope. Inside was a single sheet of paper, with "Organizacion Paris" printed at the top left; at the top right was printed an address, *Pasaje Pizarro 3B, Torremolinos.* He read the crudely typed message.

Dear Mme,
    Just today, Mr. Maseda, a man of our organization, has been having lunch with Mrs. Wilson . . .

Burnett's eyes jerked quickly up to the top of the letter. A date of September 3, 1969, was typed at the top. Three weeks ago, he thought, his heart pumping faster now. Norma Wilson was seen alive three weeks ago. Quickly, he continued reading.

    All kind of details that you wrote on your letters are O.K. In this moment, 8:30 P.M., we know something about Mrs. Wilson, and we are sure that in a very short time we will be able to know all what you can need concerning to Mrs. Wilson.
    We know where she is actually living and the kind of life she follows. But next week a complete dossier of her, will be ready for our services of information. Photos, her friends, where she eats and where she uses to dance, will be picked up next week.
    But for all this we should like to know:
1. How much are you going to pay for the full information you need.
2. Some others details that you think we can get from you apart from the ones you gave us through your last letter.

181

As you see, we use to work quickly but with all kinds of securities.

Waiting for your news R.O.P., we send you our kind regards,

Organizacion Paris
with power enough,
J. Delgado.

Burnett handed Trott the letter. "It says she's still alive," he said quietly. "As of three weeks ago."

Trott grabbed the letter.

"Then again," Burnett added, "it could be a rip-off."

"A . . . rip-off?" Mestanzas repeated.

"Yeah, a con job," Burnett said. "Fraud."

"Ah, fraud." He looked at the letter. "What does it say?"

"Some outfit in Torremolinos claims they saw Norma Wilson alive three weeks ago, and they know where she is."

"Torremolinos?" Mestanzas repeated, his brow furling darkly. "May I see the letter?"

The big man read through the letter, shaking his head angrily. *"Organizacion Paris,"* he said to Nieto. "Delgado."

"Ah," Nieto sighed. "This Organizacion Paris, I know of it."

Trott studied his face for a clue. "And?"

Mestanzas shook his head again. "It is, I think, as you say, Señor Burnett. Fraud. I do not know, but this is what I think."

"What is this outfit?" Burnett asked.

"It is run by one man. A very small organization. Señor Delgado, he has a business of finding young children who run away from their fathers and mothers. Very rich fathers and mothers, they want to find the children. There are many American runaways in Spain. Many, ah, hippies, flower children, you call them. A very big problem here at the Embassy. And so, a big problem for me."

"You saying this guy Delgado's a complete phony?" Burnett asked.

182

"Sometimes this Delgado finds the children. Most times, he does not. But he always asks very much money, and he makes many promises to the fathers and mothers. He has many contacts with those in the world of crime."

Trott looked at Burnett, then back at the big man. "Is he the kind . . . Could he be involved in Mrs. Wilson's disappearance?"

"I do not know. He is not a man of good reputation. I do not know."

Trott looked at the letter again. "And maybe he's on the level. Maybe his boy *has* seen Norma Wilson."

Burnett pulled his pipe out of his mouth. "Steve," he said, "I figure we oughta pay a little visit to Señor Delgado."

The two men walked along the winding *avenida* of Torremolinos' business district. The city was almost exclusively a tourist town, catering to sun worshippers from Germany, Scandinavia, England, France and America who came to fry their bodies on the beaches of the Costa del Sol. The only industry in Torremolinos was the moneyed visitor, and the businesses that thrived in the Mediterranean sun reflected it: glass and steel hotels, too-cute restaurants, expensive gift stores, sterile car rental agencies. But the business that the two tall Americans were now looking for was of a different kind.

Burnett looked at the paper map in his hand, then up at the blue-and-white mosaic tile street signs. He turned off the *avenida* onto a small *calle,* paved with coarse stone. The street was quieter than the *avenida,* darkened by old, deteriorating clay-and-plaster buildings that seemed to fall toward the center of the narrow street and shelter it from the tourists' bright sun. The few shops here were rundown, geared not to the tourists but to those who lived behind the bright facade of Torremolinos' playground—the cooks, the maids, the dishwashers and janitors.

Two blocks into the darkness, Burnett found the street they were looking for: Pasaje Pizarro. And a few feet down the street was number 3B, a small, worn building. The sign on the unwashed window announced the offices of an insurance broker.

Inside, a secretary ushered Trott and Burnett into the office of Juan Delgado. It was a small office, with a window at the rear looking out on a small shaded patio. The walls were covered with certificates, licenses and photographs—some framed, some simply pinned into the cracked stucco. An old wooden filing cabinet stood in the corner. Two chairs sat in the middle of the room, facing a broad, polished wood table. Behind the table sat a small man in a business suit. He rose with a smile.

"American?" he asked in English.

Trott nodded. "Juan Delgado?"

"Yes, this is my name. How do I help you?"

The Spaniard was dumpy, almost fat in his wrinkled blue suit and badly stained white shirt. His face appeared slightly swollen, and his coal-black eyes were nearly lost in the puffiness. Raven hair was swept back, gleaming with an oily sheen. The round little man looked like he had just stepped out of an old Humphrey Bogart movie.

"Organizacion Paris," Trott said simply.

"Ah," the little man said. "Yes. I may be assisting you in what type?"

"Señor Delgado, what exactly *is* the Organizacion Paris?" Trott asked.

Delgado nodded a few times in silence, his smile slowly disappearing. "It is an organization of detectives, a . . . ah . . ."

"A detective agency?" Trott injected.

"Yes. Exact. Detective agency."

"You are the owner?"

Delgado began playing with a wooden pencil. "You señores are of what, may I see?"

Burnett pulled out his wallet and displayed the silver-and-gold badge.

"This is interesting, señores," Delgado said, the smile returning, "but there is no, ah, authority in Spain, this is not so?"

"Señor Nieto," Trott replied calmly, "the chief of Interpol in Madrid, has offered his help. As has Señor Barranco, the chief of police in Malaga."

Delgado nodded slowly.

"If you prefer," Trott continued, "we can simply request that you be brought to Madrid for questioning by the authorities there." He paused. "We felt you would prefer this less . . . formal procedure."

Suddenly the smile returned. "Then, señores, let us begin."

"Norma Wilson," Trott said.

"Norma Wilson?"

"Your letter sent three weeks ago. You claimed an employee had recently seen her, and you knew where she was now living."

"Ah, yes, the Señora Wilson. Yes."

"Where is she?" Trott asked quietly.

"The señora? I do not know this. First, I must get money, then I look. This takes time, much work. I must get money first, you see."

"You wrote in the letter that you already knew where she lives."

"Ah, well, you see . . . Yes, the señora lives in Spain; this is my information. But in Spain, where exact? This takes time."

"How do you know she lives in Spain?"

Delgado shrugged. "Confidential, señores. The information of mine, it is from people very confidential."

"Where is Señor Maseda?"

"Maseda?"

"You wrote that he had lunch with Mrs. Wilson."

"Ah. Again confidential," he said.

Burnett was feeling an irresistible urge to stomp him into a grease spot.

"How much money do you need, Señor Delgado?" Trott asked.

"Ah . . ." Delgado looked up at the ceiling, as if mentally computing the costs of such a job. "This I think, in American dollars, 2,000."

"Two thousand dollars," Trott repeated. "For $2,000 you can find Norma Wilson?"

Delgado smiled. "My organization tries very hard for $2,000."

"What about this Organizacion Paris? Who runs it?"

"Detective agency, I tell you before. It is . . . I own the Organizacion."

"You are an insurance broker?"

Delgado spread his hands out. "Yes, and land, I sell. And documents, I witness. This, and detective agency."

"Have you ever seen Norma Wilson?" Trott asked calmly, almost offhand.

"No," Delgado said. "I, myself, I do not see the señora."

"But Maseda has?"

Delgado grinned.

"Okay," Trott said quietly. "Thank you, Señor Delgado. May I use your telephone?"

"But of course. You are my guest."

Trott stepped toward the phone on Delgado's desk and dialed the operator. "Hello," he said in Spanish. "Please connect me with the police department headquarters in Madrid. I wish to speak with Señor Nieto, chief of Interpol operations."

Delgado's smile dropped.

"Yes," Trott said suddenly into the phone. "Señor Nieto? Steve Trott here, in Torremolinos . . . Yes . . . Actually, we're with Señor Delgado now . . . That's correct . . . No, Señor Delgado has been very uncooperative . . . Yes, we're quite sure he knows something, but he refuses to tell us . . ."

"Señor—" Delgado said quietly.

". . . Yes . . . That sounds fine; we would appreciate it . . . We'll leave with Señor Delgado by noon and should be at your office by—"

"Señor!" Delgado hissed.

". . . Uh, excuse me for a moment, Chief." He turned toward Delgado impatiently. "Yes?"

"Ah, señor. You do not understand, I think."

"I don't understand what?"

"Ah, you . . . The police building . . . They . . ."

"Delgado, we don't have time to play games. We'll just let the police get it out of you." He turned back to the receiver. "Señor!"

Burnett could see the tiny beads of sweat forming on Delgado's dark brow and around his small delicate mouth. Trott's a real artist, he thought to himself admiringly; whatever he's saying on the phone, he's got the little Spaniard squirming.

"Señor," Delgado repeated more quietly. "I think I can maybe give you the information, yes?"

"Just a moment, Chief . . . I believe Delgado has decided to cooperate. I will certainly call you back if he changes his mind . . . Yes? . . ." Trott listened for a moment, then looked back across the room at Burnett. Finally, he said, "That's very interesting, Chief. You're quite sure? Well, we'll certainly check it out. Many thanks for your assistance, Señor Nieto. *Vaya con Dios.*" He hung up the telephone.

"Where is Norma Wilson?" he asked softly, politely.

Delgado's head sank forward, a look of misery spreading across his face. "I do not know, señores. This is the truth."

"And Señor Maseda?"

"Señores," Delgado said almost in a throaty whisper, "there is not a Señor Maseda. I . . . make him up. I do not know Señora Wilson, I do not see, hear. Nothing. I have not information."

"I see," Trott said quietly. "And the letter?"

Delgado shrugged. "I am ready to look. For money. I . . ." He looked up at Trott, then across at Burnett. "I . . . say things, so I get money to look for the señora. You understand? I read notice in newspapers, woman missing, reward is available. I write letter, say things that are not true. So I get job to look for the señora." He shrugged again. "Maybe I find her."

Trott looked at the pathetic little figure. "You answer many such notices about missing people?"

Delgado spread his hands out. "Sometimes."

187

Trott continued studying him in silence. Then, quietly, he turned to Burnett. "Let's go," he said in a low voice.

The two men walked out of the room and into the shaded street. Once outside, Burnett stopped and began tamping at his pipe.

"So much for the Organizacion Paris?" he asked.

"Yes," Trott said, "but Nieto had some information for us. He got a wire from Malaga this morning. The police there just found something in their criminal files."

Burnett continued puffing on the pipe in silence.

"Norma Wilson was thrown in jail there on November 13th."

Chapter 21

THE FOUR MEN drove down the broad, palm-lined streets of Malaga, crowded together in a small Fiat police car. Trott and Burnett sat in the back, their long bony legs jamming into the front seats. Behind the wheel was Teofilo Canete; beside him was Juan Garrido Casas. Canete was of medium height and rail thin, while Casas was short and heavyset; they reminded the Americans of Mutt and Jeff. But the men were detectives, assigned by Chief of Police Barranco to assist Trott and Burnett.

The criminal files had shown that Norma Wilson, Thomas Devins and Robert Forget had all been arrested on the evening of November 13th and taken into custody. A gun had been found in their hotel room by the maid—a .380 Star automatic pistol exactly like the one Forget had mentioned to Burnett. The maid reported to the manager that she had discovered the gun under a mattress while changing the sheets. The manager summoned the police, who then seized the gun and waited for the three Americans to return. They were quickly seized and handcuffed when they entered the hotel room later that day.

Under Spain's stiff gun-control laws, the three could have been thrown into prison for a long term. Instead, they had been hauled before a magistrate on the 14th, and sentenced to pay a stiff fine. They paid it quickly and were released.

Chief Barranco had also ordered copies of all passenger manifests for the month of November 1968, from the Arab

189

Limadet Ferry Company. The lists showed that on November 14th the following persons were transported on the *Ibnfatouta* to Tangiers: Norma "Nilson," USA; Robert Forget, Canada; and Thomas "Denins," USA.

Burnett and Trott had confirmed the identities by viewing the mug shots taken at the time of arrest, recognizing the dark surly face of Bob Forget, the clean good looks of Tom Devins, the tired, frightened face of Norma Wilson. Then they obtained copies of the magistrate's judgment, the jail release order and the property inventory. The inventory showed nothing unusual, as most of their property had been left in suitcases at the hotel. The gun had been destroyed.

In the car, Burnett glanced at his calendar watch—they didn't have much time left. Ten days. Ten days to find a body that may or may not be somewhere in Europe. And there was the A.G.'s grand jury waiting for them. Burnett bit down hard on the pipe stem. He knew she was dead; he knew Devins had somehow murdered her. But without a body . . .

The car came to a stop in front of a large modern building near the beaches. The clean lines of the architecture blended subtly with a Moorish influence, reminding Burnett of something left over from the Los Angeles of the forties.

The four men got out of the car and walked into the coolness of the lobby. They crossed the polished tile floor and identified themselves to the uniformed man at the reception desk. Quickly, the man went into another room and emerged with Juan de Dios Leon Portillo, the manager of the Malaga Palacio.

Portillo was the kind of manager one expected of an expensive, international resort hotel—dignified, polished, immaculately dressed. And he spoke perfect English.

"Yes. November 13th, I believe. Yes. The maid was cleaning the rooms, ah, numbers 312 and 311, I believe. And as she was—"

"Excuse me, Señor Portillo," Trott interrupted. "Who was staying in which rooms, and in which room was the gun found?"

"Mr. Devins and Mr. Forget registered in the double room, Mrs. Wilson in the single." Portillo coughed politely. "However, it is my understanding from talking with the maid that, ah, different arrangements were made privately. Mrs. Wilson's luggage and effects were in the double room with one of the gentlemen—I do not know which one."

"And the gun?" Burnett asked.

"In the double room, under the mattress. The maid was changing the linen and discovered the weapon under the mattress. She immediately notified me, and I, of course," he smiled toward Canete and Casas, "notified the police."

"Three officers arrived a few minutes later," he continued. "Mr. Devins, Mr. Forget and Mrs. Wilson had not yet returned. The officers searched the two rooms, in my presence. The gun was taken."

"Were there any large amounts of money found?" Trott asked.

Portillo shook his head. "No, gentlemen. No money. And no other weapons."

"Had Mrs. Wilson or either of the men used the hotel's safe deposit box?"

"No. I have double-checked this. But I would have remembered. You see, I had a pleasant conversation with Mrs. Wilson and her companions upon their arrival. We shared drinks together. I remember them quite well. And the gun incident, of course—well, it is quite unusual, is it not?"

"And they returned on the 14th for their luggage?" Trott asked.

"That is correct. The day after the arrest. Mrs. Wilson was, well . . . very upset, very worn by the experience, I am afraid. Unfortunate, was it not?"

"Yes," Trott said in his soft-spoken manner. "Did anyone mention who the gun belonged to?"

Portillo thought for a moment. "No, no, I do not believe so."

"And the gun was loaded when the maid found it?"

"Oh, yes. Filled with bullets."

"Mr. Portillo," Burnett said, "you mentioned a conversation when they arrived?"

"Yes. We had a very pleasant talk in the bar."

"What about?"

"Ah, let me see . . . Well, I believe Mrs. Wilson explained that they were stopping in Malaga because they enjoyed the coast so much. November is a lovely time, you know. And then, there was some mention of going on after a few days, on business matters, I believe."

"What kind of business, did they say?"

"Ah, I think . . . The fair-skinned one mentioned something about Africa . . . Nigeria, I believe . . . and Biafra . . . Yes, Nigeria and Biafra. I recall now because there was some mention of business with Tshombe, the prime minister or whatever." He smiled. "The gentleman was a . . . he liked very much to talk. He was . . . how do you say? Bragging, yes. He was very much bragging."

Trott looked at Burnett quickly, then asked Portillo, "Did he mention what type of business?"

Portillo concentrated again, his head slowly shaking. "No . . . But there was some mention of a civil war, somewhere in Africa. And the business had to do with politics, I believe. Dealing with politicians. I am sorry, gentlemen; it is quite a few months ago."

"You're being quite helpful," Trott said. "Do you recall if there was any mention of Switzerland, or Sweden?"

"No, of that I am fairly certain. I believe one of the gentlemen mentioned something about going to Lisbon. But Switzerland, no."

Burnett puffed on his pipe. The African thing again. The story Forget gave about knocking off the head honcho in Biafra for some oil companies. Complete bullshit. And yet—here it was again. Forget said they had all gone to Tangiers, and the Limadet passenger manifest corroborated it. So the three were heading south, into Africa, and toward Biafra and Nigeria. Coincidence? But what was Norma Wilson going along for? And why the mention of Tshombe? Vaguely, Burnett associated the name Tshombe with a deposed African ruler, Moise Tshombe, now rotting in some jail. The whole thing kept getting more involved, more entwined with cross-plots and tangent developments. And all Burnett wanted to do was find one aging blonde in a white mink coat.

Burnett absently checked his watch again, then pulled his pipe from his mouth and tapped gingerly at the glowing ashes with his finger. The stop-off in Malaga to check out the arrest had been convenient, Burnett was thinking. They had been headed toward Tangiers anyway. But at Malaga police headquarters, the two men had received a message from Nieto: the S.S. *Rafaello* would be docking tomorrow at Genoa, Italy.

Burnett and Trott could fly to Genoa and confirm Devins' presence aboard ship before unloading. Then a tail on his movements in Europe should prove interesting. Burnett was sure Devins wasn't running yet, but neither could he believe he was just taking a vacation—to the very site of Norma Wilson's disappearance. Tailing Devins would take time, time away from tracking down Norma. But the chance was too good to pass up: there was a real possibility Devins would lead them to her, or at least to some evidence of the murder. Later, if necessary, Burnett and Trott could fly to Tangiers and pick up the trail again. If there was enough time . . .

His thoughts flashed back to the grand jury room, to the grim-faced men and women studying him like a laboratory animal. He knew Huffman would be putting something together. But it was Sana that Burnett was more concerned with. The darkly intense agent had Burnett in his sights; he would do everything he could to hang his counterpart in the D.A.'s office. Somehow, Burnett knew, there would be a showdown between the D.A. and the attorney general. And then it would be Burnett and Sana, face to face.

"No," Portillo replied to a question from Trott, "I do not recall such a thing."

"When they picked up their luggage, did any of them mention where they were going?"

"I am sorry. They said nothing. Mrs. Wilson simply paid the bill. She was very embarrassed, and very exhausted. And nervous, I believe."

"I see," Trott said quietly. He thought for a moment. "Señor Portillo, did there appear to be any, well, romantic relationship between Mrs. Wilson and either Mr. Devins or Mr. Forget?"

"That I could not tell."

The man at the desk walked up to the five men, coughing politely.

"Yes?" Portillo said coolly to the man.

He explained to Portillo in Spanish that Chief of Police Barranco was on the telephone, and wished to speak with Señor Trott.

Portillo thanked him, then invited Trott to use the desk telephone.

"Señor Trott," a deep, raspy voice said. "We have a message for you from Señor Nieto."

"Can you read it over the phone, Chief?" Trott asked in Spanish.

"Of course," the voice replied. There was a pause. "Señor Nieto advises you that the Interpol agency in Bern, Switzerland, has found a hotel registration for Norma Wilson and for Thomas Devins. It is at the Hotel Astor, in Zurich. It appears they stayed at the hotel for one night, the night of November 21, 1968."

Trott listened intently, his eyes fixed on an unseen distant object. "Anything else, Chief?"

"No further information. But Señor Nieto asks you to contact a Señor . . . Buehlman. Señor Buehlman is with the police section of the Federal Department of Justice and Police in Bern. He is the head of Interpol there. He will contact the proper authorities for you in Switzerland."

Trott hung up the receiver, then turned and looked at Burnett. "Norma Wilson may have been seen alive in Zurich," he said calmly.

"When?" Burnett asked.

"Seven days after she sailed for Tangiers."

Both men were thinking the same thing. If she had made

it to Switzerland, as Devins had claimed, was it possible they were chasing the wrong man? Was it even possible Norma Wilson could still be alive?

In any event, there was not enough time to go to Tangiers. Apparently, she had finished her mysterious business in Africa, and the trail now led to Switzerland. They would pick up her tracks in Zurich and go from there.

But first the two men had a rendezvous in Genoa.

Chapter 22

TROTT WAS WAITING on the docks when the luxury cruise ship *Rafaello* slowly glided up to the huge docking area in Genoa. He looked up at the towering bow of the ship as the thick braided ropes were thrown down to the waiting men on the pier. His eyes combed the railing, lined with waving passengers. Then he looked at the hundreds of bored faces around him, the hotel representatives and tour guides who patiently awaited the stream of wealthy Americans who would soon come down the gangplank. The face he was looking for—the dimpled, boy/man looking out of the passport photo, the slender, immaculately groomed figure strolling through the surveillance shots—was not yet visible in the crowd. Trott looked away from the ship, up a street that rose slightly into a series of small buildings. He picked out one of the taller structures, squinted in the sun as his eyes swept the roof.

On the top of the building, kneeling behind a guardrail, Burnett held the camera firmly to his eye. Growing out of the camera was a long, cumbersome-looking telephoto lens, dwarfing the parent camera. Gradually, the telephoto moved across a horizontal plane as Burnett studied each of the faces in the milling crowd. Suddenly, he zeroed in on Trott's familiar baby face gazing up at him. He gently pressed the shutter button. A souvenir for Trott. Then he continued panning across the jungle of faces, profiles and backs of heads. Still, the man he was looking for did not appear in the cross hairs.

Burnett and Trott had flown into Genoa early that morning. As the plane descended on its approach past the Italian seaport, Burnett had seen the giant cruise ship inching its way through the pale blue waters of the Mediterranean. He had felt a strange surge of warmth for Devins as the ship faded from view. It was the same vague glow of affection that often develops between two boxers after they have pounded at each other for ten rounds—an almost subconscious affection born of grudging respect and a very privately shared primitive contest.

The plane landed and the two men took a taxi to police headquarters in Genoa. There, they identified themselves and explained their mission to Doctor Angelo Costa, the rotund, affable and articulate chief of police. Within minutes, Dr. Costa was in touch with the *Rafaello's* captain by ship-to-shore radio, and learned that there was no Thomas Devins aboard. However, an Adelle Devins *was* aboard, occupying a room with a Clay Kimberly. Burnett had recognized Kimberly's name as being a friend of Devins, an habitué of the gay bars along Santa Monica Boulevard and the Sunset Strip. He wondered why Devins' wife and his friend were traveling together in the same stateroom.

Trott then theorized that Devins may still be meeting the ship at the dock. Could the Chief find out if a Thomas Devins was at any of the hotels? Costa replied that their hotel control bureau would not receive the registration cards for some days yet; it would take many hours to call each hotel and wait for the manager to check the registration.

Then Burnett suggested that Devins would stay in nothing but the best hotels. The style of the Arkansas dropout was to go first class everywhere. What was the plushest, most expensive hotel in the area? The Excelsior, Costa replied immediately. The Chief had one of his men call the Excelsior Hotel. Within minutes, the man returned: a Thomas Devins, holding an American passport, had registered one hour earlier at the Excelsior, room 203.

Trott and Burnett thanked Dr. Costa, then took a taxi to the Excelsior. Located on a hill above the city, the Excelsior

197

was a remnant of the Victorian Age: huge foyers, massive marble pillars, winged statues, polished tile. At the reception desk they identified themselves to the hotel manager. At first reluctant to believe the college boy and the cowboy were for real, the manager quickly gave them his cooperation upon the mention of Doctor Costa's name. Trott had registered in the guest book two names below Devins; Devins would not recognize the newly assigned prosecutor's name if he happened to glance at the sheet. Then the manager arranged for the men to stay in room 202, adjacent to 203 and with a locked door between the two rooms.

Obviously embarrassed to be carrying Burnett's tattered old duffel bag, the porter led the two Americans up to their room and quickly left them without waiting for a tip. As Trott unpacked his suitcase, Burnett placed his ear to the door separating them from Devins' room. He heard nothing. Then the two men assembled the telephoto unit and agreed on a plan: Trott would circulate among the crowd waiting for the ship's disembarkation, since Devins would not recognize his face. Burnett would meanwhile survey the area from a nearby rooftop, through the camera's high-power lens; he could also take pictures for possible use later as evidence, should the tail dig up incriminating conduct by Devins. More than likely, Devins would just pick up his wife and friend and escort them back to the hotel. But they didn't want to miss any chances.

Burnett shifted uncomfortably under the hot Italian sun as he peered over the rail through the rectangular viewfinder: a bored man in a multicolored uniform, a long-haired little girl filled with excitement, a gray-haired old grandmother patiently searching the ship's rail, a pretty girl waving excitedly . . . Then he saw him.

Burnett almost passed over the man in the plaid sport shirt. But something caught his eye. Maybe it was the still calmness of the figure amid the surrounding tumult; maybe it was the neatly trimmed hairstyle or the freshly starched look of the clothing. But Burnett stopped cold. Quickly, he twisted the telephoto lens, zooming in on the man until it filled half of the rectangle. Carefully, he pressed the button, listening as the mechanism clicked. Then he studied the figure as it turned slowly, searching the crowd. He watched a slight smile form, watched as a slight curl in his hair drooped onto his forehead like a school kid's. Neat, trim, cool, charming, boyishly handsome . . . It suddenly occurred to Burnett that Devins and Trott were very similar in physical appearance. Trott was taller, but in their faces there was the same adolescent good looks, in their eyes the same spark of youthful energy. Each hid behind a deceptive facade of innocence, each had a quick mind that sprang from behind a cloak of naiveté. And yet, the two men could not have been more different: one a sociopathic murderer, the other an advocate of justice.

Devins' face turned toward the gangplank. Burnett panned to the line of passengers beginning to stream down from the ship. There, among the first of the departing passengers, he recognized the slim athletic beauty of Adelle Devins. Walking next to her was a tall, slender young man with long light-brown hair. He had a thin face, but Burnett could not make out the features in detail. He wore a flowered shirt with an oversize collar, opened almost to his belt, and skin-tight yellow pants. Clay Kimberly, Devins' gay friend. What was his role in all this?

Burnett clicked another picture of Devins, then zoomed in on Adelle and Clay, clicking as they walked off toward the customs area. Then Burnett backed away from the rail and walked toward the door leading down into the building. Trott had the Devins party in his sight; he would follow them in a waiting taxi and call Burnett at the hotel if Devins didn't take Kimberly and Adelle directly there.

The door opened and Trott walked in. "They're on their way up," he said.

Burnett, lying on the bed, sat up. "No stops?"

Trott shook his head. "It took a little time at customs, though. Adelle and that Kimberly guy brought a dog with them. A big German shepherd."

Burnett tried to remember if he had seen any doghouses in Devins' backyard, or any food or water dishes sitting anywhere.

"Some kind of quarantine check, I guess," Trott added. "The dog held them up for an hour or so. But then they jumped into a VW bus and drove straight up here."

"Rental?"

"Probably. Devins was driving. I'll run the license number by Costa."

Burnett walked over to the ornate chest of drawers and picked up the small tape recorder. He tested it, then set the machine for "record."

"Steve, what about the—"

"Shh!" Trott whispered suddenly, his hand in the air.

The voices, only a low mumbling, were coming closer to their door. A man's voice, then a woman's voice. A laugh. The voices passed by them down the hallway. They heard the footsteps stop, a clicking sound, and then a door opening.

Burnett grabbed the tape recorder and walked to the smaller door separating Devins' room from their own. He pressed his ear to the wood. He could barely hear the hallway door being closed. A muffled laugh, then low voices as if off in the distance, too far off to be heard.

Burnett put his ear to the wall. Nothing. He got down on his knees, then lay down on his stomach next to the door. There was a clearance of about three-quarters of an inch from the bottom of the door to the carpeting. Through it, he could just barely see a pair of black leather shoes about ten feet on the other side of the door. Devins? Or Kimberly?

He put his ear up against the opening in the door, straining to hear anything. If only he could hear Devins talking about Norma Wilson, discussing plans to thwart the investigation, to hide the body, to dispose of the money— anything that could be used in court. The beauty of this eavesdropping was that it would be admissible in court as evidence; there was no constitutional right to privacy outside of the United States, no need for obtaining a search warrant to "bug" a room.

Burnett pushed the tape recorder against the crack. He gently pushed the "on" switch, then again strained to listen.

Again, only a distant murmuring was audible—voices, but no distinct words. Burnett turned the sensitivity on the recorder to maximum, then again placed his ear to the crack. He could hear the voices shifting from one part of the room to another, between moments of silence. A drawer opened, a toilet flushed. Again there was laughter, low, muted. And again the voices, too blurred and distant to understand.

Burnett got up, shaking his head. He carried the recorder across the room and into the bathroom. Trott followed him and closed the door. Burnett placed the recorder on the sink, ran the tape back to the beginning, then flicked the "play" switch. There was a dull roar in the background, broken by a sharp crackling of static, as the small tape slowly unwound. Almost drowned by the roaring, far off in the background, the voices Burnett had heard were mumbling something. But the words were still indistinct, still a dull jangle of meaningless sounds.

"We'll have to use the tube mike," Burnett said quietly.

Trott looked at him, saying nothing. They both knew it would be risky. Burnett had brought a narrow steel tube containing a highly sensitive microphone. Hooked up to the tape recorder, they could slide it under the crack in the door and a few inches into the room. Then the conversations could be clearly heard—*if* it weren't detected. *If* Devins didn't see the thin metal tube inching under the door into his room.

The two men walked out of the bathroom. Burnett stepped over to the chest of drawers, pulled out the long, thin metallic device and quickly hooked it up to the recorder. Then he walked over to the wooden door and again lay down at its foot.

Slowly, agonizingly slowly, he fed the steel tube under the door, a quarter of an inch at a time, moving, then stopping, waiting, listening for any sudden movements or sounds in the next room that would indicate discovery. Then again, another quarter of an inch.

In five minutes, Burnett had managed to push the tube so that two inches of it projected past the door and into the room. That should be enough, he thought. He reached for the recorder.

Suddenly he froze. There was a strange sound coming from under the door, loud and close by.

Burnett glanced quickly at Trott, then back at the crack. Again he heard it: a loud whispering sound directly at the crack. It was coming from within a few inches of the mike. Burnett and Trott listened in the silence.

Again the sound came, but this time Burnett knew what the sound was: the German shepherd was sniffing at the tube mike!

Quickly, he reached for the tube and slowly began pulling it back. He could hear the sniffing again, could hear the scratching of the dog's nails on the carpeting next to the door.

Within seconds, the tube mike was withdrawn. Burnett lay there in silence, listening. He heard a shuffling sound, then a voice coming from right next to the door.

"What's wrong, boy?" Burnett could recognize the voice of Adelle Devins standing inches away from him. "Huh? You want to go in there? C'mon, boy, you can't go in there."

Trott and Burnett remained frozen in position as the sniffing finally stopped and the voice faded away.

Burnett got to his knees, then stood up. He stepped back from the door, looking at Trott.

Trott looked back at him. Slowly, a smile formed on Trott's face.

Burnett grinned. "Son of a bitch!" he said.

Suddenly the two were laughing uncontrollably, trying with all their might to hold it in. Trott held his stomach with one hand, covering his mouth with the other, fighting to keep from laughing out loud. Tears were beginning to form in his eyes.

"Son of a bitch," Burnett managed to say again, between convulsions of silent laughter.

* * *

Burnett tried three more times that day to slide the mike under the door. Each time the big dog immediately came to the door, sniffing and scratching. And each time Burnett had quickly pulled the steel tube back, waiting for the dog to tire and wander away.

On the next day, Devins, Adelle and Kimberly took a tour of the city. Trott followed the trio from a distance but noticed nothing suspicious in their activities.

Finally, on the eve of the second day, after yet another unsuccessful attempt to slide the tube under the door, Trott and Burnett decided to give it up. They had only a few days left. Time was closing in on them, and they were getting no closer to finding Norma Wilson. They had to go on.

The trail led now to Zurich.

203

Chapter 23

TROTT AND BURNETT were met on their arrival in Zurich by a uniformed officer who drove them to the headquarters of the *Kriminalpolizei* on *Kasernenstrasse,* deep within the medieval yet antiseptically modern city. There, the two men were introduced to the chief of the "Criminal Police," Paul Grob, a smooth, polished man in his early fifties.

The Chief listened as Trott outlined the purpose of their investigation. They needed to review hotel control's registration cards from the Hotel Astor for November 21, 1968, then verify the signatures. After this, they would like to check with the Bureau of Missing Persons for any reports of unidentified bodies. Finally, they wished to visit the Hotel Astor and make certain inquiries. When Trott had finished, Doctor Grob pushed a buzzer and said something in a guttural German dialect into the speaker. Within seconds, a man in his early forties walked briskly into the room and stood erect before the Chief's desk. He was solidly built but with a slender face, fair skin and efficiently short sandy-colored hair.

"Korporal Fritz Faes, gentlemen," the Chief said in English to Trott and Burnett. "Korporal Faes is from our *Mordburo.*" He looked at Burnett and smiled slightly. "Our homicide section. I am assigning him to you. He will be at your disposal for as long as you require!"

Doctor Grob handed Faes a slim Manila file, then quickly filled him in on his new assignment. A few minutes later, the three men were walking out of the Chief's office and down a long gleaming hallway.

Two officers in uniforms that vaguely reminded Burnett of the *Wehrmacht* walked down the mirrored hallway toward them. Their hair was close-cropped, their uniforms immaculately pressed, and they walked in cadence, quickly. There was a polished efficiency about them that clashed violently with the haphazard scene in the police stations that Burnett and Trott were used to. The two officers stared at Burnett as they came closer, looked almost in disbelief at his cowboy boots and his baggy gray trousers. Burnett grinned at them, then winked. The two officers continued staring as the three men walked past them.

The three men turned down another hallway, then walked through a numbered door. "Hotel control," Faes advised the Americans. He said something to a man in a crisply pressed uniform behind a counter.

A few seconds later, the man returned with two cards from the Hotel Astor. Trott and Burnett spread the two cards out on a counter, next to Norma Wilson's will, and compared the signatures.

"Can we get an expert analysis from your handwriting department, Korporal Faes?" asked Trott.

"Of course," Faes said. "Tell me which signatures you wish compared. I will have these submitted at once to Herr Erismann, our handwriting expert. It will take perhaps two hours."

Trott looked at his watch. Then he looked back at the card with "Thomas Devins" printed on the top line. "Are you sure there were no cards for a Robert Forget?" he asked Faes.

"Quite sure, Herr Trott," Faes replied. "If a Robert Forget had stayed at the Astor or at any other hotel in the canton, there would be a record." He looked at Burnett, then back at Trott. "Herr Forget did not stay at a hotel in Zurich during November of last year. Of this we can be quite sure."

Trott nodded. "Right. Well, let's get on to the Astor, huh?"

"Yep," Burnett replied.

"Herr Erismann will be finished when we return," Faes said.

The three men walked out of the building to Faes' waiting car, a silver BMW. He drove them across town to the elegantly aging hotel. Inside, Faes made an inquiry at the reception desk and was promptly ushered into the office of the *direktor,* Ewald Schlotter. The tall, elderly man rose as the three men entered. Faes showed the *direktor* his credentials, then quickly explained the purpose of their visit. Schlotter listened politely, looking very distinguished in his black suit and gray vest. "And so you have questions?" he asked in English.

Trott laid Devins' registration card on the desk in front of the *direktor.* "Herr Schlotter, we would very much appreciate it if you would go back over your records for this date and tell us if any telephone calls were made from Herr Devins' room or from Frau Wilson's room."

Schlotter lifted the receiver from the telephone and spoke into it in sharp clipped tones. Two minutes later, a young man knocked and entered the room with two sheets of paper. Trott and Burnett studied the two sheets. They were closing bills for rooms 210 and 311, occupied by Devins and Norma Wilson. Quickly, they found what they were looking for: each bill had a long-distance telephone call charged to the room. The number was identical.

Burnett pulled out a wad of scratch paper from a shirt pocket and borrowed a pen from Trott. He wrote down the number.

"We can have the number traced," Faes said.

"Is there anything else I may assist you with?" Schlotter asked.

"May we have copies of the registration and the bill?" Trott asked.

"Immediately," he replied.

Trott thanked him for his help, and the three men left.

As they drove back, Trott turned to Faes. "We have some information that Mrs. Wilson may have opened an account in Zurich on the 21st or 22nd, probably a secret numbered account. Any chance of confirming the account—of finding out how much is in it, or if there've been any withdrawals?"

"Herr Trott," he said in a low voice. "The banking laws in our country are very strict. Very strict."

"I understand," Trott said. "But this can be critical information. It may tell us if Mrs. Wilson is still alive. Possibly, our suspect had a joint account and withdrew the money by himself. Or—"

"This is very dangerous," Faes said. "There are many things I can do for you. Many ways I can help. But the banks . . ."

"Can we at least find out if an account exists in either name?"

Faes was silent, his face stoic, revealing nothing. Then he said, "I will try. I will make some inquiries. But I must clear this." He drove in silence for a moment, then added, "This is very . . . sensitive. I do not know if I can help you. But I will try."

Faes took Trott and Burnett to the office where they had left the registration card and exemplars of Norma Wilson's signature. He introduced them to Erismann, the handwriting expert, then stepped out of the room, promising to return shortly.

"You have an opinion, Herr Erismann?" Trott asked the little man, in German.

"Oh, yes," he said. "There is no question. They are the same."

"The signature on the registration card is authentic?"

"The individual who signed the documents you supplied is the same individual as the one who signed the hotel registration."

Trott looked at the puzzled Burnett, then back at Erismann. Again in German, he asked, "This is not a qualified opinion?"

"It is not qualified," Erismann replied confidently. "There is no question. I am 100 percent sure that the signatures are the same."

Trott turned to Burnett again. "We've got a match," he said in English.

A match, Burnett thought. Then Norma Wilson was alive on the morning of November 22, 1968. But where did she go next? If she stayed at another hotel in Switzerland, Buehlman would eventually discover it and notify them here. But was there time?

"Thank you, Herr Erismann," Trott said.

The little man smiled, bowed slightly, then turned and walked out of the room.

Trott looked at Burnett. "You brought the dental records?"

Burnett pulled out a small envelope, patting it.

"Okay," Trott said. "Let's head down to Missing Persons. Faes said he'd meet us there."

The two men stepped out into the shining hallway, then walked down to a stairway. They climbed to the second floor, then walked down another highly polished, antiseptic hallway. Trott kept looking at the numbers on the doors, finally stopped at one.

"Ja?" the burly man in uniform at the desk asked.

Trott identified himself in German, then handed the dental X-rays and photographs of the dental mold to him. Quickly, he also gave Norma Wilson's age and description, then added a photographic portrait of the woman. The man finished writing down the information, took the photographs and X-rays and stepped out of the room.

"He's checking," Trott said to Burnett in the empty room.

"Efficient bastards, aren't they?"

"They are," Trott answered with a smile. "I just hope they can give us something on the bank account. If there is one."

The door opened and Faes walked in. "Gentlemen," he said in English. "I have information for you. The telephone number—it is Portuguese. In Lisbon. It is registered to the Consulate of Biafra."

Burnett glanced quickly at Trott. The Biafran Consulate, he was thinking—Okuma Aikba—a trip to Africa—a meeting on a boat with foreign officials—a secret Swiss bank account—Moise Tshombe—revolution—assassination . . . Jesus! he thought. This was getting complicated. Where did a murdered millionairess fit into all this?

"The Consulate of Biafra, in Lisbon," Trott repeated slowly.

"That is correct," Faes said. "Now . . ." His voice dropped. "As to the matter we discussed in the car . . ."

"Yes?"

"There is no account at present for Frau Wilson."

"Was one ever opened?" Trott asked quickly. "Was one opened and later closed out?"

Faes shook his head emphatically. "No, I am sorry. This is all. This is what I was able to learn. It is not possible to learn more. And . . ." He looked directly at Trott. ". . . this is not official. You understand?"

Trott nodded.

The man who had walked off with Norma Wilson's photographs and X-rays returned.

"Ah," Faes said. "Gentlemen, this is Detective William Jakob."

"We've met," said Trott.

Jakob smiled. "I have checked the records," he said in German.

"Ja?" Trott replied.

"We have reviewed all discovered bodies in the canton, all discovered bodies since November 21st of last year." He shook his head. "There is nothing. There has been no body found that matches this woman's description."

Trott sighed deeply. "No match on the body," he said to Burnett. He turned to Faes. "Can we leave copies of the photos and X-rays in case a body turns up?"

Faes said something to the uniformed man. Then, to Trott, he said, "He has already reproduced these things. Herr Buehlman will be notified if Frau Wilson's body appears. And there is another matter. The automobile you mentioned—the one that Herr Devins rented in November?"

"Yes?" Trott replied.

"Avis automobile rental," Faes said simply, handing Trott a piece of paper. "November 22, 1968. Herr Devins rented a Volkswagen bus in Zurich from the Avis automobile agency. As you see," Faes continued, "Herr Devins indicated Locarno as his immediate destination. That is to the south, near the Italian border. In the canton of Ticino."

Burnett and Trott studied the document in silence. Rented on November 23rd at Geneva. So far, it checked with Devins' story that he and Norma Wilson had driven from Zurich to Locarno, stayed the night, and then driven on to Geneva.

"The mileage is roughly correct," Faes added, "for a trip from Zurich to Locarno and then on to Geneva."

Locarno, Burnett thought. He had heard of it—a sleepy picturesque Swiss village on the shores of Lake Maggiore, surrounded by the remote peaks of the Swiss and Italian Alps. The Alps, he thought; they would be a perfect place to dispose of a body. Thousands of square miles of remote, eternally snow-covered mountain ranges. Lonely, desolate roads winding for miles without a human being . . .

Locarno.

Chapter 24

Giovani Ponti's face was dark, his eyes blacker than his oily hair; yet a broad smile lent radiance to his appearance. He was a big man, but his quick, catlike movements betrayed his bulk. His thick, heavy features suggested a dull wit, and yet he spoke to the two Americans in an animated, rapid-fire English. Giovani Ponti was a study in contradictions, a ferret in the frame of a bear.

Ponti leaned back in the leather chair, propping his feet on the desk which was dwarfed by his size. As chief detective of the *Polizia Cantonali Ticinese* in Locarno, it had been Ponti whom Herr Buehlman had called to pave the way for Trott and Burnett in their search for Norma Wilson.

Upon their arrival in Locarno, they were assigned to Sergeant Alino Pedretti who would assist them in their search while in the canton. The three men had immediately gone to the Bureau of Hotel Control, requesting a registration search for Thomas Devins, Norma Wilson and Robert Forget for November 22, 1968. The canton of Ticino did not use registration cards; rather, guests at hotels signed a check-in book, and the names were then copied onto a list by the hotel management and forwarded to the police.

Within a few minutes, hotel control had located an entry on the master list for Devins: he had checked into the Muralto Hotel on November 22, 1968, and checked out on November 23. Oddly, he had listed his occupation as "student." But there were no records of a Robert Forget nor, ominously, of a Norma Wilson.

The three men then joined in the search through the records, combing the registration list for some indication that the wealthy woman had stayed at another hotel or had checked in on a later night. And while they searched, the image of the vast lonely stretches of the Alps kept passing through Burnett's mind. The two men had just driven from Zurich through the massive ranges of mountains, and Burnett's professional eye had continuously sought out—and found—small, rarely traveled roads that branched off from the highway to climb into the forbidding loneliness of the snow-covered peaks.

Then Pedretti found it. He had returned to the registration list for the Muralto on November 22 and looked for the two room numbers adjacent to Devins' room. One had been occupied by a "Mr. Urlson." Could the "Mr." have been a mistake? And Norma Wilson's handwritten "Wi" appeared to the *concierge* as a "Ur"?

Locarno's hotel control had only the master list, not copies of the signatures themselves. So Pedretti, Trott and Burnett hurriedly drove through the village to the stylish resort hotel near the lake. There, they conferred with the manager, Dario Lupi. The gracious Signore Lupi quickly obtained the sign-in book, thumbed through the pages to November 22, ran his finger down the column, down to "Thomas Devins, USA." Directly after it was the handwriting that both Trott and Burnett had come to know as if it were their own: *Norma Wilson.*

Trott handed the book to Burnett. The hotel employee had, in fact, misread "Wilson" as "Urlson"; apparently, he had concluded that "Norma" was "Norman," and added a "Mr." on his own.

Burnett looked again at Devins' signature directly above Norma Wilson's. Why would he have listed his occupation as "student"? Was it some joke he shared with Norma, or was there some sinister purpose in it?

Trott received permission from Signore Lupi to take the

book to police headquarters for expert handwriting analysis. But he and Burnett already knew what the result would be. Norma Wilson had left the Muralto on November 23 with Devins—alive.

The telephone rang on the small desk.

"Excuse me," Ponti said to the seated Americans. He picked up the phone, said something quickly, then listened, nodding vigorously every two or three seconds. "*Sì, sì, grazie,*" he said finally, and hung up. "Signore Trott, this is the department of the missing people I talk to. They find nothing. The photographs, the . . . ah . . ."

"X-rays," Trott said.

"*Sì,* X-rays . . . the teeth . . . ah, there is not such a body in all of Ticino, you see? This the records prove. Nothing since before November 23." He shrugged his heavy shoulders, raised his palms upward in helplessness. "I am so sorry."

Trott smiled. "We appreciate your help, signore."

"It is nothing. Soon, we have the writing decision."

"Can you ask Missing Persons to make copies of the records, in case her body turns up?"

"But of course," Ponti replied, waving his hand. "This will be done."

"One other thing, signore," Burnett said suddenly.

"*Sì?*"

"If you were going to drive from here to Geneva, in November, in a VW bus, what road would you take?"

Ponti raised his eyebrows. "But there is only one, signore." He rose from his chair lithely, without effort, walked across the room and opened a door. Trott and Burnett followed him out of the room and down a narrow corridor. Ponti came to a stop outside of a glass-paneled door and opened it.

It was a small office, much like Ponti's, but with a larger desk. Or did it just seem larger to the two men without Ponti sitting behind it? There were two chairs facing the desk, a small bookcase, a coatrack. Otherwise, the plainly furnished room was bare. He would have recognized the room anywhere, Burnett thought; it was the same room that police detectives throughout the world lived in.

Except for the near wall. Ponti now walked toward that wall, pointing his thick finger at it. Mounted flush against the wall was a large, multicolored and contoured relief map of Switzerland and the land immediately surrounding it. It appeared to be a solid mass of interlocking mountains, one merging into another.

"Here." Ponti jabbed at a long serpentine of blue. "Lago Maggiore. And here," he indicated the northern end of the lake, "it is where we are. Locarno. Very well, you see. You go on the road, here, through the Centovalli . . ." His finger traced the thin red line that wound through a maze of browns and greens. ". . . down into Valle Antigorio and into Domodossola." He looked up. "It is nice city, Domodossola."

"That's in Italy?" Trott asked.

"*Sì*. Italy. You go into Italy, then out again, back to Svizzera . . . Switzerland." He turned back to the map. "You see, signores, here, you climb up into mountains, big mountains. Monte Leone," he jabbed at a peak, "and Fletschhorn. Many very big mountains. Very hard road. Thin, go side to side," he said, snaking his hand through the air in a twisting motion. "And then, you go over Simplon Pass. Very high, very cold. Much snow."

"It's open in November?" Trott asked.

"*Sì*, yes, it is open November." His thick finger continued on along the winding red line. "Then into Brig . . ." He shrugged, not impressed with the city. "You are in Bernese Alps, now. You go along here, through Sion. To the south, there are very large mountains. Weisshorn. Matterhorn." His finger went on. "You go to Martigny, here. You go from Martigny to north, go past Dents du Midi, here—big mountain—and . . ." His finger stopped at the eastern end of a large kidney-shaped lake. "St. Gingolph." He smiled. "Nice, St. Gingolph. It is in France. You will like it." Then he looked back at the map, shrugged. "You see, you go along

Lac Leman, to the west, and soon you are again in Switzerland, and then Geneva."

Burnett continued studying the map in silence.

"What about this route?" Trott asked, pointing to a red line that headed north out of Locarno.

Ponti shook his head. "No, I do not think this. You must go longer way, into San Gottardo Pass. This takes more *kilometros,* more time."

The Saint Gotthard Pass, Trott pondered for a moment. "And what about this?" He ran his finger down Lake Maggiore.

"*Sì,* this is possible. But then you must go back, and to Domodossola, as before. More time."

"How long for the whole trip," Trott asked. "Locarno to Geneva, through the Simplon Pass?"

"I think, maybe, six or seven hours, no more."

Burnett pulled out a piece of paper. It was a copy of Devins' rental agreement with Avis. He walked up to the map. "How far from Zurich to Locarno, Chief?" He pointed to a red line. "Along the main road."

"I think, maybe 300 *kilometros.*"

Burnett nodded, looked down at the mileage numbers on the rental form. "So, we subtract 300 from this total, and . . ." He looked up again at Ponti. "How far from here to Geneva, through the Simplon Pass?"

"Mm . . . this is, I think, 400 *kilometros,* maybe little more, maybe little less."

"And if we went through St. Gotthard," Burnett went on, "or down Lake Maggiore, how much farther?"

Ponti shrugged. "Hundred *kilometros,* maybe."

Burnett studied the mileage figures again on the rental form. Seven hundred five kilometers. Then he looked up at Trott. "They took the main route, through the Simplon Pass."

"Are there many small roads leading off from the main road, Chief?" Trott asked.

"Oh, yes. Many small roads. But I do not advise them." He shook his head. "They are bad roads, many of them.

They go to nowhere, into the mountains, very high. Very cold, nothing there."

There was a knock on the door. Ponti opened it and spoke briefly with a young man in uniform. Then he turned toward Burnett and Trott.

"Signores," he said, "the signature on the hotel book." He smiled. "It is good. It is of Signora Wilson."

"We thank you, Chief," said Trott.

Ponti held up his hands in protest. "Nothing. I do nothing. You stay in Locarno this night?"

"Yes. We leave by car tomorrow morning. For Geneva."

Burnett continued to study the map in silence, a gloomy image of a steep, winding, deserted mountain road forming slowly in his mind.

The two lone figures stood on the high snow-covered ridge, looking down on the peaceful green valley far below. A tiny village was distantly visible—a scattering of toy chalets and farmhouses. Just beyond the village, where the Alps slowly began to rise up into lofty whiteness, a shepherd was barely visible, leading his flock down the mountain slopes and into the protected pastures of the valley.

Burnett shivered, clutching the lambs wool jacket closer to him. Swirls of fresh snow blew about his pointed-toe boots, sticking to the brown caribou hide. He ran his fingers through his hair, then pulled out a box of matches and tried to light his pipe. Three times he struck a match, and three times the icy wind quickly snuffed out the flame.

He put the matches away, then looked out again across the scattered peaks. In the distance, half hidden by a misty haze, he could see a dark form rising above the others like a brooding giant. Near its peak, a twisted black claw thrust into the ominous gray-black clouds, seeming to tear at the heavens with primeval talons.

"Meet you back at the car," Trott said suddenly. "I've had enough of the wind and the gloom." Then he turned and began walking down the narrow winding path.

Burnett watched him go down the trail. It was thinly covered with snow, the men's footprints already being disintegrated by the gusting wind. The trail clung precariously to the side of the mountain, thousands of feet above the other world far below. He could see that Trott was breathing heavily, clouds of mist shooting from his mouth, the thin cold air biting deeply into his lungs as he walked. Trott stumbled for a moment, then regained his balance and continued on down toward the road where the small Fiat was parked.

If Norma Wilson had been murdered in these mountains, Burnett reasoned, it would be unlikely anyone would ever find the body. There were thousands of square miles of unbroken mountains, with the few villages small in size and spread far apart. If a body were to be buried where he stood, it could rest undiscovered for centuries.

Burnett looked back down the narrow path. Trott had almost reached the car. The two men had decided to take one of the small roads that branched off the highway into the surrounding mountains. There had been many such roads, and they had wondered where they led. This one had wrapped along the side of a cliff, climbing ever higher into the overlying darkness, weaving its way through gorges and over small passes. Suddenly, for no apparent reason, it had ended here. It had taken them twenty minutes to drive up the torturous road, another ten minutes to hike up the steep path to the crest, overlooking the valley. During the entire time, neither man had seen a living soul—only the barely visible dot on the far valley floor that was a sheepherder.

A perfect place for a murder.

Burnett began to take a deep breath, stopped as the icy prongs dug into his chest. Three days, he thought to himself. He and Trott had to be back in Los Angeles in three days. And still they had not tracked down Norma Wilson. Was she somewhere in these lonely mountains, buried under the ice? If she was, he knew he would never find her, never be able to prove conclusively that Norma Wilson had been murdered.

Or was she really still alive? Would they open the register of the Intercontinental Hotel in Geneva and see the familiar, delicately scrawled signature? Had she really been alive in Geneva when Devins flew back to California, as he had claimed? Was it possible that Devins was innocent? And after Geneva, where did the trail go? Sweden? Africa?

Three days, Burnett pondered again. Three short days to find her. Three days, and then the two men would have to return to Los Angeles, empty-handed. And waiting for Burnett would be Sana. And Huffman. And the grand jury. And a gloating Tom Devins.

Everything depended now on whether Norma's signature rested on a ledger somewhere in Geneva. If it did, then Devins was home free.

Three days.

What more could be done? Put more pressure on Forget. Find a crack and then slam home the wedge. He was a gunrunner; there was room there for play. And the Volkswagen bus Devins had rented. Locate it, wherever it now was. Possibly a chemical test on the interior would still uncover traces of powder burns or blood. There was little pressure he could apply to Devins anymore; the wheeler-dealer had cleverly placed himself under the protection of the Attorney General. Burnett could possibly get an indictment against him for grand larceny—for the fraudulent transfer of Norma's hospital and office building. Even that would be tough, now that the attorney general was busily discrediting the D.A.'s entire investigation of Devins. The Arkansas dropout was smart, Burnett admitted to himself grudgingly: the best defense was a good offense. And somehow, he felt Devins had yet to fire his last salvo.

Norma Wilson had to be dead, Burnett once again told himself. And that little bastard had to have pulled the trigger. But how? Where? Why? And where was the body?

Burnett shook his head. He kicked at the small ridge of snow in front of him. Slowly, he turned and began walking down the steep trail. Steve Trott's words were running through his mind again. Driving out of Domodossola, Burnett had asked the young lawyer what the chances were of pinning a murder rap on Devins without a body.

"Slim," he had replied. "It's been done but not very often. The public just doesn't realize how easy it is to get away with murder—literally. If you can dump the body, you're halfway home. How can you prove—beyond any reasonable doubt—that someone has been murdered if there's no body, no witnesses, no confession? You can't even prove anyone's even dead, much less murdered."

But it had been done?

"Yes," he had answered cautiously. "It can be done. The whole case would be circumstantial, though. It'd have to be one hell of a strong case. No jury wants to convict on circumstantial evidence, especially not for murder one. And there's always the nagging doubt that, after the defendant was fried in the chair, the 'victim' would pop up somewhere, fit and healthy. No, it'd be mighty tough trying to get a murder conviction without a body."

What would it take?

"Witnesses," Trott had replied. "Or a confession."

Could it be done without a body, without witnesses, without a confession?

Trott had slowly shaken his head. "I doubt it. Theoretically, maybe. To prove murder, you've got to establish a 'corpus delicti.' The 'corpus' doesn't mean the body literally—it means the legal body of the crime itself. The corpus of murder one is the taking of a human life with premeditation and malice. So if you can convince a jury that a defendant has killed someone, and planned it out, then . . ." He had shrugged, then looked at Burnett. "But I wouldn't want to try it without witnesses or a body."

But, Burnett had pushed on, what if it could be done? Could they establish jurisdiction in Los Angeles County?

Again, Trott had shrugged. "Maybe," he had muttered. "Under California law, jurisdiction for a murder prosecution is in the state if the killing took place there, or if it were planned in the state, and the initial stages of the plan took place in the state."

If, then, it could be proven that Devins had planned the death of Norma Wilson while in Los Angeles and caused her to be flown out of Los Angeles for the express purpose of killing her, then the L.A. courts would have jurisdiction to try the case?

"Probably," Trott had said. "It's not a clear area of law. The state or country where the killing took place might insist that they had exclusive jurisdiction. And anyway, it would be hell trying to prove Devins had planned the murder in L.A., and then caused her to be flown out for the sole reason of killing her. There would have to be witnesses. And even then . . ." Trott had shrugged.

The lone figure walked slowly down the winding path, the white powder blowing past him in the cold whistling wind. A fine cake of iced snow had formed over his hair and on his moustache. There was a black briar pipe lodged between his clenched teeth, but no smoke rose from it. His eyes were moist from the biting cold. And the vague grin was gone from his face.

Chapter 25

Burnett and Trott looked up at the sign on the side of the old building on Geneva's Boulevard Carl-Vogt: *Corps de Police, Département de Justice et Police, République et Canton de Genève.* They walked quickly up the steps and through the large double doors. Once inside, the two men were directed down the main hallway and to the right.

Chief Louis Corboz rose from behind his desk, stepping forward with his arms extended in greeting. He was a middle-aged man of medium height, and wore a pair of wire-rimmed glasses that gave him the look of a studious accountant. Standing next to him was a younger man, tall, slender, and quietly polite, almost shy. Corboz introduced him as René Tomkins, an Inspector with the *Sûreté.* Corboz went on to explain that Tomkins, an accomplished mountain climber of some reputation in Geneva, was one of the *Sûreté's* best men. And he was being assigned to the two men to help them in their search for the missing Madame Wilson.

Burnett noted that, like the other plainclothes officers in Switzerland he had met, Tomkins carried no gun. In fact, in his perfectly tailored pinstripe suit, he looked more like a lawyer than a detective. Burnett suddenly felt self-conscious with the .38 Special bulging at his left side. When was the last time he had used it? he thought. Was it true that Americans were gun-happy, as the Europeans believed?

"Gentlemen," Corboz said with a smile, waving to the seats scattered around his large desk.

"Chief Corboz," Trott began, "the purpose of our—"

Corboz held a hand up with a smile. "In English, please, Monsieur Trott."

Burnett grinned. Trott wasn't getting to use his gift for languages very much in Switzerland; the Swiss all seemed to have a command of English and two or three other languages as well. Still, he had the feeling that Trott's attempts to speak the local language had been appreciated.

Trott explained the details of Devins' and Norma Wilson's trip to Zurich, the drive to Locarno, then through the Alps to Geneva. He mentioned the possibility of Robert Forget being involved, even McSpadden and Bill Wilson. And there was the mysterious Okuma Aikba. He explained that Devins had claimed he had stayed at a hotel in Geneva on November 23, but didn't recall which one; he had flown out on November 24 for the United States. Norma Wilson, he had told Burnett, had checked in on the 23rd at the Intercontinental Hotel and had stayed after his departure.

"And how may we help you?" asked Corboz. "Our facilities, they are at your disposal."

Jesus, Burnett thought. Every police agency they had contacted in Europe had bent over backwards to help them. Why couldn't agencies in the States offer that kind of assistance? Hell, he felt lucky just to get occasional grudging cooperation from L.A.P.D.

"Thank you, Chief," Trott replied. "Your help means a lot. And there are a number of matters . . ."

Corboz nodded, looked up at Tomkins. The quiet inspector was listening carefully, his eyes alert. This guy was a sleeper, Burnett decided as he studied the tall man out of the corner of his eye; there was a lot behind his silent, manicured appearance.

"First," Trott said, "we'd like a check by your hotel control. On Thomas Devins and Norma Wilson, for November of last year—specifically for November 23rd, and also for December of last year, and all of this year. It's possible that Norma Wilson may have registered under her maiden name, Bell, or her previous married name of Carty.

We'd also like a check of Forget, McSpadden, Aikba and Norma Wilson's husband William."

"This will be done immediately," Corboz said. "And?"

"Thomas Devins," Trott said. "We'll need a confirmation of his flight from Geneva on November 24th—confirmation that he was on the flight and didn't cancel out. Also, any flight manifests, train tickets, buses, car rentals—anything indicating Norma Wilson might have left Geneva after November 23rd. Under the name Bell, Carty or Wilson."

Tomkins wrote everything down calmly.

"Then," Trott went on, "we'd appreciate a check of your missing persons files. For Mrs. Wilson."

Burnett handed a large Manila envelope to Corboz. "Photographs, physical description, dental X-rays," he said.

"Inspector Tomkins, he will have the hotel control begin the investigation. And the airline, this he will also begin. And the train and automobile rental. But the bus, no, this is not possible." He sighed, lacing his fingers together. "But this Madame Wilson, I do not think she is the type to ride buses, no?"

"You're probably right, Chief," Trott replied. "Planes or trains, I'd say."

"*Bien.* And the 'missing persons,' I will personally present your records to them. If a woman's body has been found, we will know of it." He smiled. "And what else may we do?"

"We'd like to talk with the manager at the Intercontinental Hotel," Trott said. "And at the hotel where Devins stayed."

Corboz nodded. "Inspector Tomkins will personally escort you." He rose to his feet. "I will go with you to hotel control."

"We appreciate your help, Chief," Trott said. "If there's any way we can return the favor . . ."

Corboz smiled. "There is a way," he said. He looked at Trott, then at Burnett, his eyes sparkling mischievously. "In your Hollywood . . ."

"Yes?"

"You can obtain a signed photograph from the Monsieur John Wayne?" He grinned self-consciously, winked at the men. "It is for my grandson."

The Intercontinental was another of the lush, extravagant hotels that Norma Wilson had favored, filled with flashing crystal chandeliers, cold, glossy marble pillars and inch-deep pile carpeting. Tomkins immediately found the *sous-directeur*, Monsieur Volker Diewitz, and a large book was brought out and set on the reception desk for inspection.

Quickly, Burnett thumbed the pages, through April and August, through October. He could feel his heart beating a little faster, a little harder. Then November . . . the 14th, a few more pages, then the 20th . . . His throat was feeling dry now, a tightness setting in . . . What if Norma Wilson *had* stayed at the Intercontinental? The 22nd . . . He felt a coldness, a sudden feeling that the familiar delicate writing would stare up at him from the white paper . . . And the 23rd—November 23, 1968.

Burnett glanced up at Trott for a second. His partner was standing next to him, his eyes glued to the ledger. Tomkins stood on Burnett's other side, also concentrating on the large book. Slowly, Burnett ran his finger down the lines of handwriting, each unique in its own way. One boldly scrawled, another printed in clear letters, yet another an undecipherable flow of lines—Swiss, German, Swiss, French, French—and on down the page. Italian, Swiss, Swiss, U.S.—Burnett's finger froze at the U.S. His eyes looked to the left, to the erratic handwriting: James McKenna. The finger went on, slowly searching for the ornate penmanship that was burned indelibly in the investigator's mind.

Then there were no more names, only blank spaces on the page. Burnett flipped the page over. November 24th. Then he turned back to the 23rd. Once again, he slowly traced down the column of names. And once again it reached the end without crossing Norma Wilson's name or handwriting. Slowly, he straightened up and pulled the pipe from his coat pocket. He began stuffing it with tobacco, a slight grin returning to his face.

Trott looked to Tomkins. "Is it possible to—"

He was interrupted by Diewitz. "Messieurs," he said in a low, restrained voice. "A telephone call. For the *inspecteur*. If you will take it here, *merci*."

Tomkins stepped toward the telephone, said something, then listened. After a moment he again spoke briefly, then hung up.

"Monsieur," he said to Trott, "this was hotel control. They are now still in the records, they are still looking. But," he added, "they have found where Monsieur Devins stayed. The Hotel Richemond. Here in Genève. For one night, the 23rd of November, 1968." He looked at Burnett. "It is near to here."

"Let's go," Burnett said.

"Also," Tomkins added, "there is information from immigration. Monsieur Devins left Genève on November 24th, on Swissair. His destination was New York." He looked again at Burnett. "There was no cancellation."

Tomkins wheeled the small Renault through the traffic of central Geneva, then came to a stop at a red light. The cold wind coming off the lake whipped through the city, turning the faces of the pedestrians a bright scarlet. A small boy of about five, wearing *lederhosen,* walked next to his mother; his knees were a glowing red from the chill, but his eyes were on the small black-and-white police car.

Burnett sat in the back seat, the events of the day passing through his mind. The three men had driven to the Hotel Richemond where the *chef de reception,* a Monsieur Rais, had confirmed that a Thomas Devins, American, had stayed at the hotel on the evening of November 24, 1968. Room number 603. He had checked out early the next day.

Did the hotel still have a copy of his bill? Burnett asked. Five minutes later, the three men were studying a copy of the bill. On it was a charge for a long distance telephone call to the United States. Tomkins made a quick call on the hotel phone and learned that the number Devins had reached was located in the State of Washington, in a town called Sedro Woolley. Exactly as Forget had told Burnett.

While at the hotel, Tomkins had received another telephone call from headquarters. Missing Persons had found two unidentified bodies since November of last year, one of them female. However, it did not fit the description that had been supplied.

Tomkins looked across at Trott sitting in the passenger's seat. "You will leave copies of the X-rays and photographs?" he asked. "If any bodies are found in the future . . ."

"Certainly," Trott said quietly. "We'd be thankful to you for any help."

Where to now? Burnett asked himself. Assuming Corboz's boys found no evidence that Norma Wilson had stayed at another hotel, nothing showing she had left Geneva after the 23rd . . . Then what? Anyway, he thought, they had only two days left. Two days to find Norma Wilson. And not the slightest idea where to look.

Then Aikba's name flashed through his mind. The telephone calls to the Biafran Consulate in Lisbon. A talk with the mysterious African might prove interesting. Had the aging millionairess been involved in international intrigue? Had she been lured by her handsome young "adviser" into a gunrunning scheme or an assassination plot? Yes, he thought, if they couldn't find something on Norma here, then a trip to Lisbon would be a last-ditch shot.

The car radio crackled and Tomkins picked up the mike. A static-filled voice poured out of the speaker in rapid French. Linguist Trott listened, looking back at Burnett. Then the radio was silent.

"They have finished the review of files," Tomkins said in his calm, gentle voice. "There is no record of Forget, or of McSpadden or William Wilson. None of them stayed in Genève." He looked in the rearview mirror at Burnett. "For Madame Wilson, there is no record. She, also, did not stay in Genève on November 23rd. Or after this date. And she did not leave from Genève by airplane, train or hired car."

Burnett kept puffing softly on the pipe, his eyes on Tomkins in the mirror. Norma Wilson had left Locarno with Devins on November 22nd, he thought. The Avis rental agreement indicated they had taken a direct route to Geneva. But Devins had arrived in the city without her.

Norma Wilson's trail had ended somewhere high in the bleak loneliness of the Alps.

Chapter 26

Burnett and Trott flew into Lisbon from Geneva the following day. After clearing customs, they took a taxi to the American Embassy. There, Vice Consul Angel Roberto made a cursory search of records and advised them that the Embassy had no information indicating a Thomas Devins or a Norma Wilson had ever been in Portugal.

From the Embassy, the two men took a taxi to the headquarters of the Federal Police. Buehlman, their efficient Interpol contact in Bern, had again arranged a meeting for them: Assistant Director Rogerio Dias was expecting them in his office.

After a brief conference in Portuguese with Trott, Dias walked the two men to the hotel control section. A quick search revealed that neither Devins nor Norma Wilson had stayed at a hotel in Lisbon in the past two years.

With Trott interpreting, Burnett then asked the assistant director if the police had any records indicating that a Biafran by the name of Okuma Aikba was residing in Lisbon, or had stayed there—possibly as an employee or official at the Biafran Consulate.

"Ah, Senhor," Dias replied, shaking his head. "This Consulate, as you call it, it is very strange."

"How do you mean?" Trott asked.

"It has an unusual position in Portugal. The official standing of Biafra as a nation is not clear, you see. It is my understanding that independence of Biafra has not yet been recognized; it is still considered a part of Nigeria."

228

"Then what is the function of the Consulate here?"

Dias shrugged. "Officially . . . it is the voice of the Biafran Government, whatever that is. I understand that it is the only Biafran Consulate in Europe. It is, I believe, the . . . voice of the secession government in Europe—its window to the world."

"I see," Trott said.

"Officially," Dias added. "Unofficially . . ." He shrugged again, then added darkly, "I believe this Consulate is a front—a front for obtaining guns, for raising money, for hiring mercenaries to fight in the war down there."

"You have evidence of this?"

Dias shook his head. "We are told not to interfere."

"Is it possible, Senhor Dias, to locate this Okuma Aikba?" Trott asked.

"Ah, *si*. The Senhor Aikba. A moment, please?" Quickly, Dias made two telephone calls, jotting down some information on a piece of paper as he talked. Then he handed the paper to Trott. There were two addresses: *33 Rue Don Francisco de Almeida,* and *16 Avenida Torre del Belen.* The first, he explained, was the supposed Consulate of Biafra. The second was the residence of a Senhor "Ikpa," listed as living in Portugal under a Biafran passport.

The two Americans hailed another taxi, which snaked its way out of central Lisbon and into the rundown suburbs of the city. Finally, it turned onto a dirty street filled with rundown apartment dwellings. Ragged pieces of laundry hung from lines suspended between the buildings, and a faintly unpleasant smell permeated the air. A three-story building that had not seen paint in many years loomed up as the taxi came to a stop.

Burnett and Trott asked the driver to wait. They entered the building through an open door that hung limply on one hinge. A woman was mopping the hallway floor at the foot of the stairs.

Burnett glanced at the mailboxes, checking each of the six faded names of their owners. Neither an Aikba nor an Ikpa was listed there.

Trott began talking with the scrubwoman in Portuguese.

The thin, wrinkled old woman looked at him with rheumy eyes, only half-understanding what it was he wanted. Hesitatingly, in a broken voice of sandpaper, she told Trott that she had worked as a maid in the building for seven years. Yes, she said, she remembered a black man who had lived in one of the rooms. He was a small man, very quiet; he wore good clothes and never bothered anyone. Did she know where he was now? No, she answered, he had left a few months earlier. No, he told no one where he was going; the black man had no friends and kept to himself.

Five minutes later, the taxi delivered Burnett and Trott to another aging, weatherbeaten building. Dust covered the threadbare carpeting. On the third door from the end of a vacant corridor was a brass plaque announcing the offices of the Biafran Consulate.

The two men walked into a bare room with peeling paint and a window that was cracked. A lumpy couch lined the wall to the right, a shiny new desk rested incongruously in the center. Behind the desk sat a small black man.

"You are Americans?" he asked in English. He was no taller than five feet two and couldn't have weighed more than eighty or ninety pounds. His hair was short, his skin a deep, glowing black. He rose to his feet slowly, hesitantly.

"Yes," Trott answered. "Steve Trott." He nodded toward his partner. "Bill Burnett," he said. He pulled out his wallet, showed the little man the badge. "Assistant Director Dias of the Federal Police is helping us to find a gentleman."

The little man studied the badge carefully, then looked up at Trott. "My name is Uche," he said quietly, a touch of nervousness now in his voice. "What is it you wish to know?"

"We're looking for a gentleman who worked for the Consulate here, a Mr. Okuma Aikba, or Okuma Ikpa. Do you know him?"

"Yes. Mr. Ikpa was an employee here. But he has left."

"Where is he now?"

"I do not know, sir. I presume he has returned to Biafra. But I do not know."

"Biafra," Trott repeated. "What was his job here?"

Uche again looked at Burnett, then back at Trott. "He was a clerk, only a clerk."

The little guy's nervous as hell, Burnett thought. And lying through his teeth.

"And who works as the clerk now?" Trott asked.

Uche looked around the barren room, then back at Trott. "There is no clerk now. Nothing."

"This is the Consulate, isn't it?" Burnett asked. "I mean, you represent the Biafran Government?"

"That is true," Uche replied carefully.

Jesus, Burnett thought to himself. These guys must be having a hell of a time back home.

"Do you know, or have you ever heard of, a Thomas Devins or a Norma Wilson?" Trott asked. "Americans?"

"No," Uche answered, almost too quickly.

"Is Mr. Ikpa expected to return here?"

"No."

Trott studied the little man for a moment. "Look, Mr. Uche. We're from Los Angeles. We don't represent the police here. We're only interested in finding an older woman, Norma Wilson. Do you understand?"

"Yes," Uche replied. The nervousness and distrust were still in his voice.

"Now, there's a possibility that this Mr. Ikpa was involved with Mrs. Wilson and this Devins fellow in . . . well, maybe gunrunning." He looked carefully into the whiteness of the small eyes. "Or maybe something else."

"I do not think so," Uche said quietly. "This is a Consulate. It is not our business to do such things."

"Right, right," Trott said. "Frankly, we don't care. But this Mr. Ikpa—"

"He was a clerk, sir," Uche said. "Nothing more. He had no authority to be involved in such things. I am sorry, gentlemen."

"Mr. Uche," Trott persisted, "we are interested only in finding the woman. Nothing else concerns us."

"I wish I could help," Uche said politely. "I am sorry, gentlemen." He stared at Trott silently.

Trott shrugged. "Well, thank you anyway, Mr. Uche."

"Of course," he replied.

Trott glanced at Burnett, then turned and walked out into the hallway. Burnett followed him, closing the door behind him.

"Well," Trott sighed, "what do you say we get back to L.A.?"

"Sounds good," Burnett replied.

The two men walked out of the building into the sunlight, descended the stairs to the waiting taxi. They were silent as they drove across the city to the airport.

How had it happened? Burnett was wondering. Had Devins lured her out onto a deserted cliff and then pushed her off? Had he strangled her in the Volkswagen bus and then buried her on some isolated mountainside? However it had happened, he was sure now that Norma Wilson was dead.

And her murderer was Tom Devins.

Part III

THE KILL

Chapter 27

GEORGE STONER LEANED BACK in his chair as Burnett walked into the office. "You seen the papers this morning?" he growled.

"Nope."

"Page three," he said, throwing the L.A. *Times* across the desk. Burnett reached over and grabbed the paper, which was folded to the third page.

MURDER SUSPECT ANNOUNCES CANDIDACY

In a statement released yesterday at the Los Angeles Press Club, Thomas Devins, subject of a murder investigation by the District Attorney, announced that he was a candidate for state senator from the 26th Congressional District of the State of California . . .

In his statement, Devins said that he was not a politician but was scared by what is being done to the citizens of the County of Los Angeles by politicians. Devins stated that the Los Angeles County grand jury recently indicted Beverly Hills attorney Jerome Weber primarily on his testimony.

Jerome Weber was indicted because he tried to shake Devins down for $35,000 to squelch an investigation being conducted by the D.A.'s office, Devins said. The investigation revolved around a so-called murder which is alleged to have occurred in November 1968.

Devins further stated that even though he had offered

> on several occasions to submit to a lie detector test, the
> District Attorney had refused to conduct such a test . . .

Smart little bastard, Burnett thought with a grudging admiration. He had repeatedly tried to get Devins to meet with him, primarily to confront him with the possibility of a polygraph, but Devins had always weaseled out.

> Devins stated that since November of 1968, he, his
> friends and his business associates have been subjected
> to constant harassment from the District Attorney's
> office.
>
> Devins claims that he had provided the grand jury with
> information gathered by him with the aid of the Attorney
> General's office that implicated high-ranking members of
> Evelle Younger's staff in the shakedown attempt. He said
> that even though he felt that there was sufficient evi-
> dence to indict George Stoner, Chief of Investigations,
> and George Murphy, head of the special Investigations
> Division, the District Attorney had arrogantly refused to
> conduct an investigation of his two staff members.
>
> As a taxpayer and a citizen, Devins said, he was
> concerned with the breakdown of law and order at the
> District Attorney's level in the County of Los Angeles. He
> told reporters, "I call upon the citizens of the state to
> demand that the Legislature and the incumbent Attorney
> General immediately institute an investigation of the
> corruption and graft in the office of the man who now
> seeks even more power and authority with the law
> enforcement agencies of California, while he refuses to
> do anything about the wrong-doing in his own office."
>
> Devins called upon District Attorney Evelle Younger
> either to expose the corruption in his office or to with-
> draw immediately from seeking the office of State Attor-
> ney General and further to resign as District Attorney of
> Los Angeles County. He further called upon "the honest
> and concerned people of the state to support me to
> eliminate this double-edged type of justice."

"Thought you might be interested," Stoner said. "Your boy's been busy."

"Yeah, well, I haven't seen Tom for a while," Burnett replied. "I figure Sana's been sitting on him. Been kind of wondering what he's been up to."

"Real busy," Stoner repeated. "The son of a bitch." He took a deep drag on his cigarette, slowly exhaling the gray smoke. "I wonder if Sana put this state senator thing in his head. Or Huffman, or O'Brien himself."

Burnett shrugged. "Don't think so. Sounds too much like Devins—it's the way his mind works. It's his . . . style."

"Style!" Stoner snorted. "Like that goddamned shooting, I guess!"

A few days after Burnett and Trott had returned from Europe, Devins had shot two holes through the hood of his own Cadillac, then gone to the newspapers with charges of intimidation and "hit" orders put out by the D.A.'s office. There had been pictures of Devins standing next to the bullet holes of the car, and a local television station had picked up the story. A crusading TV reporter had even begun a series of stories on the Weber case, building Devins into a fearless hero of truth and justice.

Not bad for an ex-car-park jockey, Burnett mused.

"Okay. So much for the bullshit," Stoner said. "Gimme a status report."

"Well, Chief, we still got half the cops in Europe looking for Norma Wilson's body."

Stoner grunted.

"And we got some results on the VW bus Devins and Norma drove from Locarno."

Burnett had received a phone call from Giovani Ponti in Locarno a week earlier. Ponti informed him that the VW bus had been found. It had been sold by the Avis car rental agency to Fransesco Camnasio, a taxi driver in Lugano. Camnasio had turned around and resold the vehicle on the same day to a mechanic in Lugano, Giorgio Gatti. Finally, Gatti had sold it to Paulino Zambelli, a local baker. Burnett had asked Ponti to have the bus examined for any traces of blood, skin or hair; Ponti had assured him that this would be done immediately, and a technical report forwarded by air mail special delivery.

"So?" Stoner growled.

"They found blood in Devins' car." Burnett pulled a letter from the Ticino police out of his vest pocket. Stoner grabbed it, his eyes moving to the middle of the page:

> During investigations, performed on the inside of the vehicle, with the use of the solution Benzidin, we were able to obtain positive reactions on the arm rest of the door on the right side, on the profile of the seat and the back and front right side, and on the dashboard of the same side.
>
> Identical traces were found on the arm rest of the left door, that is to say on the side of the driver.
>
> Taking into consideration the age factor of the traces and considering that this great sensitivity of reaction exists only with blood, connection of reaction of 1/2.000.000 on one cubic millimeter of blood, we can say that there is a strong possibility that the reaction obtained is due to the presence of blood.
>
> Considering the age of the traces, it is impossible to proceed with a deeper examination which would give us the certainty that it consists of blood. On the other hand, both Camnasio and Gatti and also Zambelli have stated that they have never transported wounded or killed animals with the truck, and they exclude that said spots have been caused when the truck was in their possession.
>
> With the aforementioned premise, it can be concluded that the positive reactions obtained with the Benzidin method, in all probability, must be attributed to the presence of blood.
>
> Identification service
> Tsp. Casagrande E.

"Goddamn!" Stoner muttered. "So there's blood in the car. The old broad starts out on a ride with Devins and never finishes it. What about blood type? Did it match with hers?"

"Can't do it," Burnett replied. "The samples in the VW are just too old."

"Okay," Stoner muttered. "Okay. So you got the foreigners doing all the work for you. So what've *you* been doing?"

"As a matter of fact, Chief, I've got a gentleman waiting down the hall to talk with me."

"What're you talking about?"

"Yep. He's gonna tell me all about how Tom Devins killed Norma Wilson."

"That so?"

"Yep." Burnett pulled out a match and concentrated on lighting his pipe.

Stoner suddenly sat bolt upright. "Goddammit, you fucking hillbilly, what're you talking about?!"

Burnett finished lighting his pipe and carefully placed the spent match in the ashtray on the desk. "Well," he said slowly, obviously enjoying the Chief's impatience, "it seems Mr. Forget has suddenly decided that he wants to spill his guts."

"Robert Forget! Are you telling me that Robert Forget is gonna lay Devins out? How the hell . . . Where is he? Where is the son of a bitch?"

"One thirteen," Burnett answered quietly.

"One thirteen?"

"Yep."

"How the hell you get a key?"

"Well—"

"Never mind," Stoner interrupted, holding his hand up. "I don't wanna know." He shook his head, then glared at Burnett again, his eyes narrowing. "What I do wanna know, cowboy, is how you got Forget to get so cooperative all of a sudden."

Burnett's grin widened. "I don't think you want to know that, either, Chief."

Stoner sat there in silence. The French Canadian was the key to cracking the case—that much was clear. Only he and Devins—and maybe the Biafran—knew what had happened to Norma Wilson, and how it had happened. The chances of finding Aikba and extraditing him as a witness from an African nation involved in a revolution were almost nonexistent. And questioning or tailing Devins in hopes of a slipup was out; he was solidly under the A.G.'s protection now. That left Forget. Without him, they still had only a missing persons case.

But just what had Burnett said to the tough Canadian to make him talk? He had no authority to offer immunity, and Forget would have just laughed at that anyway. No, he must have scared the holy shit out of him some way. But how?

Burnett's grin didn't change as he looked back at the Chief. Smoke drifted lazily from the pipe's bowl, slowly spiraling toward the ceiling. His mind was going back to the jail cell, to the visit he had paid a certain prisoner three days earlier . . .

Through a jailhouse snitch, the County sheriffs had learned that one of the prisoners had been talking about a man he knew who had a huge green emerald. The prisoner was a tough customer, awaiting trial on an attempted murder charge. A buddy of his, he was bragging to cellmates, had a ring with an emerald stone in it the size of a small rock—worth $30,000 at least. His buddy had shown him the stone, had flashed it around the customers at a bar.

His buddy was a French Canadian, the prisoner told the snitch. And the stone had belonged to a wealthy lady who had disappeared in Europe.

One of the deputy sheriffs in the jail facility was an old drinking pal of Burnett's from the days when Burnett had been assigned to jail duty out of the Sheriff's Academy. Burnett had told him about the Devins case over a beer, mentioning the jewelry that Norma Wilson had worn on her trip. And the deputy had remembered as he listened to the snitch's story.

Burnett requested that the prisoner be removed to a cell in the isolation ward. There, no one could hear from another cell; no one could see what was going on. Then Burnett walked into the cell without his gun and locked the door behind him. The prisoner, a big man with a "rap sheet" four pages long, snarled obscenities at him.

A half-hour later, Burnett was let out of the cell.

Three hours after that, the prisoner was released on reduced bail. He was a quieter, more subdued man than the jailors had dealt with; it was as if he were afraid of something.

And on the following evening, the man visited Forget at his home. He pulled out a gun, planted it in his friend's ear, and whispered, "You talk to Burnett or I'll blow your fucking brains out! You run, and I'll hunt you down, Bobby. You got that?" Forget nodded quickly, the cold steel pressed painfully into his ear. "You go see Burnett; you tell him everything about that emerald and the old lady— everything," the prisoner whispered. "Or you're a dead man."

"Well, what in the hell you waiting for?!" Stoner snarled. "A fucking pat on the back? Get your ass on down to 113!"

Chapter 28

Robert Forget squirmed uncomfortably in the hard metal chair. He looked apprehensively around the barren room, sensing the bleak walls closing in on him. He glanced again at the young woman seated in the corner, a stenotype machine mounted in front of her. He slowly wiped his wet palms against his lap and took a deep breath. He looked down at his legs, nodded with an effort. He swallowed hard. Christ, he thought. Jesus Christ almighty.

The tomblike silence was broken by a clicking in the lock. All three looked up, startled. The door opened, and Burnett walked in.

"Hello, Bob," he said amiably.

"Mr. Burnett," Forget mumbled under his breath, avoiding the man's eyes.

Burnett sat on a chair across the table from Forget. Carefully, totally absorbed, Burnett pulled out his ever-present black briar, stuffed it with tobacco and tamped it down. Looking up at the shaken Canadian, he lit it, puffing out clouds of sweet-smelling smoke.

Forget coughed. "Can we, uh . . . can we get started?"

"Sure, Bob." Burnett signaled to the stenotypist. "Today's date is Monday, March 2, 1970. It is now 4:50 P.M." Burnett's voice seemed peaceful, serene, oddly out of place in the stark coldness of the room. "This conference is taking place in room 113 of the district attorney's Bureau of Investigations, 524 North Spring Street, Los Angeles. Present are Mr. Robert Forget, Investigator W. R. Burnett, and the reporter is Jennie Crisci." He looked directly at Forget, smiling. "Bob, you recall our talk up in Washington. This matter involves the disappearance of Norma Carty Wilson. At that time I advised you of your rights. For the record, I'm going to do it again."

Forget's head bobbed slowly up and down, eyes fixed on the hands in his lap, as Burnett read the criminal liturgy.

"Do you wish to give up those rights and speak with me?" he concluded.

There was a moment of silence. Burnett continued watching the man in the stillness.

"Yeah," Forget whispered.

"Fine. Now, when did you first meet Mrs. Wilson, Bob?"

"Uh, well . . . I think . . . I was working on her building—the one at 1017 North La Cienega, in Hollywood. I'm a carpenter, y'know? So Tom hired me to work on it."

"Tom Devins?"

"Devins, yeah. Tom Devins."

"What was your relationship with him?"

"Uh, well, uh, I met him back in '65 I guess. He was a car jockey at Frascatti's on the Strip. Parking cars, y'know? Uh, well, he met a lot of important people there, and he kinda made some money on some investments. They give him tips, like. He always said he'd make a million bucks by the time he was thirty."

He looked at Burnett trying to smile. "Looks like he made it, huh? Anyway, he started to work as a real estate salesman at, uh . . . Archer's. Yeah, Archer Real Estate on Sunset Boulevard. Well, ol' man Archer went on vacation for a while and left Tom in charge. That was a big mistake—trustin' Tom. Anyway, Norma Wilson walks in one day, lookin' for an investment. Wants to buy a hospital or something. So Tom, he starts hustlin' her. Never tells Mr. Archer about her, y'know? But he can't close any deal without the ol' man knowin', 'cause he's only a salesman. See, you gotta have a broker's license; otherwise, if you're only a salesman, you gotta work the deal through a licensed broker and split the commission. So, Tom keeps her on a line, and by God, he goes out and gets a broker's license—passes the test and everything. And he splits from Archer and takes her with him. Well, they started wheelin' and dealin', and Norma—Mrs. Wilson—kinda takes a likin' to Tom. I mean, Tom's good lookin' and young and bright and full of piss and vinegar. Hell, Tom's in the sack with the old lady, y'know? So he opens his own office in one of her buildings—the one on La Cienega. She makes him manager of the building. And they swing some deals; he's makin' a lot of money off her, y'know? Drivin' a Caddy, everything."

Forget looked nervously at the reporter, rapidly typing on the keys. Her fingers stopped.

"Uh, okay. So Tom's her broker, her adviser for four-five years after that. Anyway, I moved out of L.A. Got sick of the place—and sick of all Tom's promises about how much money I'm gonna make with him." He shook his head in disgust. "Tom's always makin' promises, puttin' together deals. I worked my ass off for him. Didn't make shit. So anyway, my wife and me—Linda was my wife then—we were gonna go back to Montreal. But we never made it past Seattle. Ran out of money."

"Early in November of 1968, did you receive a telephone call from Devins?"

"Yeah. Uh, see, he'd already told me before about some crazy deal he was workin' on. Goin' to North Africa—Algeria, I think. And rescuin' Moise Tshombe. Said if he could get him outa prison in Algeria, he could take him to Switzerland, and he'd get half of Tshombe's fortune there—twenty-four million dollars."

Burnett nodded slightly.

"Uh, so he calls me up. November 5, 6, right in there. He says, 'You wanna make twenty-five grand?' And hell, I says, 'Sure.' And he says, 'Well, remember I told you about Moise Tshombe?' And he says, 'Well, it's all worked out. It's a cinch. You and me,' he says. So I say, 'Why me?' I mean, 'cause I know I'm not so bright, y'know? I mean, I'm nothin' special. And he says, 'Cause you're tough, and you can speak French. And you can be trusted.'"

Forget took a deep breath. "So I ask what's the details.

And he says that some political party from somewhere's gonna pay him 50,000 just for tryin' to get this Tshombe out. And we'll split it. And then we'll split Tshombe's fortune in Switzerland—at least five million dollars each. And then there's something about Tshombe's attorney, and his wife who's livin' in New York, I guess. So I'm thinkin', hell, that's a lot of money. Sure, I'll do it. So he tells me to fly down to L.A. right away, and we'll go to Europe. Well, I gotta get a passport, y'know? In Montreal. So he says we'll fly to Montreal together and get it."

"What happened then?"

"Well, I said I wanted a thousand bucks. I mean, y'know I been through this shit with Tom before. I'm not leavin' till I get a thousand bucks." He looked up at Burnett. "And, damn, he telegrammed me a thousand bucks that same day, just like that! Well, I flew right down to L.A."

"Did he meet you there?"

"Yeah. And then right away we're flyin' to Montreal. And he tells me on the plane, 'Oh, by the way, Norma's gonna meet us in Montreal.' And I'm surprised, y'know? I mean what's she doin' on a deal like this? And he says, 'Yeah, I got a big real estate deal with her in Europe involving some ambassadors in Portugal or something. Big people. And it's only gonna take a few days, and then we'll go on with the Tshombe deal.' So I said okay."

"Did you meet Norma in Montreal?"

"Yeah. Well, first Tom and I drive to Ottawa. Because we could get a passport there right away. Otherwise, in Montreal, you gotta apply for one and wait to get it mailed to you. Anyway, next day we're back in Montreal and we meet Norma at the airport. And Tom, he says to Norma, 'Guess who I ran into in Montreal here,' and he points to me. And, of course, Norma knows me from workin' on her building all the time. And he tells her, 'He's coming with us. Isn't that nice?' And she says fine, y'know?"

"Did the three of you then go to Europe together?"

"Yeah. Well, we stopped off in New York. Tom said he had to have some papers signed in the States. And him and Norma signed a bunch of legal-lookin' papers, and a notary signed them and all. At the airport there. So then we fly to Spain."

"Bob, in our talk up in Washington you said Mrs. Wilson had given you $5,000 at the airport to be a bodyguard and interpreter. Was that true?"

"No, that wasn't true," Forget replied quietly, looking again at his lap. "Tom told me to tell you people that. Norma never gave me a dime."

"Did Devins have any money with him on the trip?"

"Sure as hell did. He had a briefcase with a big envelope inside that was crammed full of hundred-dollar bills."

"Okay. You flew to Spain?"

"Yeah. Madrid. And I keep asking Tom about this Tshombe deal. I mean, I want to know what kind of chance I'm takin'—am I gonna get killed or what? And Tom tells me he's got connections—that the prison guards are paid off and it's all set up. He says we'll fly in to Africa at night, with no lights, in a small plane—Tom's been takin' flying lessons, y'know?—and we'll fly low, under 500 feet, so the radar don't get us. But we never do. We just keep waitin' in Madrid 'cause Tom says they're waitin' for some people who arrived somewhere in a big yacht with a lot of cash. And they're havin' trouble clearin' customs or somethin', what with bringin' all that cash in. So one day Norma's off shopping, see, and Tom and I are alone havin' a beer in the hotel bar. And that's when he hits me with it."

"It?"

"Uh, well, Tom says to me, this Tshombe thing is only phase two. 'Phase two,' he calls it. Before we can do that, he says, we got to finish phase one."

"Did he tell you what phase one was?" Burnett asked quietly.

"Yeah. We got to kill Norma."

Forget's shoulders sagged, and his eyes gazed dully at the table in front of him.

"Go on, Bob."

"Well, I said, 'Forget it.' The Tshombe thing, okay—but not that."

"Did he tell you why he wanted to kill her?"

"Yeah. He says, 'I been playing around with paperwork and her attorney found out, and he's tryin' to talk her into pressing charges,' or somethin' like that. He took some money from her—some kind of fraud, y'know? And he had her convinced that they were great friends and all, but she was still thinkin' about pressing charges. And he didn't want to do no twenty years in prison."

"What did you do then?"

"Well, hell, I'm in a tough spot. I tell Norma, and she won't believe me against him. I go to the local cops, and I get myself in a mess in a foreign country. I just wanna get outa there—get back home, y'know. But man, I'm afraid of Tom now. Anyway, I say no deal. And he says okay, just go with them to Malaga and then I can split or whatever. But don't never mention the Tshombe deal to Norma, he says."

"Had he paid you any more money?"

"Yeah. He gave me another thousand in New York. Spending money."

"What happened next?"

"We flew to Malaga. We spent a couple of days there. Tom's always makin' phone calls, puttin' deals together. Well, anyway, Tom started gettin' upset over the fact that I wasn't goin' to help him kill Norma, y'know? And we talked and all, and I told him I wanted to split. But I didn't know if I had enough for a ticket."

"Did you or Devins have any guns at this time?"

"Yeah. Tom gave me a .380 Star automatic. Star's one of them Spanish guns, and he had a nine millimeter Browning auto. And that scared me. I got to thinkin', y'know, maybe this sneaky bastard is going to snuff me or somethin' and say I was tryin' to kill Norma. So I took my gun out of the leather shaving kit and put it under my pillow in case he tried somethin' in the middle of the night."

Forget shook his head. "Real smart. I get back from lunch and the Spanish federal police are waitin' for us. Yeah. They show me the gun. Some cleaning lady found it, makin' the bed. Shit! So they throw us in jail. Tom, he says, 'Let me handle this.' And I'll be goddamned if he didn't! Tom's one fast talker. We're in jail all night. Next day, he's tellin' the

247

judge he knows Franco and Moise Tshombe, personal friends of his, and he knows the ambassador to the United Nations for Portugal and all. And man, they bought it! I mean, he's really impressive, y'know? Anyway, they just fined us and cut us loose."

"What did you do then?"

"Well, I just wanna get back home. Tom says we gotta get out of the country fast, before the police change their minds. So me and him and Norma get on a ferryboat to Tangiers. That was the first thing out of Malaga."

Burnett tapped his pipe against the ashtray and studied it for a moment. He shook his head in amusement, then tamped it down and relit it. Casually, almost as an afterthought, he asked, "What happened in Tangiers?"

"Well, Tom tried to talk me into helping kill Norma again. Said they couldn't prosecute us in the U.S. anyway—no jurisdiction, he said. Well, I said no, and he was gettin' mad. And I was worried. 'Cause man, I didn't have the gun anymore—it was back in Spain. But Tom had that nine millimeter. But he finally gave me a few hundred bucks, and him and Norma drove me to the airport and I flew back. That's it man."

"Have you seen Mrs. Wilson since then?" Burnett asked.

"No. No, last I seen her was the Tangiers airport."

"When was the next time you heard from Devins?"

"Uh, well, few days later. I got to thinkin' maybe he's tryin' to frame me—you know, pin the murder on me. Anyway, Tom calls me up. Says he's in Switzerland or Sweden or one of those places. I forget the name of the town—they all sound the same to me."

"Geneva?"

"Could be. Something like that. So he says, 'Everything is done,' he says. 'Everything is taken care of.'"

"What did that mean to you, Bob?"

"Well, I guessed he'd killed her. And I figured he'd be back in L.A. in a couple of days."

"And when did you hear from him next?"

"In a couple of weeks. I'm still in Washington, and he calls me from L.A. He tells me to come on down and get my money! Well, I says if it's for the murder thing, I don't wanna get involved. And he says, 'No, I told you there's no crime committed in this country. There's nothing they can do to you here.' And so, hell, I'm broke, and I go down to L.A."

"What happened?"

"Uh, we meet and he . . . he says he killed her. Man, I just couldn't believe it, y'know? I mean, we're sitting in his car—a Mercedes, a little 280SL—and he reaches in the glove compartment and pulls out a handkerchief. And I see Norma's passport fall out, and I put it back in. Inside the handkerchief is this big goddamn emerald—from the ring Norma always wore. I heard it was nine carats—worth 30,000 bucks."

"Did he give it to you?"

"Yeah. He tells me to get rid of it. Wrap it in concrete and dump it off the Malibu pier or something, y'know? Well, I said okay, 'cause I'm thinkin' what if he doesn't give me my money, y'know? I can cash in the emerald. So I just hung onto it."

"Was that all he gave you?"

"No. He gave me a string of pearls, too, and a watch. All kinds of diamonds on the watch. It was Norma's—I remember it. Hard to miss, y'know? So I took them all and put them in a beer can and sealed it with white caulking compound. And I kept it."

"Didn't it seem strange to you that Devins would take the risk of smuggling all that evidence through customs just to have you dump it in the Pacific?"

Forget looked at Burnett for a moment without comprehension, wrestling to grasp the concept. "Yeah," he said slowly. "Yeah. He could've dumped the stuff over there." He shook his head and looked down at the sweating hands still in his lap. "The bastard was settin' me up, all right.

"Well, at least I made sure everybody saw me leave the airport at Tangiers, and everybody saw her there alive. I mean, you couldn't miss her, y'know? She looked like a million dollars."

"What did you do with the jewelry, Bob?"

"Huh? Oh, uh . . . I got rid of it."

"When?"

"After you guys came up and talked to me last year. I mean, I got pretty shook up 'cause you seemed to think I was some hired killer. Jesus, the night you left I had this nightmare. I was in this little green room, see, and gas pellets were droppin', and the gas was everywhere and gettin' into my throat and I couldn't breathe . . ." Tiny spots began to glisten on the man's forehead. "I woke up chokin' and screamin' and fightin' for air. And I was soakin' wet. Jesus!"

Burnett relit his pipe.

"Well, after that, I drove out the Mt. Baker Highway, and I tore the pearls apart and the diamonds, and sprinkled them all along the road, one at a time."

"What about the emerald?"

"First, I tried to smash it. I laid it down on a crescent wrench and pounded it with a hammer. Damn thing wouldn't break. So I went out another road, the South Skagit Highway out of Sedro Woolley. I knew about this pond, see? Used to hunt there all the time. The pond's got a deep silt bottom. Anyway, I threw the emerald in there."

"Could you take me to this pond?"

"Yeah, sure. Easy."

"All right. Let's go back to Devins. He told you to get rid of the jewelry."

"Yeah. He said when I got the job done, to call his answering service and say Gregory called. Then he'd know the job was done."

"Did you call?"

"Yeah. I said, 'Tell him Gregory called,' y'know?"

"When was the next contact with Devins?"

"Next day. He calls and says my money's ready. See, he was supposed to get the 50,000 from some big politicians for gettin' Tshombe out. But he was gonna pay me my half out of some escrow papers or somethin'. Somethin' about the papers he signed with Norma in New York. So I meet him, and we go to this bank on Wilshire Boulevard and get the money, and he says, 'Bob, I got good news and bad news.' He says, 'Most of the money is tied up, and all I can get my hands on is 25,000. But I can give you ten of that. And I'll pay you the rest later, when I get it.'"

"So we go into the bank, and they give him twenty grand. Then we go down to Charter Bank of London so Tom can deposit it to his account in London. And I opened an account and deposited 7,500. And I kept 2,500 cash."

"All right. Now, when and where did Devins tell you how he killed Mrs. Wilson?"

"Uh, see, we kind of hung around together for about a month after he got back from Europe. I mean, he needs a buddy, I guess. We go drinkin', shootin' pool and so on. Anyway, one time we're sittin' in his car, and we'd been drinkin', and he just all of a sudden puts his finger to my head, like that." Forget pointed his index finger to his temple. "And he just says, 'It's amazing what a nine millimeter will do. It came out the other side that big.'" He made a circle by touching the tips of his thumb and index finger. "And he smiles, y'know? And says, 'She didn't feel a thing.'"

"Where's the body?" Burnett asked quietly.

"I don't know. I mean, he never told me where he killed her or where he buried her, y'know? I mean, I really don't know. He never told me. Last time we talked, I was all pissed off 'cause he wasn't payin' me the rest of the money, and so I'm workin' on his boat doin' some carpenter work for him. See, he's livin' with this young, good-lookin' broad from Indiana on this boat he's goin' to Tahiti on. Michelle's her name. Goin' to split the States forever. And his wife, Adelle, she found out about the girl, and she wants to divorce him. Not 'cause of the Norma thing, 'cause she thinks he's innocent. Hell, he's got everybody thinkin' he's innocent. So anyway I tell him to pay me, and he says he doesn't owe me a dime. So I say I know a lot of things, y'know? Well, he gives me a look. And man, it give me the shivers. Tom's a nice, pleasant-lookin' guy, but when he puts on that look . . . man, I start thinkin' I'm next. So I split; went back to Washington. Next I hear from him, he calls—man, I don't know how he found me—he calls and tells me you guys are comin' up and to just be cool, y'know? And he said he had this attorney, Weber, who had an in with the D.A.; could get their records and knew everything that was goin' on. And he even told me there'd be two of you—you and that Murphy guy."

Burnett nodded slowly.

"And he said be careful of Burnett—the guy always smokin' a pipe. I remember that clear. Be careful of Burnett."

"Anything else, Bob?"

Forget shook his head.

"All right," Burnett said. "End of interview." He looked at the reporter. "Thanks, Jennie."

The reporter quickly walked out of the room, and for an interminable moment Forget endured Burnett's silent scrutiny.

"Bob," Burnett said finally, "we're not on the record. Just you and me."

Forget nodded, looking down in misery.

"Remember what I told you about that little green room?"

Forget's head snapped up, his eyes wide.

"I want it straight," Burnett said.

"Yeah," whispered Forget, almost to himself. "Yeah. Okay."

"Where's the body?"

"Switzerland."

"Did you kill her?"

"No!" He looked up at Burnett. "Honest to God, Mr. Burnett, I didn't! It's like I told you. I left at Tangiers, and she was still alive." He looked down again. "Yeah, I agreed to kill her. In Spain, like I told you. Tom asked me. Only I said yeah, I'd do it. Phase one. Then we'd go and do the Tshombe thing—phase two."

"What happened?"

"Well, we go to Tangiers. We figure we'd rent a car and take Norma out sightseeing in the Sahara. Only, she ain't comin' back, y'know? We'd shoot her and bury her way out in the middle of that desert, and no way anybody'd ever find her."

Burnett nodded.

"So we do rent a car, and we all drive out into the desert. But man, this real big sand storm hits us, and we gotta head back to Tangiers. I mean, it was too much; we get worried can we make it back. So anyway, back in Tangiers, I get to thinkin'. And I get cold feet. I mean, Tom's got the only gun now, y'know? The Spaniards got mine. And maybe I'm next after Norma. So I backed out. Honest to God, Mr. Burnett, I backed out. That's the truth, so help me. I can show you my passport, the stamps, everything."

"How did he kill her?"

"He says he took her up on a drive from some town in Switzerland, up in the Alps. One of those funny sounding names, y'know?"

"Locarno?"

"Yeah, something like that. Anyway, he's drivin' her to that other place—Geneva—only it's way up in the mountains, and there's nobody there and all. So anyway, he gets out with Norma for some sightseeing. And he sticks the nine millimeter to the back of her head. Blew most of the front of her face off when the bullet came out, he said."

"Where did he bury the body?"

"All over the place."

"What?"

"See, he's got a hunting knife, and he cuts her up into little pieces. Like butchering a side of beef, y'know? And then he takes the chunks and buries them in different spots all around the mountains. So's nobody'll ever identify her."

"What about the jewelry?"

"Yeah, like I said, he took all the jewelry off, and he give me the emerald and the pearls and the diamonds, and I dumped them, like I said."

"Her purse? The mink coat?"

"Oh, yeah, I almost forgot. Yeah. He says he put all her clothes in a box. A cardboard box. And then he stored it in a train station or a bus station somewhere."

"In Geneva?"

"Maybe. Geneva, Locarno—one of those foreign places. Anyway, he says to me the mink was too bloody to keep, y'know? And he had to cut the clothing off. Anyway, he put it all in some box."

Burnett once again tamped on the pipe. "Ever hear the term 'The Fox'?" he asked. The phrase had come out during Devins' recent testimony in the Weber trial.

The faint suggestion of a smile briefly crossed the Canadian's worn face.

"Yeah. The Fox. That was Tom's code name. See, he knew you guys were on him, tappin' his phone, readin' his mail and all. So he says to me never call him by name. I mean, in case anybody's listenin', I'm just talkin' to some guy named Fox. And then he got to likin' the name, y'know. Shit, I think he half sort of thought of himself as a fox. Outsmartin' the hounds, and all. Well, maybe he's right. I mean, he's one smart son of a bitch, y'know?"

"Anything else you want to straighten out now, Bob?"

Forget shook his head.

"Just one more thing," Burnett added. "The call you got from Devins—when he warned you we were coming to see you."

"Yeah?"

"Did he say who Weber's contact was in the D.A.'s office?"

"No." Forget thought for a moment. "No. Except . . ."

The jaw clamped hard onto the pipe.

"Well, he said two men are coming up. One's name is Burnett. The one who's always smoking a pipe. Be careful of Burnett, he said. But the other one . . . he said, "The other guy belongs to us.'"

Chapter 29

STEVE TROTT SAT erect in his chair, listening as Burnett and Murphy gave him the latest developments on the Devins case.

"All right," Trott said finally, looking at Murphy. "You head up to Sedro Woolley tomorrow. Take Forget with you. Locate the area in the road where he says he threw the diamonds. Go over it with a fine-tooth comb."

"Okay," Murphy said.

"Then find the pond where he threw the emerald. Set up a dredging operation. I don't care how long it takes. We've got to find that emerald.

"The whole case hangs on Forget," he added. "Everything depends on him. And the guy's a complete flake. There's just no way any jury's going to convict on the basis of his uncorroborated testimony. Fact is, I wouldn't even take it into court. So it comes down to this: we've got to corroborate Forget's story. We've got to. Without some backup, some corroboration, he's useless to us."

"If we find the diamonds or the emerald . . ." Murphy said.

"Corroboration. Maybe not enough, but it's something."

"What about the gun?" Burnett asked. They had received information that Devins had given a gun of some type to a Dr. Malzacher in a town called Wisp, in Washington State; Dr. Malzacher was Adelle Devins' father. The information was probably false—it was almost too good to be true—but it was something that had to be checked out.

Trott looked at Murphy. "George, you stop off in that town, Wisp, check it out. It's not too far from Sedro Woolley." He looked back at Burnett. "Have you checked on gun sales?"

Burnett nodded. "I've been calling around to the gun dealers. Asked them to check for a gun sale to Devins or Utter, particularly a nine millimeter. Nothing yet."

"All right," Trott said. He picked up a ballpoint pen, began playing with it. His mind was going over the memorandum he had written to Sid Cherniss, analyzing the available legal authority on proving a murder without a body, and on establishing jurisdiction. Names and case citations again began drifting through his head.

People versus Carlos Ignacio Barretto. The body had never been found, but the victim's blood was found on the floor of his apartment. In addition, a clock with the same type blood on it, had been found in Barretto's home and expert opinion established that the clock had probably been used to bludgeon the victim over the head. Most important, Barretto had confessed the murder to the police. Such a confession was not admissible, Trott knew, unless the corpus delicti had been established independently; but he also knew that a judge was human, and was more likely to rule that the corpus was sufficiently established to allow testimony of the confession if he were convinced there *was*, in fact, a murder. In the Wilson murder, there was a confession—if Forget was found credible—but there was no matching blood, and no murder weapon in the suspect's possession.

People versus Dennis Ray Bolinski: 260 California Appellate Reports Second, page 705. The court ruled that the corpus could be established circumstantially; a body was not absolutely necessary. And once death by criminal causes was shown, the question of whether the murder was first degree could be proved by evidence of the suspect's incriminating statements. But was there enough yet to prove circumstantially that Norma Wilson was, in fact, dead? And that she died due to criminal means?

The cold fact remained: the murder of Norma Wilson had

to be proved independently of Devins' statements to Forget, or Forget's testimony would be inadmissible. And on top of that, Forget's testimony would not even be permitted at all without sufficient corroboration; in California, a defendant could not be convicted on the basis of a coconspirator's testimony, unless there was legally sufficient independent corroboration of that testimony.

Then there was the L. Ewing Scott case. The prosecution had established that the victim had been in sound physical and mental health, with extensive roots in the community. Then she had simply disappeared. Her money, baggage and entire wardrobe had been left at home. And she had remained missing for a number of years, without drawing on her bank accounts or contacting anyone. Proof was offered to show that the defendant had fraudulently persuaded the victim to deed her property to him just before she disappeared. And the appellate court had ruled that a prima facie corpus had been sufficiently shown.

The parallels of the Wilson murder to the Scott case were clear: the similarities were almost eerie. But would the trial court follow Scott? It had been an unpopular decision, and there were plenty of appellate decisions to be found for the defense—decisions holding that what amounted to a disappearance under suspicious circumstances was not a sufficient corpus delicti for murder.

Trott continued studying the blue-and-silver pen, twisting it slowly in his hands. And what about the jurisdiction problem? Again, Trott had written in the memo that the prosecution would have to prove that the murder was planned in Los Angeles. Unless they could clearly establish a conspiracy before Norma Wilson flew to Montreal, the L.A. courts were without authority to try the case.

Jurisdiction—prima facie—Scott—corpus delicti—conspiracy—independent corroboration—Bolinski—256 California Appellate Reports Second, page 392 . . . Phrases began drifting through Trott's mind, conflicting precedents, vague legal authority. The Devins case was a legal nightmare. It was something he would expect to see on a law school final exam.

Trott looked up suddenly at Burnett. "What else have you got going, Bill?"

"I called Inspector Tomkins, Geneva police. I told him what Forget said about Devins hiding the clothing in a box in some station. I gave him a complete description of the clothing, and asked him to search the bus and train depots, airport lockers, anything like that. Anything in Devins' name, anything there since November.

"We've got some corroboration," Burnett continued. "The $5,000 Devins gave Forget. I'm getting records from Charter Bank showing the transaction: the check, the deposit."

"Good," Trott muttered.

Burnett paused for a moment. He was remembering the nine-millimeter bullets he had seen in Devins' house. That tended to corroborate Forget's story that Devins had used a nine-millimeter gun. But there was a problem: Burnett had been in Devins' house illegally. Thus, his viewing of the bullets would be inadmissible in court; he wouldn't be permitted to testify to what he had seen. Worse, an illegal entry and search could possibly taint the entire investigation. Better not put Trott in a bad spot, Burnett told himself; better that he just didn't know.

"Of course," Burnett continued, "you know about the safe deposit box."

"Yes," Trott said. He was still working on drafting an application for a search warrant permitting Burnett to open a safe deposit box owned by Devins. The box, number E 2083, had been located at the Security Pacific National Bank branch on Van Nuys Boulevard. There was a chance Devins was keeping something in the box that would incriminate him: jewelry, the gun, papers—something, anything.

"What about the protective custody—Forget and his wife?" Trott asked.

"We've got an investigator staying with them, Steve," Murphy said. He chuckled. "Pretty good duty, takin' care of that Colleen broad."

Trott looked at him questioningly.

"Colleen Davis, Forget's girlfriend or wife or whatever," Murphy continued. "She's a stripper." He grinned. "She works some joints on the Strip, and in El Monte, and Long Beach. Real dives. Does the thing with . . ." He looked down at his chest, twisting his large body quickly back and forth. "You know, she spins the tassels; one goes one way, the other goes the other way. That's hard to do—takes real talent, the left one goin' one way, the right one goin' the other."

Trott grinned. "I get the picture."

"Tough assignment," Murphy went on, still smiling. "He had to go out shopping with her the other day for pasties and a G-string. Honest to God—pasties and a G-string!"

"All right," Trott said, laughing. He held his hand up. "All right. So long as she's . . ." He was going to say "covered" but changed his mind, ". . . protected."

"Oh, yeah," Murphy laughed. "She's real protected."

"All right," Trott said again. "George, you're going up to Washington tomorrow. The jewelry and the gun. Bill, you're going to keep checking for gun sales, and you'll serve the search warrant on the bank. Figure on that warrant in a couple of days. But tomorrow morning I want you in the Attorney General's office."

"Oh?"

"Your buddy Leroy Sana," Trott said, smiling. "I'm going to be asking him some questions about Devins, under oath."

I'll be damned, Burnett thought to himself.

"Should be interesting," Trott added. "And besides, Compton figured it was time we stopped playing defensive ball."

Chapter 30

Burnett looked around the room again, remembering the day he had sat at the table answering Huffman's questions while the reporter took down everything he said. Now it was Sana's turn to answer the questions. And it was Steve Trott doing the interrogating, firing the questions at the A.G.'s investigator in rapid succession.

Sitting next to Trott was Harland Braun, a deputy D.A. who had been assigned to assist Trott in preparing the case for trial. And at Sana's elbow, Richard Huffman sat quietly, occasionally interrupting to voice an objection or to advise Sana on a legal matter.

". . . I was instructed by my supervisor to contact Mr. Devins, and a phone number was given to me to accomplish that," Sana was saying. "I called Mr. Devins. He briefly explained to me at that time that he had retained Mr. Weber. He told me that he was a suspect in a murder investigation being conducted by the District Attorney's office, and he alleged that certain people within the D.A.'s office were working in concert with Mr. Weber in an effort to extort from him the sum of $35,000.

"This conversation with Devins, on the phone I mean, lasted no longer than fifteen minutes at the outside. I then contacted Miles Rubin, with whom my supervisor had been in earlier contact. Apparently, Mr. Rubin had requested that I be assigned the matter.

"I went to Mr. Rubin who, quite by chance, was in the company of Mr. O'Brien, and then explained to them, in a little better detail, what I'm explaining to you now, my conversation with Devins . . ."

Quite by chance, Burnett thought as he continued staring at Sana. The number-two man in the whole state, Evelle Younger's opponent in the race for the attorney general's position. And he just happened to be with Rubin during the initial briefing on possible corruption in Younger's office.

". . . and that Devins had a two o'clock appointment that afternoon with Mr. Weber, and this would be an opportunity, if this office elected to do so, to wire Mr. Devins up to see if, in fact, there was some corroboration to his story."

Sana paused for a moment, then continued. "I was given approval to wire Mr. Devins up. I met with him about one-thirty at the Continental Hyatt Hotel. I think he went into greater detail at that time regarding his contacts with Weber and the promises made by Weber to get him out from behind the murder investigation being conducted by your office. We did not discuss in detail at that time the Norma Carty Wilson disappearance."

"Did you discuss it at all?" Trott asked.

"It must have been a part of the conversation but only that he went to Europe with this woman, and that he came back, she didn't come back. He wound up with some of her property, the consequence of which was that he was being considered as a murder suspect."

"Didn't you—" Trott began.

"If what you're looking for," Sana went on quickly, "is my conversation where we went into some detail about his trip to Europe with this woman, it was on the late afternoon or early morning, as I recall, the 27th of June. It was in his vehicle, where I removed from him the recording device that I had placed on his person. We were parked in a residential area nearby Weber's office."

"What vehicle were you in?"

"His Cadillac."

"All right. What did he tell you about the trip to Europe?"

"As it relates to Forget, I believe that Devins explained to me that Forget accompanied them on the trip at the request of Mrs. Wilson. Mr. Devins explained to me that either

Mrs. Wilson had or was going to receive—and I don't know which at this time—a large amount of cash. And that she wanted a bodyguard, wanted Forget as a bodyguard, and he inferred without saying that Mrs. Wilson apparently had something, or had some sexual involvement, or wanted some sexual involvement with Forget."

Trott nodded. So far, it had not been difficult; Sana was talking freely, and the best tack to take was to give him free rein, shifting direction occasionally to keep him off balance.

"Devins went through the itinerary with me, which I'm not able to recall in detail at this time. But he mentioned such countries as Morocco and Spain and France and Switzerland, and one other country which I forget right now. He explained how Forget took sick in Tangiers and had to go back home. Then he, Devins that is, and Mrs. Wilson flew on Air Maroc to France and then on to Switzerland, and that he could corroborate his position with hotel receipts, car rental slips, and so on." Sana paused. "I'm trying to think of that other place in Switzerland, other than Geneva."

"Zurich?" Trott offered.

"Zurich. Yes. They went to Zurich first, I believe. At some point in time, Devins had given to Mrs. Wilson a large amount of cash, something around a hundred thousand dollars. I don't recall exactly. And they went to a bank in Zurich."

"Did he say which bank?"

"I don't recall. And she was out of his presence for a while, and he concluded that she had opened up a numbered Swiss bank account, because there had been earlier conversations about this, with some people they met during the course of their trip."

"Who was that?" Trott asked.

"I couldn't tell you who this was. I just don't know. Anyway, he said they rented a vehicle then and drove to Locarno."

"He told you they drove to Locarno?"

"That's correct. And from there, they drove to Geneva. He left her at one hotel in Geneva and he went to another hotel."

"Did Devins explain why they stayed at different hotels?"

"He said because they had been staying together all the course of the trip, and he explained that the trip wasn't meant to be as long as it turned out to be, that she was beginning to wear on him."

Trott nodded. "Mr. Sana, I understand that you suggested that Mr. Devins call Mr. Burnett and talk with him about the case, and he agreed. How did you get him to agree to talk if he believed that our office was corrupt in this investigation?"

Sana stared at Trott for a moment. "I feel bad about having him talk, now," he said slowly. "I had an open mind at that time, which I don't have now." He looked at Burnett. "He informed me that he had not killed this woman and was willing to take a polygraph examination and give you a statement. But he was afraid of certain people within the structure of your office, the District Attorney's office, and I don't really recall exactly what I said to him at that time. Basically it was what I would have said to anybody, that you're not involved, so what have you got to lose by coming on in?"

"Mr. Sana, do you know a Clay Kimberly?"

Sana was quiet for a moment, then said, "Yes, I had an occasion to meet with Mr. Kimberly. I was trying to corroborate a story Devins had told me about going back to Europe a second time to look for Norma Wilson. Kimberly had been with him, he said."

"All right," Trott said. "Now as I understand it, your investigation concerned strictly the question of corruption in the D.A.'s office, involving Weber."

"Yes."

"And you were not concerned with whether Devins was guilty of murder or not; that, for your purposes, was irrelevant?"

"Yes."

"All right. What changed the situation so that you were now attempting to corroborate Devins' statements concerning his involvement with Norma Wilson's disappearance?"

"Curiosity," Sana replied.

"Just curiosity?"

"Yes. I recognized that he was a murder suspect in the eyes of the District Attorney's office. It was certainly a very interesting case, to say the least."

"I see," Trott said. "Now, getting back to Clay Kimberly. How did you first meet him?"

"Well, Devins mentioned Kimberly to me in a telephone conversation. Apparently, Kimberly was standing next to Devins at the time. And Devins told me over the phone that Kimberly had been told by a bartender, Gary Fountenhaut, that Devins had put out a contract on his life as a result of information Kimberly had about Devins and Mrs. Wilson."

Jesus, Burnett thought. Tom Devins was quite an artist when it came to laying smoke screens.

"So I talked to Kimberly on the phone. He said his apartment had recently been torched and that these hit men had done it. Ultimately, that turned out not to be the case. Kimberly was a homosexual. He lived with another homosexual who had in turn lived with a third homosexual, and it was a fight over who got who. I contacted the sheriff, and the apartment had, in fact, been torched, but it was over this love triangle.

"But Kimberly also told me that this Fountenhaut told him that if he would tell him where Norma Wilson's body is buried, he would get a letter of immunity from the District Attorney's office and put some dough in his pocket.

"Then I got a phone call from Mr. Devins, and Huffman and I went over there and met with Devins and Kimberly. Kimberly was genuinely frightened and informed me he was leaving town. I told him I couldn't see any need of it, but I couldn't convince him and he left. I don't know where."

"You haven't seen him since?"

"No."

"All right. Is there anything else that Devins told you

about Norma, or where he got the money, or anything at all that might be of some significance?"

"I'm sure there must be, but I just don't have the ability at the moment to recall." He looked directly at Trott. "I've been in the business long enough to know what you're searching for, and if there were any admissions made by Mr. Devins, anything like that you could use in court, I'd volunteer them to you, but I know of nothing that would benefit you in your prosecution."

"Did Devins mention anything to you about an Okuma Aikba?"

"Yes," Sana said. For the first time there was a slight smile on his face. "He told me that was a name he made up."

Burnett blinked. He continued studying Sana, trying to read something in his eyes. Devins had made up Aikba? But the man at the Biafran Consulate, Ikpa . . . The telephone calls . . .

"It was a fictitious name," Sana continued. "He made it up. Tom Devins was Okuma Aikba."

"When did he tell you that?"

"In a conversation I had with him."

"Did he mention any African countries: Biafra, Nigeria? Did he mention any African names like Moise Tshombe?"

"Yes, I think he either stated or implied that he had, in fact, had conversations with Tshombe's wife."

Trott studied the pen in his hand. "Did he tell you that one of the reasons why he and Forget were going to Europe in November was to see about getting Tshombe out of an Algerian prison?"

"No. He mentioned something about a previous trip involving something to do with Tshombe, with Forget. But not on the trip with Mrs. Wilson."

Was it possible Devins *had* manufactured Aikba? Burnett pondered. The notary public, Rochelle Rishe, had never seen Aikba sign the document. In fact, no one had seen him with Devins or Forget. But what about the Ikpa at the consulate? Had Devins just used his name, creating a fictional and nearly untraceable character to use in his wheeling and dealing? But then why had Devins, Forget and Norma Wilson gone to Africa? And if he had created "Aikba" just to lure Norma to Montreal and then Europe, why the telephone calls to Lisbon? Why the later forged signature notarized by Rochelle Rishe? Why . . .

Suddenly Burnett became aware that Sana was getting angry. There was something Trott had said, something Burnett had missed.

"Devins explained to me that he had now found himself in a position where he was afraid that if he didn't pay, he would be indicted," Sana said in a forced calm. "And in addition to that, he was appalled by the whole thing. So he came to us."

"He was appalled by it for $35,000 but not for the $3,000 Weber originally mentioned?"

"Well, I didn't . . ." Sana looked at Huffman, then back at Trott. "See, he's my witness, Trott, like Forget is your witness. And I didn't wish to squeeze on him. I wasn't going to cross-examine him as to why he was willing to pay three or four but not thirty-five."

"What about the shooting?" Trott said, once again shifting the questioning to a different subject. "The alleged shooting into Devins' car. Did you ever determine who shot the holes in Devins' car?"

"No," Sana replied. "Not personally. Devins said it was . . . Well, let me back up. The day that happened, Devins and I, and a couple of friends of his, were walking to the Redwood over on First and Broadway for lunch. I noticed there were two or three tough-looking guys following us. When we got into the restaurant, they took a nearby table. I asked Devins if he knew them; he said he didn't. Then, that evening, I got the call from Devins; he'd been shot at in the car."

Trott nodded. "Where did he get the name 'The Fox'?"

"That was when Devins was on the stand, testifying against Weber at the trial. Weber's lawyer, Cantillon, had called him a fox on the stand, and Devins replied by calling him a mongoose." Sana smiled slightly. "Cantillon asked him why he called him a mongoose, and Devins said because a mongoose keeps company with snakes. Referring to Weber, I guess. And Cantillon called him The Fox in newspaper interviews after that. Why, I don't know. He figured Devins was pretty clever in framing Weber, I guess."

"Why didn't you tape any of the conversations with Devins? Or take any notes? Why isn't there any evidence of what he told you?"

"What's the question?"

"Well, I'm just curious as to why you didn't take any notes on the conversations about Norma and why you remained ignorant intentionally as to the murder aspect."

Sana glared at Trott. "I didn't remain ignorant intentionally. I asked the questions. I was curious as to the trip. There was no reason I didn't take notes. But . . . As I said in the beginning, I just don't know of anything that Devins has said to me that you people in the pursuit of your prosecution would benefit by. I guess I concluded anything he did tell me would be self-serving. He didn't cop out to me; he didn't acknowledge having killed the woman."

"Did Devins tell you anything about his relationship with Norma Wilson?" Trott was continuing his tactic of suddenly shifting his line of inquiry.

Sana took a short breath, then went on, once again calm. "I concluded that Mrs. Wilson had some kind of a problem, and that she was growing old and didn't want to grow old. She was going for her second face-lift over there. I heard she was a platinum blonde, that she dressed extravagantly and, well . . . I think it's all pretty obvious, isn't it?"

Trott looked up from the pen in his hand directly at Sana. "The newspapers have been carrying some stories, and the TV news. Did you ever tell a reporter that Tom Devins would be killed by the District Attorney's office if he was arrested by them?"

"Definitely not. I think it's ludicrous to believe or even entertain such an idea."

"Did you ever tell Devins that you were afraid if he was arrested by the D.A.'s office, he would never make it downtown alive?"

"Never. Quite to the contrary, Trott."

Jesus, Burnett thought, where was Trott getting all this from?

"Did Devins ever express any fear of, or animosity toward, anyone in the D.A.'s office?"

"Sure. He was afraid of everyone in the D.A.'s office. And animosity, you bet. Trott, he referred to you as the son of a bitch . . . ," he looked toward the young woman, "with apologies to the reporter, and Burnett was the asshole." Sana paused, looked across the table at Burnett. "He had expressed a real fear of Burnett, a genuine fear."

Thomas Devins, AKA Thomas Utter, Burnett repeated to himself as the questioning continued. Quite a guy. The Arkansas dropout still had the two biggest prosecuting agencies in the West tearing at each other's throats.

Chapter 31

Yes, WHAT CAN I do for you, Mr. Burnett?" the manager of Van Nuys Security Pacific National Bank asked pleasantly.

"I'd like to take a look into the safe deposit box rented by Thomas Devins," Burnett replied quietly.

The manager looked at the figure in the rumpled gray suit and dirty brown Western boots, trying to comprehend the request. "I . . . I beg your pardon?"

Burnett handed him the document. The manager continued looking at Burnett for a moment, then began reading the papers.

"A search warrant," he said quietly.

Burnett grinned. "Yes, sir."

The manager seemed slightly shaken, as if his orderly world of finance had suddenly been jarred. Then he turned to a slim, elderly woman whose black-rimmed glasses were attached to a chain around her neck.

"Sally, this is Mr. . . ."

"Burnett," the investigator said.

"Mr. Burnett." The manager looked quickly around him, making sure that the chapel-like serenity of the bank was not being violated. "Mr. Burnett has a search warrant," he added, almost in a whisper.

The woman looked quickly at Burnett, appraising him over the upper rim of her glasses.

"Please take him to the vaults. Box number . . ."

"E2083," Burnett said quietly. "Devins."

The woman reached into a drawer and pulled out a ring of keys. Then quickly, crisply, she escorted Burnett to the vault.

The vault was lined along its three walls with different sizes of hinged, brushed-steel safe deposit boxes. Burnett watched as the woman found box E2083 and inserted the key into the box. Then she began to insert the master key into the slot next to it. Suddenly, she hesitated, looked up at the man in the baggy gray suit. Something in her, something in the years of ritual and sanctity that she had observed in this room, rebelled. She was destroying a trust—a deeply held trust—by permitting this violation of a customer's innermost confidences.

She bit her lip, then looked back at the box. Slowly, she twisted the two keys. Even more slowly, she swung the small rectangular steel door open. Then carefully, she pulled out the long dark gray metal tray and hesitantly handed it to the man with the pipe.

Burnett nodded, thanking her. He placed the covered tray on a shelf in the vault. He began to raise the lid, then looked at the woman. She quickly turned her back to him. Burnett returned his attention to the safe deposit box. Carefully, he raised the lid, rested it against the wall and looked inside.

The box was empty. Or almost empty. A small folded piece of paper lay inside the gray steel walls. Burnett picked up the piece of paper, unfolded it and read the erratic handwriting:

> *Sorry . . . The Fox*

So the little bastard had a sense of humor.

Burnett looked at the newspaper rack as he started to walk into the Hall of Justice. He stopped suddenly, backed up. The headlines stood out, as if in relief.

**JEROME WEBER SENTENCED TO PRISON
IN BRIBERY CASE**

He reached into his pocket, pulled out a dime and dropped it into the slot. Then he pulled a copy of the paper out and quickly began to read the underlying story.

> Prominent Beverly Hills attorney Jerome (Jerry) Weber yesterday was sentenced to one to five years in prison for his conviction for soliciting another person to offer a $25,000 bribe to quash a district attorney's investigation.
>
> Superior Court Judge Charles H. Older stayed the sentence indefinitely until Weber has exhausted his appeals. The judge ordered the prison term despite appeals by Weber's attorney, James P. Cantillon, that Weber was falsely convicted and that he has suffered enough because of publicity in the case . . .

I'll be damned, Burnett thought as he read. He had heard the jury verdict a few days earlier, but everyone expected that the influential lawyer would succeed in getting probation. Judge Older was a tough old bird.

> Weber, 58, of 9917 Sunset Blvd., Beverly Hills, was charged with the April 1969 solicitation of Thomas Devins, 30-year-old former real estate man, to offer a bribe to quash an investigation into the disappearance of Mrs. Norma Carty Wilson, 57, of West Los Angeles.
>
> Devins now faces possible charges for the alleged murder of the woman whose body has not been found.
>
> Cantillon blamed Devins for the charges against Weber. Devins' motive, Cantillon claimed, was to discredit the district attorney's investigation of him in the Wilson case . . .

Burnett chuckled. Score another one for The Fox, he thought. Then his eyes caught a paragraph near the end of the column.

> Despite the fact that Devins claimed Weber said he wanted the $25,000 to influence "friends" in the D.A.'s office, Dep. State Attorney Gen. Richard Huffman said the

case is "closed, unless something new comes up." Authorities previously said there was no evidence that anyone in the District Attorney's office was actually involved. . . .

Burnett slowly folded the newspaper in half, walked into the old building and punched the elevator button. So it was over, he thought. It was finally over. The grand jury had done its work, and there would be no further indictments.

The elevator doors opened and he stepped inside. No more indictments, he thought again. But there had been a leak. And, maybe, a bribe deal. Weber had a connection; there was no question about it. But who? Had it been a secretary? Had she gotten his report from a friend in the office's typing pool? He was confident it was not Stoner. Murphy? No, he couldn't believe the big Irishman was dirty.

His mind drifted back to Tom Devins, to the information he had just received. Surveillance reported that Devins had been visiting various yacht brokers in the Marina del Rey area and had been taken out on a number of yachts that were up for sale. With him had been a beautiful young woman, and it wasn't Adelle. She had been seen with him more and more over the past few days, and the two spent a lot of time at her newly acquired apartment in Marina del Rey. Her name was Michelle Verpillat, and the striking young brunette had been telling neighbors that she and Tom Devins were engaged to be married.

The information about Devins' romantic interludes hadn't concerned Burnett, but his shopping for a yacht had. The types of boats Devins was looking at were big, deep-hulled, blue-water sailboats, designed for long distance cruising. Did he have plans to leave the country on a yacht, to sail far off into international waters? Or maybe to anchor in the safe harbor of a country without extradition treaties? Normally, the fears would seem farfetched, but Burnett knew that with Devins they were not. The wily investor had carefully orchestrated a murder so that jurisdictional problems would complicate any attempt at prosecution. Wasn't it likely that he would now try to thwart an arrest by throwing more legal roadblocks in the way? And what better way than on his own yacht? No customs or immigration to clear at borders, no airline flights that could be traced, no trains that could be followed. If he wanted to leave a country, he simply set sail for the high seas. How long did it take to wade through the red tape of extradition proceedings? And by the time the paperwork was nearing completion, off Devins would sail for yet another unknown country, with no transportation records anywhere for Interpol to trace his movements.

No, Burnett thought, it would be just like Devins to have a yacht ready to take off when the investigation got too hot. He could sail for years, hiding and dodging futile extradition proceedings, until finally the case faded in importance and was eventually forgotten.

Or am I getting paranoid? Burnett wondered. Seeing conspiracies where there are none? Isn't it more likely that the wealthy young investor is simply looking for a yacht for weekend jaunts to Catalina with his shiny new mistress?

The elevator opened and Burnett stepped out. He walked through the glass doors of the District Attorney's office, winking at the receptionist as he continued on past the front desk and into the drab corridors leading to Steve Trott's office.

Trott was sitting behind the desk, wearing a crisp, short-sleeved white dress shirt and an Ivy rep tie. Seated in front of him was George Murphy. In Murphy's hand was an automatic pistol.

"We got it," Murphy said. "Devins' gun. Nine-millimeter Browning."

Burnett lifted the blue steel automatic from the detective's hand. It was heavy, still loaded. He pulled the clip from the bottom of the stock; a live round projected from the top of the steel slip. He snapped the clip back into the handle, jammed it home. "Prints?" he asked.

"Naw," Murphy replied. "Everybody and his mother's handled the damn thing."

"Got it up in Washington?"

"Yeah. That Dr. Malzacher. Adelle Devins' father. Tom Devins asked him to keep it for a while." He grinned. "I wonder why ol' Tom didn't want to keep the gun in L.A.?"

I wonder why Devins didn't dump it in the ocean, Burnett said to himself. Or was there a reason Devins wanted to keep the murder weapon?

"Another thing," Murphy went on. "When I got the gun, Forget remembered something Devins had told him when he was bragging about blowing her away."

Burnett looked at Murphy, waiting.

"Yeah," Murphy continued. "He said Devins bragged about how clever he'd been. He'd shot the ol' lady with the gun, but he'd also bought an interchangeable barrel."

"A second barrel," Burnett repeated quietly.

"Yeah. A second barrel, Browning. Fits just like the original."

So that's why he hadn't dumped the gun, Burnett suddenly realized. To buy the gun, Devins had to fill out a lot of paperwork. The authorities would eventually discover he had bought a gun. And if he became a suspect in Norma's disappearance, it would look mighty suspicious if he couldn't produce the Browning. But with a switched barrel, he could produce it and prove it was not the weapon used in the murder: the grooves of the new barrel wouldn't match the marks on the bullets. It was Devins' insurance in case any part of Norma's body was ever found with a bullet in it.

"Clever bastard," Burnett said. "By the way, I found where he bought it."

"The gun?" Trott asked.

"Yeah. The Hollywood Gun Shop. They've got receipts: one nine-millimeter Browning sold to Thomas Devins. Not too long before the trip to Europe."

Trott looked at the two men from behind his desk. "Bill, I want you to contact the Browning factory. It's in Belgium somewhere—it's called the *Fabrique National,* or something like that. Ask them if they can tell from the markings whether the barrel has, in fact, been switched. If we can prove that, we'll have more corroboration on Forget. And Devins is going to have to explain to a jury just why he wanted to change barrels on his gun."

"Okay," Burnett said, then looked back at Murphy. "What about the diamonds and the emerald?"

Murphy shook his head. "We went over that highway a hundred times, me and Forget. Nothing. Those diamonds were too small; they could be anywhere. And we were covering a half-mile of road."

"The emerald?"

Murphy again shook his head. "I set up a dredging operation, worked that whole pond over, real careful. Hell, there's three feet of silt at the bottom. It could take years, and then we'd never find it. Needle in a haystack." He continued shaking his head. "No way."

"But a thought occurred to me," Trott said. "In the transcript, Forget said he tried to smash the emerald. Hit it with a hammer."

"Yeah," Murphy said. "He told me he laid it down on a wrench, a crescent wrench, and then pounded on it with a hammer. But it was too hard—harder than the forged steel."

"Exactly," Trott continued. "The emerald is harder than the steel in the wrench and the hammer. So it wouldn't give." He looked back and forth between the two men. "Something had to give, and it had to be the softer steel."

"I don't get you," Murphy said.

"An imprint," Burnett muttered.

"Exactly." Trott looked again at the pen that always seemed to be in his hand. "An imprint. The crescent and the hammer must have some kind of scratches on their surface from the emerald. And just maybe, those scratches are identifiable."

"Identifiable?" Murphy asked.

"Like a diamond, an emerald has its own unique characteristic. Each is cut slightly differently. And the insurance companies want records of those characteristics, to identify the jewel being insured. It's like a fingerprint. Norma's emerald has its own fingerprint."

"But we don't have the emerald," Murphy protested. "It—"

"I've contacted Norma Wilson's insurance company," Trott continued. "We have the figures on the emerald."

Burnett nodded. "That imprint, or scratch or whatever— it's going to be pretty slight. And maybe a scratch isn't enough."

"Maybe," Trott replied. "But they've got a newly developed electron scanning microscope over at Jet Propulsion Laboratories. It's so sensitive, it can pick up disturbances in molecular structure."

J.P.L., Burnett thought. He remembered reading about J.P.L. It was located next to CalTech and involved in the space program, somehow. "I'll get on it," he said.

"Good."

Burnett looked at Murphy. "Forget still have the hammer and wrench?"

"Yeah," Murphy answered. "He showed 'em to me. Has 'em down here; brought 'em down to L.A. in case he got some work here."

"All right," Trott said, leaning back in his chair. "Then that's it." He looked at Murphy, then at Burnett. "It's beginning to look like we may have a case."

Chapter 32

DEVINS HAD BOUGHT the yacht.

Burnett hung up the phone. The boat dealer had confirmed what the surveillance unit suspected: Devins had completed the purchase of an expensive forty-eight-foot sailboat, large enough to cruise anywhere in the world, sturdy enough to be self-sustaining for months.

Was Devins making his move? He must realize that the noose was tightening. And he must know it was just a matter of time now before Burnett would be looking for him, armed with an arrest warrant for murder. Time . . . Was there enough time left? Enough to lock up the case and get a warrant, before Devins was gone—perhaps for good?

Burnett looked down at the long telegram he had received from Interpol in Washington that morning. For the third time, he read the message:

REF YOUR TELEX 30TH SEPTEMBER PLEASE NOTE THAT 9 MM PISTOL SERIAL NUMBER T182632 WAS SENT TO BROWNING IN THE USA ON 6TH MARCH 1967. AS THE BARRELS ARE NOT SERIAL NUMBERED IT IS NOT ALWAYS EASY TO ASCERTAIN THAT A PISTOL IS EQUIPPED WITH ITS ORIGINAL BARREL.

HOWEVER ON THE LOWER BARREL PROJECTION A FIGURE IS ALWAYS STAMPED WHICH SHOWS THE YEAR OF MANUFACTURE OF THE BARREL. IN THE PRESENT CASE THE FIGURE USED WAS 8. TO BE ABLE TO RECOGNIZE A BARREL MANUFAC-

TURED IN 1948, 1958, OR 1968, A DIFFERENT FOUR-SIDED
GEOMETRICAL FIGURE IS USED FOR EACH OF THOSE YEARS.
MOREOVER AFTER EACH TRIMESTER ONE SIDE IS REMOVED
FROM THE GEOMETRICAL FIGURE. THEREFORE A FOUR-SIDED
FIGURE MEANS THAT THE BARREL WAS MANUFACTURED
DURING THE FIRST TRIMESTER, A THREE-SIDED FIGURE
MEANS THE SECOND TRIMESTER, ETC. FOR THE YEAR 1968 A
DIAMOND WAS USED AS GEOMETRICAL FIGURE.

AS THE BARREL IN QUESTION HAS THE FIGURE 8 STAMPED
AND IS ENCLOSED IN A THREE-SIDED DIAMOND, THIS MEANS
THAT THE BARREL WAS MANUFACTURED DURING THE SEC-
OND TRIMESTER OF 1968. ALL THE OTHER MARKS ON THE
BARREL ARE ONLY CONTROL MARKS AND GIVE NO INDICA-
TION REGARDING THE YEAR OF MANUFACTURE.

CONSEQUENTLY IT SEEMS TO BE OBVIOUS THAT THE BARREL
WHICH IS PRESENTLY ON THE PISTOL SERIAL T182632 IS NOT
THE ORIGINAL ONE SINCE THE PISTOL WAS SHIPPED IN 1967.

Solid proof from the Browning factory. Now Trott could
show in court that Devins had bought a nine-millimeter
Browning automatic shortly before taking Norma Wilson to
Europe and that the barrel on the gun was switched after he
returned. Would Devins claim the new barrel was already
on the gun when he bought it?

Burnett sorted through the stacks of files, notes, letters
and messages on his desk. Finally, he found the photocopy
of the sales slip from the Hollywood Gun Shop. The serial
number of the gun was listed, but no other identifying
markings were included.

He dialed the number for the Jet Propulsion Laboratory
in Pasadena.

"Mary Ann? This is Bill Burnett."

"Oh, yes . . . they've finished the testing on the crescent
wrench and the hammer."

"What's the story?" he asked quickly. Was there a match?
Could they tell whether the emerald had been struck by the

hammer as Forget had claimed? It would be solid corroboration of their key witness and it might prove tough for Devins' lawyer to explain to a jury how Forget came into possession of Norma's jewelry.

"The testing on the hammer was inconclusive, I'm afraid."

"Inconclusive?"

"Yes, I'm afraid so. There simply were not sufficient impressions from which to draw a pattern. A certain number of points are necessary to extrapolate a total pattern, you see."

"So they can't match the emerald to the hammer."

"No."

"And the wrench?"

"According to the report, yes . . . apparently so."

"A match?"

"Yes. A total pattern was extrapolated; photographs were taken through the electron microscope. These will be forwarded to you."

"And they match? The emerald and the wrench?"

"Yes. . . . The pattern was compared to the geometric description of the emerald from the insurance company. And the impression from the wrench matches one segment of the emerald. In the doctor's opinion, the emerald was lying on the wrench when it was struck by some object, and the impact imbedded a partial but identifiable pattern on the wrench."

They may never find the body, Burnett was thinking, but that little bastard's still going to take a trip to the gas chamber.

Did they have enough evidence now? he wondered. It was Trott's decision. Only Trott could decide when the evidence was sufficient to insure a reasonable chance of success in trial. Only Trott knew all the legal technicalities involved in the case; he could analyze which evidence would probably be admitted and which stood a risk of being suppressed. He understood what had to be shown for jurisdiction, what had to be proven to establish a corpus delicti. And then he knew what hurdles had to be faced in presenting Forget's story, and how to overcome them. Burnett knew the case better than anyone. But in the complex world of the courtroom, nothing seemed to make sense. Only Trott would know what was necessary to work their way past the myriad of obstacles to a murder conviction. And when there was enough evidence, Trott would give Burnett the green flag: bring Devins in.

"Hey, Bill."

Burnett looked across the room at Murphy. "Yeah?"

"I think I found the man who sold the barrel to Devins. Just talked to the guy. Gun shop over in West L.A. Says he sold a replacement barrel to a guy a year or so ago, for a nine-millimeter Browning." He grinned. "I ask him, was it to a Tom Devins, and he says, yeah, that sounds right to him."

"You going to get the records?"

"The guy says he looked and couldn't find any record of the sale. But he says he remembers well enough."

"Sounds good."

"Yeah. But wait till you see these." Murphy walked over to Burnett's desk and threw three postcards down in front of him. "Forget give 'em to me—says Devins mailed 'em to him."

Burnett looked at the first postcard. On one side was a color photograph of a statue in Stockholm. He flipped it over. It was addressed to Forget and postmarked Stuttgart.

Dear Bob,

I am in Germany en route to Switzerland to attempt to locate Norma. If you can remember the name of town it will help me get those jerks in Los Angeles off my back. If they contact you, just tell them to stop bugging everyone and find her or shut up—dig?

Best, Tom.

"Yeah," Murphy said. "Forget tells me Devins mailed them to him that time he went back to Europe to look for Norma Wilson. Maybe he figured the postman or the cops or someone would read the postcards and think he sounded pretty innocent."

Burnett turned to the second card, a color photograph of an Arab snake charmer holding up a viper. He turned it over. It was dated September 26, 1969, and postmarked Reggio Emilia, Italy.

Dear Bob,
   Just a short note. I've had to leave Los Angeles because of the problems I've created by reason of my testimony before the Grand Jury against the corruption within the Los Angeles District Attorney's office. When they took a shot at me on the freeway. I felt my life was worth too much than to just let them kill me. Interpol has cleared you of any conspiracy with me over Norma's disappearance.
   Best, Tom.

The second card had been sent about the time Burnett and Trott were tailing Devins in Genoa. Murphy was probably right: he was just sending postcards that anyone could read, in the hopes that it would tend to establish his innocence in their eyes. He probably figured Forget would eventually turn the postcards over to the D.A.'s office.

He looked at the third postcard, a photo of an oriental tea garden. It was postmarked San Francisco. He flipped it over and read the familiar writing.

Dear Bob and Judy,
   Good luck on your new house. Sorry we didn't get a chance to say goodbye, but I guess you were late in leaving. I'm en route to Europe to find information about Norma after I left her. Someone must have seen her. I'll write or call when I get back. Bob—keep cool—all is okay.
   Best to you both, Tom.

Burnett kept looking at the handwriting on the card. Maybe Devins had felt Forget was under surveillance, his mail being checked. Maybe he thought Forget was a pipeline to Burnett. Or maybe he was just setting Forget up. Why would the clever manipulator send three cards to Forget during his "search for Norma"? Why would he be reporting periodically to the not-too-bright "bodyguard"?

Burnett read the message over a second time, stopping at the last sentence. *Bob—keep cool—all is okay.* Had Devins simply been worried that Forget might crack? Maybe the postcards were simply intended to reassure the volatile French Canadian?

"By the way," Murphy said, "did we ever get confirmation from the L.A. customs people on Forget?"

"Yeah. His story checks. Their records show he tried to smuggle in a watch without paying duty, like he said. He was fined and released. The dates match."

"What about the—"

The telephone rang. Burnett answered it. "S.I.D., Burnett."

There was a faint clicking on the line and the sound of static reverberating in a long hollow tunnel. "Mr. William Burnett please. Overseas operator for Mr. William Burnett."

"This is William Burnett."

The operator said something in French. Suddenly, a man's voice broke through. "Monsieur Burnett?"

"Yeah."

"René Tomkins."

"How are you, Inspector? Good to hear from you again."

"Very well, thank you."

"How's everything in Geneva?"

"Very well." He laughed. "Very dark now." There was a short pause. "Monsieur Burnett, I call on a very important matter."

"Yeah?"

"We may talk like this?"

"Sure. What do you got?"

"The clothing, monsieur. I find the clothing."

"The—"

"The clothing of Madame Norma Carty Wilson."

Burnett sat bolt upright. He looked up at Murphy, then back at the phone. "You found Norma's clothing?"*

Oui, monsieur. As you say, I have my men look at the train station. Other places also, but it is at the train station that they find the box."

"A box?"

Oui. A large box. It has not been, ah, claimed for much time now. We open the box, and inside is the clothing that you describe. Some of the clothing—not all."

"Which clothing, Inspector?" Burnett could feel his heart accelerating. This could be the final link.

"The white coat of mink; this is in the box. There is much blood on the coat, much blood. Dry, powder—very old. But we check: it is blood, human blood."

Forget had said Devins told him he had shot her in the head from behind, and the bullet had torn off the front of her face. If the story were true, most of the blood would have spilled down the front of the mink coat. "What part of the coat was bloody, Inspector?"

"There is some blood in many places. But most of the blood is on the front of the coat. We check the blood. It is type A."

"Type A," Burnett repeated. Norma Wilson's medical records reflected that she had type A blood.

Oui. Also, there is in the box the, ah, panties and the . . . on the legs?"

"Stockings."

Oui, stockings. These have also blood on them. Also, the panties and . . . stockings are torn, cut. We believe cut—by a knife. The edges are sharp, clean. The panties and stockings are cut off Madame Wilson, we believe. Someone cuts them off with a knife."

---

*One of the mysteries of this case is why Devins did not simply burn Norma Wilson's clothing, destroying this evidence once and for all. My own theory is that he was setting Forget up somehow, that the clothing was a part of his original frame-up, but that in the long run his plans fell through.

Burnett was remembering Forget's gruesome recounting of how Devins had bragged about butchering the older woman into pieces, and then burying them in scattered locations.

"There is a . . . dress, also," Tomkins continued. "Also with much blood. And . . . a brassiere."

"Was Devins' name on the box?"

"No," he replied. "No, there is no name. Nothing. Ah!" he added. "Also, there is in the clothes many leaves, pieces of grass, pieces of wood. It is like they are dragged through trees and grass and plants, I think."

Burnett nodded, thinking. "Inspector, can you forward a detailed summary of what you found, where you found it and so on? With photographs?"

"But of course. At once."

"And you will be available to come to Los Angeles with the clothing . . . to testify?"

"It is my pleasure, Monsieur Burnett."

"Many thanks, Inspector." Burnett barely heard the click, the following static and the voice of the operator. Norma Wilson's coat. Exactly where Forget said it would be. They still hadn't found her body. But maybe now they didn't need to.

Burnett leaned back in his chair, stretched his arms high above his head. He was suddenly feeling good, very good—as if a heavy weight were being lifted from his shoulders. It had been nearly two years now that he had been digging away, trying to solve the mystery of Norma Wilson's disappearance. Two long years. And now the end of the road was in view.

"Burnett!"

Burnett looked up, saw Chief Stoner hurrying toward his desk.

"Just came in over the radio," Stoner growled. "It's Devins. The son of a bitch suddenly took off like a bat out of hell. The surveillance units lost him."

Chapter 33

STEVE?"

"Yes," the voice answered over the phone. "Is this Burnett?"

"Yeah. Steve, Devins just shook the tail. He took off at high speed; the unit couldn't keep up. Out near Tarzana, heading east."

"He's in the El Dorado?"

"Yeah."

The line was silent. Trott was trying to weigh the situation, his mind rapidly calculating the competing factors. Was there enough evidence to justify an arrest at this point? There was no question that they had Devins on theft charges, for the fraudulent transfers of Norma's real estate holdings. But the murder charge was the big one, and he was still hoping for her body to be found. Without it, a conviction would be difficult. And arresting him now would mean going to trial with what they had so far. If he were acquitted because the jury thought Norma might still be alive somewhere, Trott wouldn't get a second chance: double jeopardy would prevent further prosecution even if her body were found.

Do we go now? Trott was thinking. Or do we hold off, waiting for more evidence—for, maybe, Norma Wilson's body. And was Devins just playing games with the surveillance units? Or was he running—was this the last chance they would have to grab him?

"Steve," Burnett said into the telephone.

"Yes?"

"I called J.P.L. They got a positive match on the wrench."

There was a pause. "Then, they'll testify Norma's emerald was lying on Forget's wrench when it was struck?"

"Yep. But here's the big one. Tomkins called me from Geneva. He found Norma's clothes." Again, there was silence on the line. "In a box, at a railroad station—just like Forget said. The clothes had blood all over them, human blood, type A. And the clothes had been cut up, probably by a knife."

"Go," Trott said suddenly. "Murder one."

"You'll transmit the warrant?" Technically, Burnett could arrest Devins for murder without a warrant, on the basis of his own reasonable suspicion that Devins had committed a felony. But the D.A.'s office preferred to use arrest warrants whenever possible in the more important cases; that way, the legality of the arrest was less susceptible to later attacks by defense lawyers.

"Yes," Trott replied. "But either way, you haul him in." It would take nearly a half-hour to draft a proper arrest warrant and have it typed—a half-hour of waiting that Burnett couldn't afford if he was going to catch Devins. So instead, Trott would radio Burnett in his car, reading the contents of the warrant to him; legally, that would be the near equivalent of Burnett's physically possessing the warrant. And if that didn't work out, then Burnett would just make an old-fashioned, flat-out arrest without a warrant.

"Got it," Burnett said. He dropped the receiver into the cradle, grabbed his rumpled gray flannel coat and sprinted for the door. He stopped for a second, quickly walked back to the desk and shuffled through the stacks of papers. He found the leather pouch filled with tobacco, stuffed it into his pocket. Then he turned and ran for the door.

Within minutes he was heading south on the Harbor Freeway in the Ford station wagon, weaving through traffic at eighty miles per hour.

A crackling voice came over the radio speaker. "Wildflower, Wildflower, this is Daisy Three. Over."

Burnett grabbed the mike. "Daisy Three, this is Wildflower. Over." Daisy Three was the L.A.P.D. helicopter, called in for the chase.

"Wildflower, we have made contact with Rabbit. Repeat, we have made contact with Rabbit. Over."

"What is your ten-twenty, Daisy Three?"

"Southbound, San Diego Freeway, near intersection of Mulholland."

He was heading south, over the pass from the Valley into West L.A., Burnett thought. "Daisy Three, what is Rabbit's speed?"

"Fifty-five, sixty, Wildflower. I don't think he's made us yet. He was hitting ninety or a hundred when he left Daisy One."

Burnett swerved the station wagon to the right, merged into the transitional lane. Then he was on the Santa Monica Freeway, heading west toward the juncture with the San Diego. If Devins stayed on the San Diego, Burnett would hit the southbound juncture about fifteen miles ahead of him. That was a lot of distance to make up.

"Daisy One, Daisy One," Burnett said into the mike. "This is Wildflower, do you read? Over."

The radio continued to spit in empty static. Then a voice came over the speakers. "Wildflower, this is Daisy One. Over."

"Daisy One, what is your ten-twenty?"

"Wildflower, we are now on San Diego Freeway, southbound, nearing Mulholland Pass. Estimate ninety miles per hour. Over."

"Are you reading Daisy Three?"

"Affirmative, Wildflower," the voice replied. "We read Daisy Three loud and clear."

"Daisy One, where did you lose Rabbit?"

"Ventura Boulevard, near Reseda."

"Was he alone in the El Dorado?"

"Affirmative, Wildflower."

Burnett swerved to miss a car, then jammed on his brakes. The station wagon fishtailed down the lane, the tires screaming and black smoke pouring from the wheel wells. Quickly, he evened the car out.

"Daisy One, did Rabbit make any stops before losing you?"

"Affirmative, Wildflower. Rabbit stopped at a Marine Supply store, then at a bank. Over."

That was it, then, Burnett was thinking. Devins stopped to pick up a pile of money, or possibly to convert money into traveler's checks. And at the boat store, some last minute equipment. He was heading southbound. The freeway would take him to Marina del Rey. He could get to the boat before Burnett, and before Daisy One. But Daisy Three in the helicopter could follow him out to sea, and Burnett could radio the Coast Guard.

"Wildflower," a voice said.

"This is Wildflower," Burnett answered into the mike.

"Wildflower, this is Daisy Three. Rabbit has just left the freeway, is now eastbound on Pico. Over."

What the hell? Burnett thought. Devins was heading away from the Marina now, and on slow surface streets. What was he doing?

"Wildflower, Rabbit is entering a parking structure, multilevel parking structure at May Company."

"Daisy One," Burnett said. "What is your ten-twenty?"

"Wildflower, we are nearing Pico turn-off. Will proceed to May Company parking structure. Over."

"Ten-four, Daisy One." Burnett swerved sharply to the left, narrowly missing a Volkswagen loaded with kids. What the hell was Devins doing? he pondered, clamping down on the pipe stem. He shakes off a tail at a hundred miles an hour, then calmly goes shopping at the May Company. What was he up to?

Five minutes passed, and Burnett had slowed the big station wagon down to seventy. He maneuvered it into the far right transition lane, approaching the San Diego Freeway. So far, the helicopter had not seen the El Dorado emerge from the parking structure.

"Wildflower, Wildflower, this is Daisy One. Over."

"Daisy One, this is Wildflower."

"Wildflower, we are in the parking lot, in view of the El Dorado. The vehicle is empty. The driver's door is wide open. Do you want us to go inside the May Company? Over."

"Negative, Daisy One," Burnett replied. "Maintain present position, wait for Rabbit to come out. Out." He put the mike back in the cradle. What the hell was Devins doing? It didn't make sense. Unless . . . Suddenly, he grabbed the mike. "Daisy Three, Daisy Three, come in."

"This is Daisy Three. Over."

"Daisy Three, how many other cars have come out of the parking structure since Rabbit went in?"

"Uh . . . ten, maybe fifteen. Over."

Jesus, Burnett was thinking. What was the car his girlfriend drove? Michelle Verpillat. One of those American pony cars . . . a Cougar. A Mercury Cougar. "Daisy Three, have you seen a Mercury Cougar come out of the structure? Over."

There was silence for a moment, only the sharp staccato of static coming over the speaker. Then: "Wildflower, we don't know. Over."

Burnett swerved onto the transition ramp, rose in a gentle arc over and onto the San Diego Freeway, then quickly headed south toward Marina del Rey.

"Maintain surveillance," he said quietly into the mike. "Out." Then he again replaced the mike in its cradle. Could Devins have set up a switch? He knew he was being tailed, had known for weeks; the surveillance units didn't even try to hide themselves anymore. Had he set up a car switch with Michelle? Had she been waiting in the structure with her car? Or was Devins once again playing games, trying to prove himself smarter than his pursuers? Was this just another message from The Fox?

Burnett pushed down on the accelerator. The marina was four miles away. He wouldn't call off the helicopter or the ground unit; chances were Devins was showing off his cool by doing some casual shopping in the department store. And if his hunch was right, there would still be plenty of time to call the Coast Guard.

Burnett suddenly bit down on his pipe. Or had Devins switched boats, too? He must know that Burnett was aware of his new sailing yacht. Had he arranged some deal for a boat switch? Marina del Rey was the largest private yacht harbor in the world, with berths for thousands of boats. At any time during the day, dozens of vessels left or entered the harbor. And Burnett couldn't have each of them stopped and searched. Was the forty-eight-foot sailboat just a dummy? A blind? Jesus, Burnett kept thinking, it was just Devins' style.

Three more minutes, and Burnett wheeled the big Ford off the freeway and onto Washington toward the marina. He jammed on the brakes, swerved, then slammed down on the accelerator. The black briar stuck straight out as the raw-boned investigator bit down hard on the stem.

The car hurtled through the red traffic signal at Lincoln, causing four cars to skid to a stop, horns blaring. Burnett threw the wheel over hard to the left, felt the big machine slide sideways, then suddenly right itself and come out of the drift in a lazy rocking motion and again bite into the asphalt, black rubber screaming.

Burnett covered the next five blocks in no time, leaving a wake of jangled traffic and yelling drivers. He threw the steering wheel to the right, sending the station wagon into another four-wheel drift, then straightened out and shot into the marina.

There was relatively little traffic on the streets, and Burnett was at the forty-eight-footer's slip within seconds. But the big boat was empty, buttoned up. And there were no cars in the nearby parking lot—no Cougar, no El Dorado.

Then Devins really was back at the department store, Burnett thought. There was no car switch, no boat switch—nothing. Devins was calmly doing some shopping, while Burnett was tearing around the city on half-cocked paranoid theories.

Burnett pulled out of the parking lot, headed the car back toward Lincoln Boulevard. Slowly, he turned left onto Mindanao Way, past the grocery store. Then Burnett saw it.

In the parking lot of the grocery store was a bronze-colored Mercury Cougar with a brown vinyl roof.

Burnett wheeled the station wagon over sharply, bounced

into the parking lot. He drove past the Cougar. Empty. He continued on across the lot to the farthest parking space, stopped and killed the engine.

Could it be Michelle's car? he thought as he pulled out his .38 Smith and Wesson and quickly checked the load. Then he replaced the gun into the cross-draw holster. He was remembering what he had heard from some vague source: Sana had told Devins he would never survive an arrest by the D.A.'s men. And Burnett knew Devins had bragged on more than one occasion to his friends that he would never let Burnett take him alive. Theatrical, Burnett thought—but maybe true. Devins was known to carry a revolver. And one thing was for sure: he had already proven himself capable of killing.

Burnett got out of the car and began walking toward the grocery store. He realized there wasn't enough time to call for backup units. And besides, there was nothing to indicate the bronze Cougar belonged to Michelle Verpillat. Chances were still that Devins was back at the May Company. But if he *were* in the grocery store, how should Burnett take him? He had to figure there would be shooting, and that was no good in a store with innocent citizens. Jesus, Burnett thought, you're getting jumpy; you see a Mercury Cougar and right off you—

Burnett froze. Devins was twenty feet away, his arms wrapped around a brown paper grocery bag filled with food. He was alone, walking toward the car, unaware of Burnett's presence.

Burnett whipped out the .38. "Stop," he yelled at Devins as he leveled the gun.

Devins suddenly looked up, saw Burnett. He stopped in his tracks, staring at the crouching investigator.

"Don't make a move, Devins," Burnett yelled. "You're under arrest for murder."

Devins' eyes were fixed to the steel barrel pointed at him. His mind was flashing through the possibilities, his muscles tensed for the lightning-quick decision.

Burnett was still set in a semicrouched position, his right hand holding the revolver, his left hand bracing the gun under the butt. The pipe was still clenched in his teeth, but his eyes were sighting along the gun barrel at the frozen figure with the grocery bag.

Neither man moved in the midday sun, as the seconds ticked slowly by.

Then, Burnett straightened slightly and began walking forward, the barrel of the gun still pointed directly at Devins' chest. "Don't even think about it, Tom," he said in a low voice. "Put the bag down real slow; then put your hands behind your head, real slow."

Devins didn't move. He just stood there, his eyes locked now on Burnett's eyes, trying to guess the man, trying still to weigh the chances.

"Now," Burnett whispered as he approached Devins.

Slowly, Devins shook his head. "You're lucky, Burnett," he said. "You're one lucky son of a bitch."

Chapter 34

Burnett stepped out of the elevator and began walking down the hallway toward Department 102. The jury had finally been chosen, and Trott was going to begin presenting evidence today. It had been a long, tough grind—months of courtroom battles, preliminary hearings, pretrial suppression motions, delaying tactics by the defense. Joe Reichman was representing Devins, and he was a respected and dangerous adversary, a courtroom brawler who went for the jugular. But Trott had met all the attacks; he had blocked the voluminous legal motions, overcoming them with his own stacks of legal precedents cited to the judge. And now it was time for the showdown: trial by jury.

Burnett squeezed through a crowd of milling reporters in the hallway. Most of them, he knew, were waiting for testimony to resume in another trial just down the hall from Department 102: People versus Charles Manson. Someone was being interviewed just outside Judge Older's courtroom. It was difficult to see in the blinding light of strobes and flash bulbs, but Burnett thought he recognized the bulldog face of Irving Kanarek, the cantankerous old lawyer who was succeeding in stretching the Manson case out one month after another.

Burnett grinned. Kanarek could push the patience of the most temperate judge beyond the breaking point. But in Judge Older he may have met his match; Older just refused to be rattled. And Burnett had firsthand knowledge of that: Older had been the trial judge when he had testified in the attorney general's prosecution of Jerome Weber. And the elderly judge had earned Burnett's lasting respect when, in the face of considerable pressures, he had denied probation to the influential lawyer and sentenced him to prison.

The doors of Department 102 drew near. Judge Malcolm Lucas presiding. Another good judge, Burnett thought as he entered the courtroom. They had been lucky to draw a judge as sharp and tough as Lucas.

The spectators' gallery was filled with witnesses, reporters, and the general thrill-seekers who had been unable to work their way into the Manson courtroom. Judge Lucas hadn't taken the bench yet, but the jurors were seated in the jury box, waiting. Burnett counted four women, eight men. And six alternate jurors. Usually, there were only two alternates, but then the Devins trial could take a long time, so Lucas was playing it safe.

Near the jury box was the prosecution's counsel table. Steve Trott sat to the right, staring intently at the empty judge's bench, his mind going over the opening statement he was about to present to the jury. Seated next to him was Harland Braun, the deputy D.A. who would assist Trott throughout the trial in preparing witnesses, researching legal precedents and conducting some of the direct and cross-examination.

A few feet away from the jury box was the defense counsel table. Reichman sat behind it, pouring over a stack of legal papers. To his left, Tom Devins sat expressionless, dressed in a sport coat and tie.

So the stage was set, Burnett thought as he walked down the aisle toward Trott. After two years of investigation and months of legal maneuverings, the day had come.

"All rise!" the bailiff's gruff voice bellowed. There was a clatter of chairs, a series of coughs, as everyone in the courtroom stood up. Quickly, the conversation subsided. Then Judge Lucas stepped out through a door, black robes flowing behind him, and rapidly mounted the steps to the bench.

"Department 102 of the Superior Court of Los Angeles is

now in session," the bailiff announced. "Honorable Malcolm Lucas presiding. Please be seated and come to order."

"Well, gentlemen," Judge Lucas said. "People ready?"

"Yes, your honor," Trott replied.

"Defense?"

"We are, your honor," Reichman said.

"Fine. Mr. Trott, do you wish to make an opening statement?"

Trott rose to his feet. "Yes, if it please the court." He walked toward the jury box, put his hands on the old wooden railing. He looked at each of the jurors in turn. "Ladies and gentlemen, this is my opportunity to present to you a preview of this case, the State of California versus Thomas Edward Utter. I am going to tell you what I expect the evidence in this case will be to support the charges of murder, robbery and grand theft. Bear in mind that what I am telling you now is not to be considered by you as evidence in this case."

He turned away from the jury box. "The evidence will show that some time during the morning of November 23rd, 1968, the defendant, Thomas Utter, under the alias Thomas Devins, shot Norma Carty Wilson in the head with a nine-millimeter Browning automatic pistol, causing her death."

He walked to the counsel table and picked up a color photograph of Norma Wilson. He walked back to the jury, holding up the photo. "This is Mrs. Norma Carty Wilson. This is the woman whom, we will show, Thomas Devins murdered in cold blood. . . ."

"The tape-recording machine was working at that time?"

"It was."

Burnett shifted his position in the chair. He had been sitting on the witness stand now for more than three hours, undergoing intensive cross-examination by Devins' attorney.

"Then," Reichman continued, "later on, at the conclusion of the conversation, you mentioned the little green room to Mr. Forget?"

"I did," Burnett replied.

"But when you mentioned the little green room to Mr. Forget, you had already turned off the tape recorder."

"I had."

"Why?"

"We were getting ready to leave the room, and as I picked up the briefcase I turned the switch off."

"Mr. Burnett, isn't it true that you had decided to mention the little green room to him after you had turned off the tape machine? That you made that decision before you turned off the machine?"

"I don't believe so."

Reichman stepped away from the witness box, walked toward the jury. "Weren't you simply trying to terrorize Mr. Forget—to scare him into helping you set up Tom Devins?"

"No."

"Wasn't it part of your technique not to mention the little green room until after the tape machine was turned off?"

"I don't recall whether I'd made up my mind to ask him that question. I think it was just a parting shot as we were leaving."

"A transcript has been prepared of that conversation, has it not?"

"Yes."

"And there is nothing in that transcript about a little green room?"

"There is not."

Reichman looked back at Burnett. "All right. Now, you prepared a written report concerning this trip to Sedro Woolley, did you not?"

"Yep."

"Had you given that report to anyone?"

"Just within the Bureau."

"When you say within the Bureau, you mean the District Attorney's Bureau of Investigations?"

"That's right."

"Those reports aren't released to the public?"

"No."

"And during the conversation you later had with Mr.

Leroy Sana, did it appear to you that Mr. Devins, or his lawyer, Mr. Weber, had come into possession of the contents of the report?"

"It sure did."

"Was there some language that indicated to you that somebody outside the Bureau had seen the report—somebody who shouldn't have?"

"I'd definitely say someone had been informed as to the contents of the report."

"And only you and two or three of your superiors in the Bureau had access to it?"

"That's right." Burnett's mind was beginning to wander. After three hours of crossing swords with the clever lawyer, he was exhausted, and his throat was dry. All he saw was the image of a frosted, ice-cold bottle of beer.

But Burnett couldn't afford to let his mind drift. If his guard dropped for a second, Reichman would find an opening and thrust home. It was becoming obvious that Devins' defense was based not so much on contesting the evidence directly as on accusing the D.A.'s office of framing him in order to cover up internal corruption. The best defense was a good offense: Reichman was putting Burnett on trial. And the jury was intently looking for any indication that there was truth to the accusations. A temporary lapse on the stand, a mental slip, could be disastrous.

"Did you ever call Mr. Devins at his home?"

"Yes."

"You knew at that time that he had an attorney, Jerome Weber?"

"Yes."

"But you called Mr. Devins at his house?"

"I did."

"Is it your practice to call people directly when they are represented by an attorney?"

"I wanted to verify that he was still in town."

Reichman began walking back to the witness stand. "Mr. Forget was an addict, wasn't he?"

"I'm sorry?"

"Mr. Forget—didn't he tell you once he used heroin?"

Like Trott, Reichman was adept at suddenly switching subjects, hoping to catch the witness off-guard. It was more difficult to keep up your guard when you didn't know which direction the next blow was coming from.

"He never said a thing about heroin to me."

"Didn't he tell you anything about his use of drugs?"

"He mentioned that at some time in the past he'd played around with bennies—amphetamines. But that's all."

Reichman stared at Burnett for a moment in silence, then turned and looked at the jury. "Mr. Burnett, we have discussed the accusation made by Mr. Devins concerning Mr. Weber's solicitation of a $35,000 bribe. Twenty-five thousand of this was to go to . . . certain people in the Bureau?"

"That's what Mr. Devins said."

"And in return for the $25,000, these . . . people would squash the case against Mr. Devins?"

"That's what he said."

"And he said that to a grand jury?"

"I wasn't there when he testified."

"And the grand jury indicted Mr. Weber."

"Yes."

"And he was later convicted and sentenced to prison."

"That's what I understand."

"And the investigation that Mr. Weber was going to have stopped was *your* investigation, was it not?"

"The Devins investigation was mine, yes."

"The prosecution of Mr. Weber was done by the attorney general, not by the district attorney, isn't that so?"

"It is."

"And in connection with this, you were investigated by the attorney general—*you* were a suspect?"

"I was questioned."

"And to date, it is not known with *whom* Mr. Weber was going to share the bribe in the D.A.'s office." He looked directly at the jurors. "It is only known that there *was* such a bribe arranged—on *your* case."

Trott jumped up. "Objection, your honor. Argumentative. Calls for conclusion. Speculation."

"Sustained," Judge Lucas said.

Reichman smiled. "Nothing further of this witness." He began walking back to the counsel table.

"Any redirect, Mr. Trott?" the judge asked.

"A few questions." Trott remained standing at his table. "Mr. Burnett, were you indicted after the grand jury investigation into the Weber matter?"

"No."

"And you freely testified before the grand jury?"

"I did."

"Was Mr. Stoner indicted?"

"No."

"Was Mr. Murphy indicted?"

"He was not."

"Were you ever formally charged with anything concerning the Weber matter?"

"I was not."

Trott sat down. "Nothing further."

Judge Lucas looked at the defense table. "Mr. Reichman?"

"No more questions, your honor."

"You may call your next witness, Mr. Trott."

"De Wayne Wolfer," Trott said.

"De Wayne Wolfer," the bailiff repeated loudly.

The scholarly looking man seemed relaxed as he walked toward the stand; he had testified in such courtrooms hundreds of times before.

"What is your occupation, sir?" Trott asked, standing at the table.

"I am a criminalist for the City of Los Angeles Police Department, assigned to the Scientific Investigation Division, where I am in charge of the laboratory."

"How long have you been . . ."

Burnett listened as Trott led Wolfer through the preliminary questions that established his expertise in the area of criminalistics. Trott was mainly interested in corroborating Forget's story of how Devins told him he had shot Norma Wilson. From the bloodstains on the clothing, Wolfer would attempt to re-create how she was killed.

"Mr. Wolfer," Trott asked, "with **respect** to the clothing and the items you examined in the box marked 'Exhibit 50,' did you find any stains or large quantities of foreign material on any of them?"

"I did, yes."

"What exactly did you do?"

"I took samples and by preliminary examination, what we call preliminary field testing, I made a benzidine test of all the areas to determine if it was blood. It was. I then went to the biological precipitating tests to determine if it was human blood. Finally, I went to the human sensitization series and did the tests where I determined that this was human blood, Type A."

"You then mounted the clothing on a mannequin—a dummy—is that correct?"

"Yes, I did."

"For what purpose?"

"I wanted to study the flow of the bloodstains to see the position the body was in at the time the blood was flowing and depositing on the clothing."

"And what clothing was on the mannequin?"

"Let's see, there were the stockings, the, ah, undergarments . . ."

"Undergarments?"

"Panties and bra. And the wool suit or dress. And . . . the coat, the mink coat."

"All right. And what did you determine in making the examination? From what area of the anatomy did the blood come?"

"The blood came—when it was fresh—from two head wounds. It flowed down the body of the person wearing the clothing, from an entrance wound and an exit wound."

"Would you please explain how you came to that conclusion?"

Wolfer nodded. "If we were to draw a line through the center of the blood area, this would show the train or the flow of the blood. In this case, it showed that at the time of hemorrhaging, or flow of blood, the body was more or less in an erect position. Now, if you look at the bloodstains, you will notice that the largest amount of blood is up in the shoulder and neck area. So you know the origin of the wound was above the shoulder and neck area, the blood flowing directly down by gravitational forces, to the lower areas where it then goes into serous stains."

"What's a serous stain?"

"The blood is in two conditions, liquid and solid. Serous is liquid, and is indicated by the lighter stain areas."

"I see." Trott pulled out a large, cardboard-mounted photograph of a mannequin clothed in stained woman's garments. "Your honor, may this be marked Exhibit Number C-1?"

"It may," Judge Lucas replied.

Trott walked toward Wolfer, holding up the large photograph so that the jury could see. "This is a photograph of the mannequin and clothing you have referred to?"

"It is."

"Now," Trott said, pointing to a spot on the photograph, "there is a darkened spot on the left breast area of the wool suit, isolated. How did this occur?"

"This didn't flow from the neck down, obviously, or the whole area would be darkened. But if you draw a perpendicular line through that stain also, it will indicate the body was erect. Again, the source had to be the head area—the shape indicating that rather than flowing down, it dripped down, directly onto the breast area."

"I see."

"Now, directly below this stain area, there are spots of dry or partially coagulated blood—partially coagulated at the time the blood was deposited on the dress—and this would indicate that blood had—"

"Objection," Reichman yelled. "The witness is testifying in the narrative. He is not answering specific questions."

"Overruled," Judge Lucas said quietly. He turned to Wolfer. "Please go on."

"It would indicate the blood had flowed down from the head, partially forming a clot or coagulating, before coming to rest."

"What does this signify?"

"Actually, it signifies two things. It indicates movement of the body, because the large darkened area is liquid, very fluid blood. The spotted area here," he pointed to the photograph, "shows that it is no longer fluid, but is now partially dried blood. And this means that the body was moving somewhat while it was still bleeding."

Trott walked back to his table, picked up another cardboard-mounted photograph of a mannequin in stained clothing, this time taken from the back. "Your honor, may this be marked 'People's Exhibit C-4'?"

"It may."

Trott showed the photograph to the jury, then to Wolfer. "This is a photograph of the same mannequin and clothing?"

"It is. A back view."

"Now, I notice stains on the clothing of the mannequin's back."

"That's correct. You will notice the flow of blood, the pattern, coming down from the back of the head."

"And what does this indicate?"

"That there were two wounds to the skull."

"Two wounds?"

"That's correct. Two wounds."

"What does this indicate?"

"A gunshot wound, entering at one point of the skull and exiting at another. From the blood patterns, entry of the bullet was from the rear of the skull and exit was through the facial area. The exit wound is, of course, much the larger wound, causing a larger flow of blood. Hence, the larger stains on the front portions of clothing."

"Why does there appear to be such a large quantity of blood involved, as indicated by the extensive stains?"

"You see, the heart continues to pump after the brain has been penetrated by a gunshot wound. For a short while. And as long as there is pressure in the system, the blood will come out of the head wound. In this case," he looked at the two photographs, "I would say the owner of the clothing lost several pints of blood before bleeding stopped."

"Did you find any indications of any other wounds?"

"No."

"Then, in your expert opinion, the cause of the stains to the clothing you studied was a head wound?"

"Yes."

"Caused by a single gunshot?"

"That's correct."

"Administered from behind the person wearing the clothing."

"That's correct."

It all seemed so smooth, so effortless, Burnett thought as he listened to the criminalist testify. Yet, he knew what had gone on behind the scenes before the orderly testimony of one witness after another. Once Devins had been arrested, there had been long hours of preparation for trial—weeks and even months of legal research, continued investigations, locating witnesses, briefs, attending strategy meetings, protecting and preparing key witnesses . . . Arranging for the testimony of the witnesses alone had been a back-breaking task. First, they had to be located—dozens of witnesses, many of them having moved in the past year or two, many of them reluctant to testify. Then, subpoenas had to be legally served upon them, followed by a call to soothe ruffled feelings and arrange for appearances in court that would not conflict with work or plans. Witnesses from Washington State, from Washington, D.C., from New York, from Spain, Morocco, Switzerland, Portugal. Witnesses who required official releases from their agencies through a jungle of bureaucratic red tape. Witnesses who could not speak English and would require translators. And for each of these witnesses, travel arrangements had to be made, accommodations found, fees paid after computing times and distances. All of this and more was necessary so that the orderly "natural" flow of testimony during trial would continue without interruption.

And while the headaches of witness logistics were being dealt with, the prosecution would find itself defending against a never-ending myriad of pretrial motions. The defense would challenge the probable cause for the arrest, question the jurisdiction of the court, argue that venue be changed due to the extensive publicity. There would be motions to suppress evidence, motions to dismiss for lack of evidence, motions to produce documents, motions, motions . . . And each of these, often designed simply to harass or delay, would have to be met. Manpower would be diverted; time would be lost.

Thousands of hours of preparation for each hour of testimony—this was what the jury never saw. Slowly, painfully building the case, overcoming the legal roadblocks, building a structure that would withstand the expert ravages of a defense lawyer. Foreseeing the attacks, shoring up the defense, and preparing one's own cross-examination—for witnesses who may never testify. Yet, only a small fraction of all the facts would ever be heard by the jury. And what they did hear would inevitably be a filtration of the truth; the case had been strained through a filter of motions, objections, legal constrictures, conferences at the bench and meetings in chambers. What emerged would inevitably be a kind of pap—a mangled, unrecognizable version of what had really happened.

The trial—the evidence actually heard by the jury—was just a surface performance. The tip of the iceberg. And it suddenly occurred to Burnett, as he sat there listening to Trott addressing the jury, that preparing for trial was very much like producing a play. The attorneys were the directors, the witnesses the actors, the jury their audience. Everything had been carefully rehearsed before the actual performance—the attorneys orchestrating, the witnesses carefully coached. And the roles that were being played, the lines being read, were only a sort of puppetry.

"Mr. Wolfer," Trott was saying as Burnett's mind again drifted back to the testimony of the criminalist, "did the clothing contain any other foreign materials besides blood?"

"Yes. The clothing was contaminated with botanical material, particularly in the case of the stockings."

"Botanical material?"

"Yes. Leaves, twigs, dirt."

"What does this indicate?"

"That the body had been dragged through a wooded area, or an area with natural vegetation. Particularly in view of the condition of the stockings, I would say the body was taken under the arms, face up—or what was left of it—and dragged along through an area of dirt, grass and leaves, the legs dragging along the ground. The tears of the nylon stockings were rolling in a downward direction, at the back."

"Now, Mr. Wolfer, did you find any other damage to any of the clothing?"

"Yes. The lower portion of the dress was torn where you would unhook or unbutton it. The seam had been ripped out. And, the bra—it had been cut."

"Cut? Like with a knife?"

"Probably by a knife. The pattern was elliptical, unlike one made by scissors. But sharply made—not the rough, frayed edge that would be made if it was torn."

"Any other damage?"

"The slip—there was a slip I didn't mention—it was also cut by a knife."

Trott nodded. The criminalist was substantiating every detail of Forget's story: the single gunshot, the mountainous area, the hunting knife. If only there had been fingerprints on the box. But Wolfer had checked, and there were none. Devins was too smart for that.

"Now," Trott continued, "another subject, Mr. Wolfer."

"Certainly."

"It is possible, is it not, to determine whether a particular bullet had been fired from a particular gun?"

"If the spent bullet is in good enough condition, yes."

"How is this done?"

"As the bullet goes down the barrel of a gun, it is scratched by the series of lands and grooves of the barrel, as well as by minor imperfections in the barrel. These scratches on the bullet will be unique: no two barrels will ever scratch in the same pattern. Each barrel has its own unique striation marks."

"Then it is the barrel, not anything else in the gun, that gives the telltale marks?"

"Yes."

"And if an individual did not wish a bullet he fired from his gun traced to that gun, how could he prevent it and still keep the gun?"

"Change the barrel."

Trott looked up at the jury, then across the courtroom at the seated figure of Tom Devins. Devins was staring straight ahead at the draped flag of California, apparently bored.

Burnett checked his watch. Four-thirty. They would be recessing soon, and he had an interview at five with a witness to a Hell's Angels rape-murder case. But it looked like Trott had things under control.

He quietly eased his way into the aisle and out through the swinging doors. Yes, Trott was getting his licks in now. But no matter how carefully the young prosecutor wove his case, it still all came down to whether the jury believed Forget. And Burnett could already see Reichman's defense: if Norma Wilson were really dead, it was Forget who murdered her. The corroboration of Forget's story could backfire: the jury could believe that Forget knew of the details of the killing not from Devins but from firsthand knowledge.

And Forget would take the stand tomorrow.

Chapter 35

W<small>HEN WAS THE</small> first time you met Mr. Devins?" Reichman asked, leaning toward Forget.

"That was way back in late '58 or early '59."

"What were you doing at that time, sir?"

"Nothing."

"You had no profession, no job, nothing—is that correct?"

"Yeah."

"What was Mr. Devins doing?"

"He was a parking lot attendant, best I can remember."

"But he then became a real estate agent, isn't that right?"

"Yeah, that and a mercenary," Forget replied. He shifted in the witness chair.

"What do you mean by mercenary?"

"He was going to help Moise Tshombe escape, going to fight for Biafra. There was a lot of money to be made, he said."

Reichman stepped back from the witness stand and walked toward the jury. It was the sixth week of trial, and even the energetic Joe Reichman was beginning to suffer from combat fatigue. But Forget was the primary target, and Reichman knew the jury would decide on the basis of this man's testimony.

Burnett looked over at the jury box from his seat in the audience. Four hours of cross-examination so far, and it was difficult to see what the jurors were thinking. Certainly, Forget gave a less-than-favorable impression. He constantly shifted in his seat, rarely looked the examining attorney in the eye, and consciously avoided looking at the jurors at all. He nervously licked his lips, massaged his chin, and coughed—the body language of the lying witness. And the jurors were not blind.

Forget would not break. Unlike the Perry Mason television shows, witnesses never broke down sobbing on the witness stand. Burnett had been through hundreds of criminal trials, and he had yet to see a single case where a lying witness made the dramatic confession E.G. Marshall and Raymond Burr routinely obtained during their brilliant but legally impermissible cross-examinations. No, Forget would not break—particularly since most of what he was testifying to was true. But he was also a habitual liar, a man who could not tell the truth without adding a few false details. And Reichman was an artist at finding those details.

Reichman understood—as the television-drugged public never did—that cross-examination was laborious, methodical, usually dull work, with very few isolated moments of inspiration or drama. The prosecutor had most of the tools and materials, and with them he carefully built a towering structure on a solid foundation, one plank at a time. And just as he was a creator, so was the defense attorney a destroyer. Armed with fewer tools, his job was now to whittle away at the towering structure, shaving a little off this plank, chipping a piece off that brick, until finally, during the closing argument, he could collect the chips, shavings and slivers that had fallen from the structure. He would pick these up from the ground, and just as carefully and methodically as the prosecutor, he would begin stacking them into a shaky pile until, finally, he will have built for the jury a small, flimsy shack that barely stood on its own. This he would call "reasonable doubt."

"Now, Mr. Devins worked his way up from parking cars to where he was managing an office building, didn't he?"

"Yeah."

"And then he passed the test and became a real estate salesman?"

"Yeah."

"And then he became a full broker, with his own business?"

"Yeah. Tom was always real smart."

"And he expanded his business and became a successful investment consultant?"

"Yeah."

"Now, Mr. Forget, during all this time, what were *you* doing?"

"Carpentering."

"Carpentering. And as the years went by, it seemed like Tom Devins was doing better all the time?"

"Yeah."

"You were doing what?"

"Not much, I guess."

"Did it ever bother you that this man was getting ahead while you weren't?"

"You might say it did, yeah."

Reichman looked directly at Forget. "This emerald that you say was given to you by Mr. Devins, you tried to smash it with a hammer?"

Forget again shifted his weight. "Yes."

"And at that time you thought it was worth $30,000."

"That's right."

"You decided to smash $30,000 into little pieces?"

"Yeah."

"Why?"

"Why not?"

"You tell us why, sir."

"Because it was trouble to me. I never have liked that kind of trouble. Maybe she paid $30,000 for it, but that don't mean I can get $30,000 for it. And if it was hot, it could do me a lot of harm."

"When did you take the pearls off the strand?"

"The pearls? I think . . . I don't remember."

"How did you do it?"

"How?"

"How."

"Well, the string holding the pearls . . . I just cut it with a knife, a pocket knife."

309

"Were they all the same size?"

"To the best of my recollection, they were."

"Are you sure?"

"No, I . . . I'm not sure, no."

Reichman nodded. "On the trip to Europe, you say you saw Mr. Devins with an envelope full of money."

"Yeah."

"What denominations?"

"The envelope was full of one-hundred-dollar bills."

"Did you ever see any other money in the envelope?"

"No."

"The only money you saw during the trip were the hundred-dollar bills?"

"Yeah."

Reichman walked quickly back to his table, picked up a paperbound volume. "Directing your attention to your testimony at the preliminary hearing, sir, at page 692, did you not testify that the envelope was full of, quote, singles, fives, tens, twenties *and* hundreds?" Reichman crossed back to the witness stand, showed Forget the opened page.

Forget read for a few moments, then looked up, shrugged his shoulders. "It was mostly hundred-dollar bills."

"Mostly? You just testified under oath that there was *nothing* but hundred-dollar bills!"

Forget shrugged again.

"Mr. Forget, you testified under direct examination that you saw Tom Devins and Norma Wilson sign some real estate papers before a notary in New York, did you not?"

"Yeah."

"You specifically saw that they were real estate papers?"

"Yeah."

Reichman turned the pages of the bound transcript. "Again, Mr. Forget, quoting from your testimony at the preliminary hearing a few months ago, didn't you state under penalty of perjury the following: 'Question: Did you see what kind of papers were signed? Answer: No.'" He showed Forget the opened page.

Again, Forget read it, then looked up.

"Well, sir?" Reichman demanded.

"I guess I just figured they were real estate dealings, you know, because that's all they ever did."

Reichman turned to the jury, letting the answers sink in. "You testified, did you not, at Jerome Weber's trial for attempted bribery?"

"Yes."

"And you observed Mr. Devins testify at the Weber trial?"

"Yes."

"All right. Now, when you were in Tangiers, you were very concerned about people seeing that you were leaving, and that Mr. Devins was staying with Mrs. Wilson."

"That's right."

"You wanted there to be witnesses to your leaving while she was still alive?"

"Right."

"Well, Mr. Forget, can you give us the name of one single person who can testify that you left that day?"

Forget shook his head slowly.

"Answer for the record," Reichman added.

"No."

"And you flew not to the United States but to Paris, is that correct?"

"Yeah."

"Do you have any witnesses, any way of verifying what you did while in Paris?"

Forget shook his head. "No." He looked up. "But I got stamps on my passport."

"How many passports do you have, Mr. Forget?"

"One."

"It's illegal to have two, isn't it?"

"I guess so."

"So you wouldn't tell us if you had two?"

"Objection!" Trott said from his chair.

"Sustained."

Reichman continued. "Can you show us anything to prove that you didn't return to Europe under another passport after setting up your alibi?"

"Objection!" Trott yelled, jumping to his feet.

"Sustained," Judge Lucas replied. He looked toward the defense lawyer. "Please move on to another subject."

But Reichman was satisfied. The question had been asked, the idea implanted in the jurors' heads. And nothing could stop them from thinking about it.

"Mr. Forget, what type of work have you done since coming to Los Angeles at Mr. Burnett's request?"

"None."

"How have you been living?"

"Colleen's been supporting me. Colleen Davis."

Reichman looked at the jury. "And what does she do?"

"She's a dancer."

"What kind of dancer?"

"A . . . topless dancer."

"Where?"

"Everywhere."

"All right," Reichman said, walking toward his table. "Mr. Forget, you received a couple of traffic tickets sometime ago, didn't you? Tickets you didn't pay that went to warrant?"

Oh, Jesus, Burnett thought. How did the son of a bitch find out about that?

"Yeah. One, a couple of years ago, up in northern California. I had a windshield wiper that didn't work and I just forgot about it."

"And the other?"

"Speeding, on my bike."

"Your motorcycle?"

"Yeah."

"Well, what happened to these tickets that had arrest warrants on them?"

"I got them taken care of."

"You mean, fixed?"

"Yeah, I guess."

"And, Mr. Forget," Reichman said, turning slowly toward the jury, "who fixed these warrants for you?"

"Uh, Mr. Burnett."

"William Burnett of the District Attorney's office?"

"Yeah."

Reichman turned to the audience, pointed an accusing finger at Burnett. "Are you referring to that gentleman as the man who fixed your tickets?"

"Uh, yeah. Yeah."

"I see," Reichman said. "And what other little favors has Mr. Burnett done for you to get you to testify here today?"

"Objection!" Trott yelled.

"Sustained."

"All right, Mr. Forget. You say you saw Norma Wilson's passport in Devins' car. You saw her photograph in the passport?"

"That's right."

"You recognized her photograph?"

"Yeah."

"Well, now, Mr. Forget, let me again direct your attention to your testimony at the preliminary hearing." He flipped some pages of the transcript to a marker, then opened the volume to Forget. "Page 680, line 18, to page 681, line 4."

Forget read in silence. Finished, he took in a deep breath. "Yeah?"

"Did you not testify at that time, under oath, that you couldn't recall positively seeing the photograph?"

"See, there was a lot of questions being asked back then, just like now, and—"

"Yes or no?"

"—and it gets to be real confusing."

"My question, Mr. Forget, is: did you testify before that you couldn't definitely recall seeing Mrs. Wilson's photo in the passport?"

"Well, yeah. I guess that's what I answered."

"Then, sir, which time were you lying under oath, then or now?"

Burnett's mouth was locked rigidly in place, his jaw muscles quivering perceptibly. Forget was being destroyed, he realized; and with him, the case against Tom Devins.

Reichman walked to the far end of the jury box, then turned and stared at Forget in silence. "Mr. Forget, isn't it true that you've been given immunity in this case?"

Forget looked down at his hands in his lap, nodded.

"Out loud, please," Reichman said.

"Yes. Yes."

"What kind of immunity did you get?"

"Well, I'm not sure, but I wanted immunity in this state, and all countries involved in this case. But all I know for sure is I got immunity, but I don't know if it's good for France or Spain or any of those places."

"This immunity was given to you by the District Attorney's office?"

"Yeah."

"Yet, you testify here that you did nothing wrong—nothing for which you would need immunity!"

"Objection!" Trott yelled, jumping to his feet.

"I made an agreement with Tom, a conspiracy, and I—"

"Did you kill Norma Wilson?" Reichman suddenly yelled at him.

"Your honor," Trott yelled, "I have an objection pending."

Judge Lucas slammed the gavel on the bench. "Gentlemen!" He looked at the two lawyers, then around the courtroom, suddenly silent. "I think this would be a good time for a recess."

But Burnett was looking at the twelve men and women in the jury box. And every one of them was looking directly at Forget.

"Court is again in session," Judge Lucas said. He looked at Forget on the witness stand, then across to Reichman seated at the defense table. "Mr. Reichman, you may continue your cross-examination."

"Your honor," Reichman replied. "I have no further questions of this witness."

"Any redirect, Mr. Trott?"

"No, your honor," Trott said, as Forget stepped down from the chair, "the People rest."

"Well," Judge Lucas said. "Fine." He looked toward Reichman. "You have motions?"

"Yes, your honor," the defense lawyer replied.

The judge looked at the jury. "Ladies and gentlemen,

there are some technical matters that I must discuss with counsel, now that the People have rested their case. You are free for . . . shall we say thirty minutes. Please be back promptly at three o'clock sharp, and we will begin hearing the defense. Also, please bear in mind the admonition against discussing this case with anyone."

The jurors filed quietly from the box and out of the courtroom. When they were all gone, Judge Lucas looked at the two lawyers.

"In the matter of the People versus Thomas Edward Utter," he said, "let the record reflect that we are proceeding in open court and that the defendant is present, all counsel are present, but that we are proceeding outside the presence of the jury." He looked at Reichman. "Gentlemen?"

"Your honor," Reichman said, "I make a motion under Section 1118.1 to dismiss all charges on the grounds of insufficiency of the evidence."

This was the test, Burnett thought as he watched from his seat. At the end of the prosecution's case the defense could move to dismiss, and the judge had to grant the motion to any counts he felt were too shaky to justify a conviction. He doubted that the judge would throw the case out on the evidence. But the kicker in this case was jurisdiction: Reichman might succeed in convincing Judge Lucas to dismiss the case on the grounds that the prosecution's own evidence established jurisdiction on at least the murder charge in Switzerland.

"Proceed," the judge said.

"Your honor, it has been our contention all along that California does not have jurisdiction to try the defendant for a murder that allegedly took place in Switzerland.

"Now, the law in California is clear: there must be facts sufficient to establish an independent charge of attempted murder within California's boundaries, in order to obtain jurisdiction over a murder culminating outside of California. In other words, under People versus Buffum, the prosecution for the murder within the state must be supported by facts of an attempted murder within the state.

Here, we have only the buying of tickets and, at most, a conspiracy.

"Now, Mr. Trott can stand before this court and tell us that California has the primary interests in prosecuting, that the victim and the perpetrator are California citizens, and so on. And he may be right. But the law is clear on jurisdiction, and it is spelled out by the legislature."

Reichman picked up a book, opened it to a marker. "The Buffum case relies heavily on a New York case, People versus Werblow, where Justice Cardozo said, 'We think a crime is not committed either wholly or partly in this state unless the act within this state is so related to the crime that if nothing more had followed it would amount to an attempt.'" Reichman closed the book.

"Now, I think that's the point. This court has got to sit down and forget what happened in Switzerland, or in Spain, or Tangiers, and just view what took place in the state of California. And then ask itself if these were the only facts it had, would the court in good conscience convict this defendant of attempted murder?

"A conspiracy is not attempted murder. Stealing property is not attempted murder. Buying tickets to Canada is not attempted murder. Even if it could be proven that the defendant planned out the entire murder in Los Angeles, that would still not be legally sufficient for attempted murder.

"And, your honor," Reichman said with a deep sigh, "if there are no facts for attempted murder within California, then, quite simply, the court has no jurisdiction over the murder itself. That is the law." Reichman slowly sat down.

"Mr. Trott?" Judge Lucas asked.

Trott rose to his feet. "Your honor, Mr. Reichman has talked a lot about People versus Buffum. But he has failed to mention People versus Anderson, which states in unequivocal language that California has jurisdictional interest in proceeding criminally against persons who would lure people from this state for the purpose of stealing their property. And I think the reasoning of Anderson is applicable to the situation in this case."

Go to it, Burnett thought. He rarely understood all the intricate, nitpicking legalese thrown around by lawyers during these motions, but he was always amazed at how completely in the right each side seemed.

"First, the Anderson case is more recent than Buffum and should therefore control.

"Second, the facts here are completely, totally distinguishable from Buffum. The facts are much more parallel to Anderson.

"Finally, I believe the Buffum case is extremely bad law. Now, I have submitted to this court a lengthy brief on this issue, anticipating Mr. Reichman's motion."

"I have read it," Judge Lucas said.

"And contained in the brief is extensive reference to authority which criticizes and contradicts the Buffum decision. Therefore, unless the court wants further argument, I will submit my argument on the basis of the brief. As your honor can clearly see, the only government concerned with this murder is California. The murder was planned in California, for the purpose of covering up thefts in California. The victim was a citizen of California, and the murderer was a citizen of California. And the plan was set in motion in California with the acquisition of a gun and airplane tickets. There is no other jurisdiction interested but California."

"Thank you, Mr. Trott," Judge Lucas said. "Submitted, gentlemen?"

"Yes, your honor," Trott replied.

Reichman nodded.

Burnett felt his breathing becoming shallower. It would be all over, he thought, if Lucas rules against us. If he decides there's no jurisdiction, then Devins will be a free man. The chances of Switzerland's extraditing him to face murder charges were minimal; the Swiss authorities looked on the Devins case as a strictly American matter that happened to take place in the Swiss Alps. No, if Lucas follows the Buffum case, then Devins had committed the perfect crime: a murderer with no one able or willing to prosecute him.

"Gentlemen," the judge said finally in a firm tone, "I've considered your arguments. And I deny the motion to dismiss charges."

Devins stared at the judge almost in shock, then turned to his lawyer. There was anger in his face.

"Bailiff," Judge Lucas continued, "bring in the jury."

Burnett breathed a small sigh of relief. Another hurdle overcome. Another in a long line. And there would be more.

The jurors began filing out of the deliberation room, taking their assigned seats in the railed area of the jury box. Soon, the twelve men and women were seated, with alternate jurors at the end.

"In the matter of Thomas Edward Utter," the judge recited, "let the record reflect that the defendant, all counsel and all members of the jury are present." He looked to the two lawyers. "Mr. Trott, the People have rested their case, is that correct?"

"Yes, your honor."

"Very well. Mr. Reichman, you may proceed with the defense."

Reichman rose slowly from his chair at the counsel table. He looked at the jury, then back at the judge. "Your honor," he said quietly, "the defense rests."

The courtroom was dead silent. Burnett couldn't believe what he had just heard. Reichman was offering no testimony, no evidence—no defense of any kind. He wasn't even putting Tom Devins on the stand. What was his plan? What tactics was the clever lawyer using now?

Judge Lucas studied the attorney for a moment. "Mr. Reichman, you will offer no defense?"

"No, your honor," Reichman replied, shifting his gaze to the jury. "In view of the weakness of the People's case, it will not be necessary."

Chapter 36

Trott was giving a good argument to the jury, Burnett thought. Not flashy, no theatrics—but thorough, steady, methodical. The facts were there, and he was laying them out for the jury, one after another, refreshing their minds after weeks of testimony. Calmly, he was organizing the evidence into a logical, cohesive pattern—a pattern that was becoming a noose around Devins' neck.

". . . The primary distinction between first-degree murder and second-degree murder is premeditation and deliberation. In other words, murder is the unlawful killing of a human being with malice aforethought. Malice isn't like a biblical term; it means ill will—it means, in this case, an express intent to take a human life.

"Premeditation means it is thought up and planned and deliberated. It means planned in advance, a deliberate killing. And all of the evidence in this case points to the fact that Norma Wilson was lured out of Los Angeles—as part of Phase One. All of this was an attempt to commit a perfect crime."

Trott leaned on the jury railing with both hands. "Tom Devins killed Norma Wilson in Europe. Only your imaginations will tell you exactly what was done with her body. She intended to come back from Europe. She intended to be buried someday near her first husband, Roy Carty. Instead, what was left of her came back in a gruesome cardboard box.

"You've seen hundreds of documents, listened to dozens

319

of witnesses. And all of this evidence adds up to only one reasonable conclusion: that Devins took her to Europe, and there murdered her in one of the worst fashions imaginable. And then he returned to Los Angeles to enjoy the fruits of his labor.

"Now, on this evidence, to find him not guilty would be to give him a ticket, to say, Yes, Mr. Devins, you have committed the perfect crime. I hope you will deny him this request. I hope you will refuse him that status among the world of sharks in which he moves.

"Now, you will have to decide whether or not he is guilty of this crime. This, in the final analysis, is your decision. I know your decision will be based on the evidence and the law. Thank you very much for your consideration."

Trott slowly walked back to the counsel table.

"You may proceed, Mr. Reichman," Judge Lucas said.

Joe Reichman rose, quickly walked across the courtroom to the jury box. He saw Burnett, smiled slightly. Burnett winked back at him.

"Now," Reichman said slowly, looking at the jurors. "Ladies and gentlemen, I almost didn't stand up to speak to you. I gave very serious consideration to not saying anything and just letting you decide the case. Because, you see, you *must* find this defendant not guilty based upon the evidence that has been presented to you.

"I believe some of you were somewhat surprised when the defense rested and didn't call a single witness. But the burden is on Mr. Trott to prove that the defendant is guilty beyond a reasonable doubt. The burden isn't on me to prove that he's innocent.

"Now, I don't know what reasonable doubt is. We talk about moral certainty. I kind of like to think of it: if I were a juror, and I voted guilty, then could I look at myself in the mirror while shaving two weeks later and ask myself, Did I do the right thing? and answer, Yes, and be sure of it. Because that's a question you're going to have to ask yourself the rest of your life.

"So, first, you must decide if Mr. Devins has been proven guilty—beyond any reasonable doubt. But second, you must determine for yourselves the interpretation to be given the evidence. You will be instructed that when a case is based upon circumstantial evidence, and there are two reasonable interpretations that can be given to the evidence: one pointing to guilt and one to innocence, you *must"*— Reichman slammed his fist on the jury railing—"you must adopt the one that points to innocence. This is not a decision: it is a duty, something you must do, under orders of the court. And ladies and gentlemen, as you recall this duty, bear in mind that this is a circumstantial case. The prosecution's evidence is based *entirely* on circumstantial evidence!"

Reichman paused. "There is absolutely no direct evidence of Mr. Devins' guilt. He was not seen committing murder, and he has certainly not confessed to such a thing. In fact, the prosecution has not even produced the body of Norma Wilson. We aren't even sure she is dead! For all we know, it could be an elaborate insurance hoax.

"Now," he continued, walking away from the jury box, "this case has not been an ordinary one. The District Attorney's office is a legal agency. It is not normally an investigative agency. In Los Angeles, investigations are normally done by the Los Angeles Police Department, or the Sheriff's Department, the Highway Patrol, or one of the local police departments. But in this case the investigating unit is not any of these police agencies—it is the District Attorney's office." Reichman walked toward the audience, stopped at the railing, looking directly at Burnett. "And you must keep that in mind when you review the evidence."

He turned back to the jury. "You see, the district attorney is in a unique position. He is supposed to be independent of the investigating agency. His duty is to protect not just the interests of citizens, but also those of the defendant. If he sees a wrong being done, he must correct it—regardless of the source. He must be on guard to prevent perjured testimony. He has a duty to present all evidence that is relevant, even if some evidence is exonerating.

"But this case is unique, as I said. All of the evidence has been produced by investigators from *within* the District

Attorney's office. The neutral role of the prosecutor has been removed. There is no longer the motive to prevent perjury, for the perjury comes from within!"

Reichman turned toward Trott, pointing his finger at the deputy D.A. "And on top of having the investigator come from the D.A.'s office, we have the prosecutor deprived of his neutral status by becoming actually involved in the investigation. Mr. Trott went to Europe with Mr. Burnett. And I say to you, ladies and gentlemen, that perhaps the thinking of Mr. Trott is not the thinking of the normal prosecutor, which you would see in a normal trial. He has become completely involved in this case. He is in the investigation and has a close comradeship with the investigators involved.

"And you can bet your bottom dollar that the D.A.'s office wants to see Mr. Devins convicted more than anything else in this world. If they had their choice, he would be the one they'd want. They want Devins before Sirhan Sirhan. They want Devins before Charlie Manson. And you know why!" He pounded the jury railing, staring at each of the jurors in turn. "Because he has cast a shadow on that office. He has cast a shadow on that office, and that shadow has not been removed!"

Burnett kept glancing at Trott, waiting for him to jump up and object to Reichman's inflammatory accusations. But the quiet young lawyer sat in oblivious silence.

"Mr. Devins didn't pay the $35,000," Reichman went on. "Instead, he went to the Attorney General's office and worked with them, and they began to investigate and take statements from Mr. Burnett, from Mr. Murphy—and eventually Jerome Weber was convicted through the testimony of Mr. Devins.

"There are friendships involved. The friendships of Mr. Murphy with Jerome Weber. There is a shadow, and it pains me to think of it, but there is a shadow on the District Attorney's office. And I ask you to keep that in mind when you evaluate this testimony because things are not always the way they seem to be."

Clever son of a bitch, Burnett admitted to himself. He

knows the evidence is all solidly against him, so he just ignores it—and attacks the prosecutor and investigator. He's working to shift the issue from murder to corruption. But would the jury buy it? Would they start taking a closer look at him and Trott, forgetting that it was Devins who was on trial? It was a clever tactic, used successfully on many occasions in the criminal courts.

Reichman stepped back for a moment, his head bowed in thought. He walked slowly toward the witness stand, stopped in front of it. "Ladies and gentlemen," he said in a low voice, "the prosecution's whole case rests upon the testimony of Robert Forget. Without that testimony, there is, of course, no case. If you do not believe this man, then there is no case. If you even harbor a reasonable doubt as to the honesty of this man, then there is no case. For Mr. Trott's case, Mr. Burnett's case, depends entirely on the solitary testimony of this 'star' witness, this fine citizen: an illegal immigrant, a gunrunner, a man who quickly agreed to a crazy scheme to take part in an African revolution, a man who says he agreed to murder an elderly woman, a man who admittedly lied at length to investigators, a drug addict . . ."

Burnett sat in his chair, listening to Reichman as he paced back and forth across the courtroom, alternately pounding on tables and pointing accusing fingers. He was entertaining, Burnett thought; you had to give him that. And the first job of any trial lawyer was to make sure the jury didn't go to sleep. But was he scoring points?

Burnett looked across at Trott seated behind the counsel table. His face was without expression; if anything, he wore a look of polite attention. Burnett chuckled silently; it took a certain aptitude to sit quietly as someone else called you a no-good skunk in front of a crowd.

Reichman walked back toward his table, then turned. "Now, we know Mr. Trott here has tried to hide things from you. As I said, the whole case really hinges on Forget. Mr. Trott had Forget on the stand for a whole day, but he never once told you Forget had been granted immunity." He looked at Trott. "I think it's pretty important for all of you to know that Forget had been granted immunity, but he didn't bring that out. He may say that he forgot to . . .

"And what about Mr. William Wilson? If I were the prosecutor on this case, I could make a pretty persuasive argument to you that Mr. Wilson had something to do with the demise of his wife—if she really is dead. Yet, I am astonished to hear Mr. Trott tell you that Mr. Wilson got almost nothing out of all this. Just take a look at the will: he gets everything!

"And he wasn't honest, was he, about his treatment of her? 'Well, we have our little differences,' he said. But we know he beat her! Regularly! And he was about to be divorced by Norma Wilson, cut off without a penny. Who has the motive to kill her?

"Obviously, the finger of suspicion points to William Wilson. You've all seen the kind of a man he is—or isn't. And if I could, I would present to you the person who killed Mrs. Wilson. If I could. But it isn't my job. It's the prosecution's job. And instead, they've attacked Tom Devins, to cover themselves up from charges of corruption. And William Wilson watches from the sidelines, gloating."

Maybe not too far off at that, Burnett thought as Reichman rambled on. He had kept tabs on Norma's husband, more out of curiosity than any real suspicion. Bill Wilson had been named trustee of Norma's estate, and stood to inherit the whole bundle. His lawyers had immediately filed suit against Kates, Rosen and Zukin in an attempt to recover the Malibu properties, and there was a strong likelihood of a big-money settlement there. Meanwhile, Wilson was still as far from a job as ever, but he had found a new paramour—a well-to-do widow living in the plush Comstock apartments on Wilshire Boulevard. The west side would always be a happy hunting ground, Burnett thought, filled with wealthy older women desperately looking for the companionship of a man—any man.

Reichman's voice cut back into the investigator's thoughts. "Now, as I said, the prosecution's case depends entirely on Robert Forget. And if in the next world there be such a thing as a book of infamy, his name will be on the first line of the first page. He is a despicable character. Yet, Mr. Trott is asking you to convict on his word alone.

"And consider. Mr. Burnett goes up to Sedro Woolley and talks to him, and they start talking about his income tax problems, child support problems, whether he should be permitted to have a gun since he's an alien, whether he's a legal citizen. Then Burnett leaves him with an arrow sticking out of his chest by telling him about the little green room.

"Now, I think this is perfectly terrible for a law enforcement officer to be talking that way to anybody, suspect or not. But you must consider the effect it had on his testimony. You must ask yourselves why Forget decided to testify. And if those same reasons would be enough for this proven liar to lie to you.

"All right," Reichman said, his voice dropping slightly as he walked toward the jury. "So what about all this supposed testimony from Forget? Well, there would be two ways to establish that Forget was telling the truth: produce the jewelry, or produce Mrs. Wilson's body. Forget's done neither. Oh, you've seen scratches on a wrench, and clothing dramatically covered with blood—but neither confirms Forget. Either could have been set up. Is it really believable that the greedy Robert Forget just threw away a fortune in diamonds? And if Devins really told him what Forget says, then why hasn't the prosecution found the body?"

Reichman turned away from the jury again, walked toward the part of the audience where Burnett was sitting, his eyes riveted on the investigator. "And what about the testimony of Mr. Burnett? This business of the little green room horrifies me, and it becomes particularly obnoxious when he turns the tape recorder off before that happens.

"And why hasn't he tape-recorded other witnesses? Why hasn't he produced orderly notes? For two years he's been working on the case, and yet his only records are a pile of little jottings on pieces of scrap paper, kept here and there. Could it be that Mr. Burnett doesn't want any records kept?

"It might be a good trial tactic, but it isn't good law enforcement. You should ask yourselves, also, whether

Burnett is an impartial witness. Is he really reliable? Is he viewing this whole thing impartially, or with only one thing in mind: convict Devins? You are asked to believe Mr. Burnett, but I ask you to consider his motives for not telling the truth."

Reichman turned around, again facing the jury. "But it is still Robert Forget upon whom the entire case hangs. It is upon his word that you must decide guilt beyond a reasonable doubt.

"Ask yourself a question. If you were Thomas Devins and you had killed Norma Wilson, would you be telling someone like Forget about it? Would you be giving Forget the fruits of your crime? Mr. Trott tells you how clever and how shrewd Mr. Devins is. But that doesn't seem to be a very clever or shrewd thing to do.

"And if you had killed her and some lawyer came to you and said he could bury the case for $35,000, wouldn't you pay it? If you had killed her, would you reject it and go to the Attorney General's office?"

Reichman again breathed in deeply, studied the floor in front of him. "What about that gun?" he said suddenly. "Mr. Murphy went to pick it up, he said. Can you believe the D.A.'s office would send Murphy up to get the gun? Murphy—the man Devins has accused of being in on the $25,000 bribe? Murphy, the man who was investigated by the attorney general? This is the man whom the district attorney continues to allow to work on the case. It staggers the imagination!

"I don't know whether Murphy changed the barrel on the gun. It is certainly in the range of possibility—I hate to think it is true—that Murphy changed the barrel. I don't like to say that. The District Attorney's office should be beyond reproach. Unfortunately, in this case they have not been."

Reichman stood still in the middle of the courtroom. His head was slightly bowed. He waited for a moment in silence. Then, in a hushed voice echoing through the quiet room, he said, "God sees the truth, but waits." He looked up slowly at the jury. "He reveals the truth when He wants to—maybe in a week, maybe in a month, maybe in a year, maybe in a decade. But, as sure as you are sitting here and listening to me, there will come a time when we will know the whereabouts of Norma Wilson. And as sure as you are sitting here and listening to me, there will come a time when we will know who put the bloody box into the train locker. And there will come a time when we will know who, if anyone, killed Norma Wilson.

"As sure as I am of that, I am also sure that nobody is going to rush God—not even Mr. Trott."

Reichman bowed his head in the silent courtroom, standing before the jury without speaking. Then, very slowly, he walked back to the defense table and sat down.

Chapter 37

THERE WAS A VERDICT.

The court bailiff called Trott at his office at 10:00 A.M. and notified him that the jury had finally reached a decision; he was ordered to be in the courtroom within one half-hour for the reading of the verdicts. Reichman had also been contacted.

Trott had then called the Bureau, told Burnett of the news and agreed to meet in the lobby of the Hall of Justice. Fifteen minutes later, Burnett walked into the old criminal courts building and spied Trott nervously sipping coffee from a paper cup.

Burnett walked across the lobby to the young baby-faced prosecutor. Lighting his pipe, he said casually, "How's it look, Steve?"

Trott shrugged. "Who knows?" He took another sip from the cup. "Could go either way. No body, no eyewitnesses . . ."

Two months of trial, Burnett thought. And nearly two years of hard investigation—two years of frustrating days and sleepless nights. Two years of living with the gentle smile of Norma Wilson burned into his mind. And now it was all riding on a piece of paper that bore the jury's decision: guilty of murder, or not guilty. There would be a number of verdicts, of course—the robbery and grand theft counts—but they were insignificant. The name of the game was murder.

"Educated guess?" Burnett asked, grinning.

Trott shook his head. "No way. This one's up for grabs."

Burnett continued trying to light the bulky pipe. "You don't think they bought that line Reichman gave them about the D.A.'s office trying to cover up?"

Trott shrugged again. "Who knows?" he repeated, gazing absently down into the brown liquid in the cup. "Maybe they think it's a frame. Maybe they think Bill Wilson knocked her off. Maybe they think Norma's still alive. Maybe . . ." Trott looked up. "Come on, we'd better get up there."

Trott threw the half-filled cup into a trash can, and the two men walked across the lobby toward the opening doors of an elevator. As the two men stepped in, a third man ran across the lobby and jumped in, just beating the doors as they clanked shut. He was slightly built, with piercing blue eyes and quick energetic movements. His name was Vincent Bugliosi, Charles Manson's prosecutor, and he was still in trial down the hall from the Devins courtroom.

"I heard you got a verdict, Steve," Bugliosi said to Trott.

"Looks like it," Trott replied.

Bugliosi nodded. He knew better than to ask a fellow prosecutor to second-guess a jury. The moments before the reading of the verdict was a tense time for trial lawyers, and there was a lot of superstition involved. "Well, good luck," Bugliosi said quietly.

The elevator jerked to a stop, and the antique doors slowly opened. The three men stepped out into the hallway. Immediately, a swarm of reporters and cameramen rushed across the hall and surrounded Bugliosi.

"Well, here we go again," Bugliosi said. He waved to Trott and Burnett as they pushed their way through the mob.

The two men walked down the hall. As they approached Department 102, three reporters descended on them.

"Any comments, Mr. Trott?" one asked.

A flashbulb ignited the air for a split second.

"Nothing," Trott said, opening the door. "No, no comments."

"Do you expect the—"

"No comments," Trott repeated. Then he entered the

329

courtroom, followed by Burnett. The two men walked up to the railing separating the audience from the court. Devins and Reichman were already seated at their table.

"Let's grab a beer after, huh?" Trott said.

"Yeah," Burnett answered. He took a seat in the audience.

Trott walked over to the prosecution table. Deputy D.A. Harland Braun was already there, gazing at the empty jury box. He looked up at Trott, managing a sick smile. His stomach, too, was twisted into knots; he, too, had devoted months of his life for the moment that was about to come. The moment of truth.

Trott sat down, began sifting through the stacks of paper on the table. Then he stopped, realizing he was looking for nothing.

The two prosecutors sat in their chairs, not looking at each other, not saying anything. Each man was lost in his own thoughts, lost in a world of agonizing doubts. A thousand "ifs" were streaking through their minds as the weeks of trial flashed in review, the decisions now made, the course now taken. Was the brutal murder of Norma Wilson going to go unpunished? Was Tom Devins going to walk out of this room, free to find another Norma Wilson somewhere in the future?

The door to the jury deliberation room suddenly opened, and a man walked out. Burnett recognized him as juror number twelve. James Pyburn. Behind him was Printle Russell, another juror. Then Walter Fuller and Kei Oshiro. Each of the jurors filed out of the room, one at a time. And each found his designated seat within the rectangular oak box. Finally, all twelve were seated.

Burnett studied their faces in the hushed silence of the courtroom, searching each of their faces for some sign, some clue to the life-and-death secret they alone held. Juror number eight—was that a slight smile he saw? Who was he smiling at? What did it mean? And number two—an almost imperceptible nod? Why was number three staring at Trott?

"All rise," the bailiff bellowed.

Judge Lucas walked through the door leading to his

chambers, as everyone rose to their feet. Quickly, he ascended the steps to the bench.

"Department 102 of the Superior Court of Los Angeles is again in session, the Honorable Malcolm Lucas presiding. Please be seated."

"In the matter of Thomas Edward Utter," Judge Lucas said, "let the record reflect that the defendant, all counsel and all members of the jury are present." He looked toward the jury. "Mrs. Greenberg, you are the forewoman, is that correct?"

A middle-aged woman rose to her feet. "Yes."

"Has the jury arrived at a verdict?"

"Yes, we have."

"Please hand all the verdict forms to the bailiff."

The uniformed bailiff walked to the jury box, accepted the pieces of white paper from the somber-faced woman. Slowly, agonizingly slowly, the bailiff walked across the courtroom toward the judge's bench. He looked up at Judge Lucas and gradually lifted the papers up toward him as if they were made of lead.

Judge Lucas took the verdicts, then silently read the first one to himself. He coughed. As if in a slow-motion replay, he lifted the piece of paper up, set it down, and began reading the second verdict. His eyes looked up for a moment, glanced briefly at Trott, then at Devins. The only sound in the tomblike courtroom was the deafening rustle of paper as Judge Lucas slowly read the verdicts to himself.

Burnett could feel his heart hammering against his ribs now, his throat beginning to swell. The judge seemed blurry to him now, drifting out of focus.

Judge Lucas looked up, then handed the papers down to the clerk. "The clerk will read the verdicts."

The clerk took the forms from the judge's outstretched hand. She shuffled them, dropped one.

Burnett felt something screaming inside, something clawing to get out, to hit, to smash. *Read* the damn things! he was shouting inside. *Read* them! Tell me if Devins walks out a free man!

Burnett took in a sudden breath, dropped his head

slightly, stared at the floor. Jesus! he thought. Sadistic goddamn ritual! He concentrated on his boots for a moment, staring at them without seeing.

"Ahem," the clerk cleared her throat. She glanced at Devins.

Reichman rose to his feet, motioned Devins to do the same. Slowly, like cold molasses, Tom Devins uncoiled from his chair and stood erect, confident.

"Ladies and gentlemen of the jury," the clerk said, turning to the jury box, "as I read each verdict I will be polling you. I will call your name and ask if this is your verdict. If it is, please say yes. If it is not, say no."

She looked back at the two standing figures. "Title of Court and Cause. We, the jury in the above-entitled action . . ."

Burnett's heart was pounding louder, and suddenly he saw the gently smiling face of Norma Wilson flash before him.

". . . find the defendant, Thomas Edward Utter, guilty of murder as charged in Count I of the Information, and further find it to be murder in the first degree. This 8th day of December, 1970. Lois Greenberg, Foreman." The clerk looked at the jury. "Mrs. Beetz?"

"Yes."

"Mrs. Hamilton?"

The voices were fading now, merging into a distant drone, as the thin man in the baggy gray flannel suit and brown cowboy boots quietly stepped out into the aisle and walked toward the swinging doors. His shoulders were sagging slightly, and the grin on his face was a weary one; it matched his strangely sad and empty eyes.

He pushed open the doors and walked out into the dimly lit corridor. A group of reporters was still standing down the hall, waiting outside of Judge Older's courtroom. They glanced at him for a moment, then returned to their vigil.

Slowly, he began walking toward the creaking elevator. He did not know if the face of the smiling, silver-haired woman would return to haunt him. He only knew that he was tired, very tired.

Epilogue

On February 4, 1971, Judge Lucas reviewed Probation Officer Doris Feldman's report on her background investigation of Tom Devins. Feldman noted that her subject was "confident that his conviction will be reversed for lack of jurisdiction and for this reason presented no defense . . . The defendant apparently sought to commit the 'perfect crime' by arranging the murder so that no governmental agency, in his opinion, would be authorized to have the legal power to try him for the offense." She then concluded by observing that: "The personality of this defendant has been so molded as to prevent him from acquiring the conscience that would restrain an ordinary person from committing the ultimate crime. He displays the charm and glib tongue often associated with what is described as the sociopathic personality. It is felt that when and if defendant is returned to the community he would pose a continuing danger to life and property."

One week later, Devins stood in Department 100 awaiting sentence. The jury had deadlocked as to the death penalty; as a result, the worst he could receive was a life sentence. Judge Lucas imposed the life term, then added additional imprisonment "for the terms prescribed by law" as penalty for the crimes of robbery and grand theft.

But on March 29, 1972, the California Court of Appeals reversed the murder conviction. There was simply insufficient evidence to establish jurisdiction in California, the court said; the trial should properly have been conducted in

Switzerland. The robbery-theft counts were left standing, however, and Devins was left with a short prison term remaining to be served.

On January 9, 1974, Steve Trott received an urgent message from Buehlman in Switzerland. Interpol had received a report that a Swiss citizen, while picking mushrooms high in the Alps, had discovered a partly buried human jawbone. The local authorities had contacted Interpol, and Buehlman had then compared the jawbone with the X-rays and dental mold left by Burnett. "In the opinion of our technicians," Buehlman advised Trott, "the jawbone is that of Norma Carty Wilson."

Two months after this discovery, Trott notified the warden at the Susanville Correctional Facility that attempts were being made by his office to have Devins extradited to Switzerland to stand trial for murder. Due to the minimal security at Susanville, it was suggested that he be watched closely.

On March 30, 1974—one month after this warning was sent—Devins escaped from Susanville while conducting an interview as a reporter for the inmate newspaper. He was later joined in his flight by a young woman. Beth Greenhouse, a graduate of New York University and the daughter of a wealthy New York builder, had met Devins while visiting a friend in the prison facility. She had quickly fallen in love with him, and had spent large sums of money retaining Melvin Belli to seek a reversal of the remaining robbery-theft convictions. "I was fascinated by the man," she later explained. "I petitioned the courts to let me marry him. When he wasn't released I decided I loved him too dearly to let him rot in prison."

Two weeks after his escape, a man answering Devins' description was picked up while hitchhiking in the Hollywood area. The driver reported that he had dropped the man off, as requested, in an area near the home of Bill Burnett. Burnett and his family were away from home on vacation at the time.

Devins was next reported in Vichy, France, where he was living with Ms. Greenhouse at the home of a close friend of her parents, Michelle Chonac. Interpol reported that Devins had then stolen $700,000 worth of jewelry from Mme. Chonac and fled to Australia.

At the Sydney airport, Devins was arrested for attempting to enter the country with a forged passport bearing the name "Leo Schultz."

Ms. Greenhouse who had accompanied Devins to Australia, hired a prominent Australian solicitor, Bruce Miles, to fight extradition proceedings, and again retained Melvin Belli to assist Miles in preventing Devins' return to California. Miles argued to the Australian courts that Devins was seeking asylum as a political prisoner: he was, Miles said, a refugee from political persecution by corrupt members of the Los Angeles District Attorney's office. If Devins were returned to California, Ms. Greenhouse added, he would be killed because "he knows too much."

The Australian courts granted a postponement of extradition proceedings to study the matter. Meanwhile, the case had become a *cause célèbre* in Australia. The Sydney *Sunday Telegraph* ran the story under front page headlines:

FUGITIVE IN BIZARRE TANGLE FEARS FOR HIS LIFE

An American jail escapee seeking asylum in Australia believes he will be murdered if he is sent back to finish his sentence.

He is Thomas Edward Utter, 34, who this week became the centre of a bizarre international legal battle. The case involves the disappearance of a wealthy woman in Switzerland, charges that she was chopped up and fed to the sharks, allegations of legal corruption and a political vendetta, and high-speed car chases with machine gun bullets riddling one vehicle . . .

As Trott awaited the verdict of the Australian courts, he received further word from Buehlman: his Interpol contacts reported that the jewelry described by Mme. Chonac had very recently been sold to a "fence" in Australia.

Finally, the Australian authorities discovered what

335

Devins always knew: their treaty of extradition with the United States did not cover the crime of escape from prison. Devins could not be extradited. The Sydney police, however, took a pragmatic approach: they simply put Devins on an airplane bound for Los Angeles and then placed a discreet phone call to Trott's office.

On October 11, 1974, Tom Devins was re-arrested at Los Angeles International Airport. He was placed in County Jail, and soon thereafter transferred to Folsom Prison. One of his new fellow inmates was Eddie Wein—the man who had raped Adelle Devins.

The Lassen County District Attorney's office quickly filed felony charges against Devins for escaping from Susanville. Strangely, however, the case was eventually dismissed—for reasons still unknown. Officially, there is no record of any involvement by the California Attorney General's office in the dismissal.

Meanwhile, Burnett learned from confidential sources in Switzerland that the Swiss authorities did not intend to extradite Devins on the murder charge. The government felt that a sensational trial involving an American tourist murdered in their country would only hurt the tourist trade; in any event, no Swiss citizens were involved in the killing. At the same time, French authorities appeared to show no interest in extraditing Devins on the $700,000 jewelry theft; the French Sûreté was content that Devins had been recaptured and was serving time in prison.

Trott filed a formal request with the California Adult Authority, instructing them to notify him in the event Devins was granted a parole hearing. The D.A.'s office, he explained, wanted to offer critical evidence establishing compelling reasons why Devins should not be given an early release.

Nevertheless, on February 14, 1977, Devins was released from Folsom Prison on parole. He requested that his parole be transferred to Massachusetts, and this request was granted.

Trott did not learn of the parole hearing and grant until

five weeks later. The official excuse given by the Adult Authority for the failure to notify Trott was that his request had been "misfiled." Again, there is no official record of intervention by the Attorney General's office.

Tom Devins was discharged from parole by the Massachusetts authorities on July 1, 1978—a free man.

About the Author

LAWRENCE TAYLOR is a criminal attorney with his own practice in Los Angeles. He has been a deputy public defender, a deputy district attorney, and a deputy county counsel; in the latter capacity, he represented the Sheriff's Department and advised the trial judge in People v. Charles Manson. As a defense attorney, he successfully argued to the Supreme Court for a reversal of the death penalty in the case made famous by Joseph Wambaugh's *The Onion Field.*

In 1975, Mr. Taylor was privately retained by the Attorney General of Montana to investigate and prosecute high-level political corruption; Bill Burnett served as a special investigator during this prosecution.

Mr. Taylor serves periodically as Judge Pro Tem, lectures in criminal law at universities, and contributes broadly to the field of legal literature; his most recent textbook is *Criminal Appeals.* He is an ex-Marine, was briefly a professional light-heavyweight boxer, and is an ardent boater—having once single-handed his sailboat through the Bahamas for six months.